"Alain Hunkins brings years of experience to the topic of leadership, and has important insights into the process of becoming someone whose influence brings greater success, heightened communication, and larger empathy to the whole organization. *Cracking the Leadership Code* is a great book for those starting out on the leadership journey or managers who need a refresher in what connected, effective leadership really means."

—*Daniel H. Pink, author of* When *and* Drive

"One of the most practical books on the planet when it comes to leadership and how to make a difference. Full of great examples, truths, and insights readily accessible and applicable on both an individual and organizational level. Highly recommend."

—*Barry Z. Posner, PhD, Professor of Leadership Leavey School of Business, Santa Clara University, coauthor,* The Leadership Challenge

"*Cracking the Leadership Code* is a valuable and enlightened guide for anyone with the courage and passion to lead with an open mind and open heart. Alain Hunkins writes from rich personal experience with conviction and credibility."

—*Danny Meyer, founder and CEO, Union Square Hospitality Group*

"The pace of change and the ever-present threat of disruption pose daunting challenges for business leaders. *Cracking the Leadership Code* offers clear, real-life advice to help navigate these tumultuous times. Seasoned CEOs and first-time managers will benefit from its practical wisdom."

—*Frits Dirk van Paasschen, former CEO of Starwood Hotels & Resorts and The Coors Brewing Company and Amazon bestselling author of* The Disruptors' Feast

"Leaders need to continuously improve their fluency in the language of leadership. *Cracking the Leadership Code* is a magnificent guide to help you translate leadership ideas into action. It manages to be smart, engaging, practical, and authentic all at the same time. If you're a leader who wants to grow your effectiveness and impact, get Cracking!"

—*Marshall Goldsmith, New York Times #1 bestselling author of* Triggers, Mojo, *and* What Got You Here Won't Get You There

"Alain Hunkins is a supremely gifted communicator, and through engaging stories and effortless prose he brings to life essential lessons of leadership in *Cracking the Leadership Code*. Alain's framework is at once elegantly simple, but at the same time well-grounded in research and highly applicable in practice. It's also just plain fun to read—one of the most enjoyable leadership books I've read all year. I found myself eagerly turning the pages for more of Alain's wit and wisdom, and I am confident your experience will be the same. Five stars for *Cracking the Leadership Code*."

— Jim Kouzes, *coauthor of* The Leadership Challenge, *and the Dean's Executive Fellow of Leadership, Leavey School of Business, Santa Clara University*

"How to lead well shouldn't be a mystery. *Cracking the Leadership Code* lives up to its title — it shares a wealth of real-world information that's valuable for leaders at all levels in any organization."

— Sydney Finkelstein, *Professor of Leadership at the Tuck School of Business at Dartmouth College and author of the bestselling book* Superbosses

"This wonderful book shows you how to communicate, influence, and persuade others faster and more effectively than ever before. Get more things done, faster and easier than ever."

— Brian Tracy, *chairman and CEO of Brian Tracy International, author of* How the Best Leaders Lead

"This book really does help crack the leadership code in a way that is practical, easy to understand, and easy to apply. I am a proponent of the concepts of connection, communication, and collaboration as the primary tools of leadership. You'll be a better leader for reading this book."

— Mark Sanborn, *president, Sanborn & Associates, author of* The Fred Factor *and* The Potential Principle

"In an era of uncertainty and change, leadership is all the more vital and its personal mastery all the more essential. The formula for doing so can seem elusive, however, and Alain Hunkins has given us a practical roadmap. For learning to be self-consciously courageous, for taking charge even if you are not fully or formally in charge, *Cracking the Leadership Code* is the driver's manual."

— Michael Useem, *Faculty Director, Wharton Leadership Center, Professor of Management at the Wharton School of the University of Pennsylvania, and co-author of* Mastering Catastrophic Risk *and* Go Long

"Leadership excellence starts with fully understanding the fundamentals. *Cracking the Leadership Code* shines a brilliant spotlight on the fundamentals of Connection, Communication, and Collaboration. Blazing with insights, inspiration, and instruction, it's a comprehensive guide on how to become a better leader."

— Pat Williams, *Orlando Magic founder and senior vice president, author of* Character Carved in Stone

"Alain Hunkins has written an excellent guide for aspirational leaders. Filled with practical advice and wonderful stories, *Cracking the Leadership Code* is a must-read primer that cuts to the core of the challenges most leaders face. Hunkins' emphasis on the them-versus-me side of leadership is inspiring."
—*Allen Morrison, PhD, CEO and Director General, Thunderbird School of Global Management*

"Well written and well researched—a practical guide for leaders who want to improve on the fundamentals and be better at what they do."
—*Bruce Tulgan, CEO of Rainmaker Thinking and bestselling author of* It's Okay to Be the Boss

"Not many leadership books make you laugh and cry and then compel you to take an honest look in the mirror. Alain Hunkins will gently but expertly help you reflect and ask yourself, "What kind of leader do I want to be?" And then, he'll tell you how to do it."
—*Suzanne Bates, CEO of Bates Communications and author of* All the Leader You Can Be

"*Cracking the Leadership Code* delivers the fuel you need to propel your career forward quickly. Hunkins shares great insight and useful tools to becoming the leader you've always wanted to be."
—*Jon Gordon, bestselling author of* The Energy Bus *and* The Power of Positive Leadership

"If you're a time-starved leader looking to amp up your effectiveness, put this book on your reading list. With actionable tips and practical tools, *Cracking the Leadership Code* delivers a roadmap for propelling your career forward."
—*Lisa Bodell, CEO of Futurethink and bestselling author of* Why Simple Wins

"In *Cracking the Leadership Code*, Alain Hunkins raises the bar on what a leadership book should be. With an authentic voice gained from walking his own leadership path, Hunkins weaves together ideas from business, psychology, neuroscience, and behavioral economics in a surprisingly engaging way. You'll be inspired not just to think differently, but to act differently."
—*Kevin Kruse, New York Times bestselling author of* Employee Engagement 2.0 *and founder and CEO of LEADx*

"*Cracking the Leadership Code* is a treasure chest of leadership insight that will help you personally and professionally. Told in a refreshingly candid style, you'll benefit from Alain Hunkins' 20+ years working with thousands of leaders. The stories opened my heart and the principles apply to my daily leadership practice. I'm delighted to recommend this book."

—*Dan Rockwell, author of* Leadership Freak *blog*

"What a terrific book on leadership. It is substantive and useful to anyone who wants to create capacity in others."

—*Dr. Nido R. Qubein, president, High Point University*

"Most people want to be good leaders—but what does that actually mean? With warmth and good humor, Alain Hunkins reveals that being a great leader comes down to the small choices we make every day. *Cracking the Leadership Code* will open your eyes to the obvious and not-so-obvious reasons why leading today is so difficult, help you better think about and interact with everyday challenges, and provide tools you can employ right away."

—*German Herrera, Industrial Practice Leader, North America, Egon Zehnder*

"*Cracking the Leadership Code* is an insightful guide for leaders. Alain Hunkins offers sage advice for leaders on connection, communication, and collaboration rooted in decades of his leadership coaching and consulting experience. His examples and stories provide memorable lessons for leaders to create more productive and healthy organizations."

—*Christine Porath, Professor of Management, Georgetown University and the author of* Mastering Civility: A Manifesto for the Workplace

"Brimming with hard-won wisdom and practical tools, I will be returning to *Cracking the Leadership Code* for years to come in my journey to be a more conscious and effective leader."

—*Jonah Sachs, founder of Free Range Studios and author of* Winning the Story Wars *and* Unsafe Thinking

"*Cracking the Leadership Code* is as enjoyable to read as it is practical to apply. Hunkins engages the reader with wit, wisdom, and timely insights gleaned from his decades of experience successfully guiding leaders through challenging situations."

—*Arthur Carmazzi, bestselling author and ranked as one of the Global Top-Ten Most Influential Leadership Gurus 2018 by Global Gurus*

"It is with pleasure that I endorse Alain Hunkins' perceptive and revealing book, *Cracking the Leadership Code*. As the third-generation CEO of my own business, I found his writing to be particularly resonant, and I was quick to share Hunkins' insights with my sons, who I hope will one day be fourth-generation leaders of my company!

Hunkins' voice is deceptively simple as he delves into the complex communication issues that plague organizations today. In a straightforward manner he shares why companies need to integrate—and implement—greater empathy, collaboration, listening techniques, understanding, etc. into their corporate culture. His message is on-target and valuable. In fact, Hunkins imparts so many words of wisdom—combined with so many excellent tools—I had to stop highlighting them all before I ran out of ink! This book is a must-read for anyone in leadership or contemplating leadership in today's world."

—*Mitchell Kaneff, CEO and chairman, Arkay Packaging*

"An enlightening book on bettering meaningful and purpose-driven leadership traits in everyday life—home and workplace. Almost immediately I began to reflect on interactions of communication with those in my world. Hunkins has nailed it! A must-read for those learning—which is everyone in a position in life of influence and persuasion. Moms, dads, executives, clergy, political leaders, community organizers, and many more will be well served reading *Cracking the Leadership Code* and evolving as a result."

—*John Ohanesian, president & CEO, Lear Capital*

"Superb book! *Cracking the Leadership Code* does much to simplify leadership for all of us who practice it and teach it. Alain Hunkins' work is extraordinarily narrative—I am inspired by how much of his life he shares with us, and you will be, too. He pulls together so many ideas in the leadership space, and does so in a such readable, engaging format, that this book represents real value. This book will not exhaust you, but it will activate you and stimulate your desire to lead as it builds your capacity to lead. Hunkins' framing of leadership as Connection, Communication, Collaboration is among the most useful structures I've seen used in books that develop leaders. I enjoyed every minute and every page of this book."

—*Thomas A. Kolditz, Brigadier General, US Army (ret) and executive director, Doerr Institute for New Leaders, Rice University*

"I truly enjoyed this book! With the world changing at such a rapid pace, this is a book every leader must read. Through entertaining storytelling of situations we can all relate to, Alain Hunkins reminds us that leadership is a journey of constant and never-ending improvement. By using a framework of Connection, Communication, and Collaboration, he reminds us of the fundamentals of great leadership. Alain's exposure to a wide array of industries and leaders going through times of change has allowed him to see where some leaders have gotten this right

and others have not. This book is a gift for anyone interested in being a great leader to be able to benefit from Alain's insights he has collected over the years."
— *Terri Pearce, head of Learning and Talent Development, Human Resources,*
HSBC Bank USA

"*Cracking the Leadership Code* offers a refreshing, practical approach to leadership that will help you develop both personally and professionally."
— *Dr. Tasha Eurich,* New York Times *bestselling author of* Insight *and*
Bankable Leadership

"Written expressly for today's leader who is too busy to read it! The world of work has changed as have all the motivators for working in it, and the philosophies underpinning the old ways no longer serve anyone. Hunkins acknowledges leaders face challenges on multiple fronts in this faster, flatter world: ever increasing pace of change, increased expectations of workers, and customers' equal access to information and platform to share their views. Today's leader must be willing and able to face those challenges with empathy, as a human."
— *Cheryl Reich, senior director, Organizational Effectiveness, Broadridge Financial*
Solutions

"*Cracking the Leadership Code* brings us a down-to-earth, experience-rich guide for how to make leadership both impactful and effective. Hunkins presents the challenges of today's leadership coupled with three guiding principles for leadership that directly meets these challenges: Connection, Communication, and Collaboration. The book is chockfull of useful examples and pragmatic tools, tips, and techniques for making these principles a real part of your leadership signature. *Cracking the Leadership Code* is an essential element in your leadership library to both inspire and engage in effective leadership actions for today's business world."
— *Jane Dutton, Robert L. Kahn Distinguished University Professor Emerita of Business*
Administration and Psychology, Ross School of Business, University of Michigan and
author of Energize Your Workplace

"Leadership is a deeply human endeavor, and Hunkins' *Cracking the Leadership Code* reflects that critical idea while offering very practical ideas and tactics to bring your humanity into your leadership. It's a worthwhile read for leaders wanting to show up as their best, most impactful selves."
— *Peter Bregman, bestselling author of* Eighteen Minutes *and* Four Seconds

CRACKING THE
LEADERSHIP
CODE

CRACKING THE
LEADERSHIP
CODE

THREE SECRETS TO
BUILDING STRONG LEADERS

ALAIN HUNKINS

WILEY

Published by John Wiley & Sons, Inc., Hoboken, New Jersey.
Published simultaneously in Canada.

For general information on our other products and services or for technical support, please contact
our Customer Care Department within the United States at (800) 762–2974, outside the United
States at (317) 572–3993 or fax (317) 572–4002.

Wiley publishes in a variety of print and electronic formats and by print-on-demand. Some material
included with standard print versions of this book may not be included in e-books or in
print-on-demand. If this book refers to media such as a CD or DVD that is not included in the
version you purchased, you may download this material at http://booksupport.wiley.com. For more
information about Wiley products, visit www.wiley.com.

Library of Congress Cataloging-in-Publication Data
Names: Hunkins, Alain, 1968- author.
Title: Cracking the leadership code / Alain Hunkins.
Description: First Edition. | Hoboken : Wiley, 2020. | Includes
   bibliographical references and index.
Identifiers: LCCN 2019051506 (print) | LCCN 2019051507 (ebook) | ISBN
   9781119675549 (hardback) | ISBN 9781119675563 (adobe pdf) | ISBN
   9781119675556 (epub)
Subjects: LCSH: Leadership. | Communication in management.
Classification: LCC HD57.7 .H856 2020 (print) | LCC HD57.7 (ebook) | DDC
   658.4/092–dc23
LC record available at https://lccn.loc.gov/2019051506
LC ebook record available at https://lccn.loc.gov/2019051507

Cover Design: Wiley
Cover Image: © 3D_generator/Getty Images
Author Photo: Maurice Jager © Alain Hunkins

Printed in the United States of America

V10017411_020620

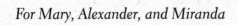

For Mary, Alexander, and Miranda

CONTENTS

CONTENTS

INTRODUCTION

Deciphering the Code: Why I Wrote This Book

In 2007, a large, well-known organization had a problem. Their service wasn't keeping pace with their customers' expectations. The organization's leadership had to act.

And did they ever. As part of their 87-page strategic transformation plan, they wrote:

> Customers form expectations on critical attributes such as waiting time in line based on their experience with other similar services, and compare (our) performance to best-in-class providers.[1]

In other words, customers were complaining that they had to wait too long in line. The organization's leadership knew, however, that defining the problem was not enough. They had to do something about it. In a declaration of intent, they confidently pronounced that they were

> committed to changing with its customers, designing new products to meet new needs, and creating new solutions that customers value.[2]

It all sounded good.

These published promises mirrored the organization's published "core set of enduring goals that guide all of (our) strategic initiatives and continuous improvement efforts."[3]

They were using all the right words. So what did they actually end up doing?

One of the biggest customer complaints was long wait times to talk with a customer service representative at their 37,000 retail locations.

To address the issue, these bold leaders executed their most innovative idea:

They removed the clocks from the walls of every location.

No, really.

That's what the United States Postal Service did.

Shockingly, the clock removal did not make customers happier about their wait times. There were 87 *pages* of strategic planning, and removing the clocks was the best solution leadership could come up with.

Maybe the United States Postal Service thought people would forget they carried their own timepieces and wouldn't notice how long they were still waiting in line. Maybe they thought that without clocks on the walls, people would act as though they were in a casino and put all their money on Forever stamps. We really don't know what the leadership at the U.S. Postal Service was thinking.

The clock removals set off a customer backlash.[4] Leadership tried to contain the outrage, saying this was part of a national effort to have all post office lobbies look the same. Yet no matter what the spin, removing clocks to address long wait times is absurd.

It's easy to blame the Postal Service blunder on poor strategy or bad execution. But who creates the strategy? Leaders. Who maps out the execution? Leaders.

If you work in an organization, this clock-removing story may not seem all that surprising. Leaders do strange things all the time that leave employees scratching their heads in disbelief and muttering, "What were they thinking?" Although we don't know for sure, there's one thing we do know: the state of leadership is poor.

MIRED IN MEDIOCRITY

Ketchum, Inc. is a nearly 100-year-old global public relations firm. Every year, Ketchum interviews more than 25,000 people from 22 industries on five continents to ask them what they think about their leaders. They've found the following from their research:

- **Only 23%** believe their leaders are leading well. (This number has not been above 25% in the last five years.)
- **Only 31%** believe leaders communicate well.
- **Only 17%** have confidence that leadership will improve in the upcoming year.[5]

Ketchum's findings are not the exception, but the rule. Other research corroborates the shoddy state that leadership is in. Only 37% of the population believes CEOs are credible,[6] and less than half (48%) of employees report their top management does a good job of providing effective leadership.

It gets worse. Bad leadership has a ripple effect—particularly on those being led. Worldwide 87% of employees are not engaged,[7] 54% of employees claim they don't regularly get respect from their leaders,[8] and less than half of full-time workers place a great deal of trust in their employers.[9]

The future of leadership also looks bleak. More than half (55%) of organizations are struggling with a talent shortage.[10] Only 18% of HR professionals rate their leadership bench strength as strong or very strong,[11] and 71% said their leaders are not ready to lead their organizations into the future.[12]

No leader sets out to be mediocre. No one shows up to work and thinks, "Today I want to make someone else's life miserable." No one says, "Today, I'm going to be a crummy communicator. None of my direct reports will trust me, and they'll assume that my overall leadership will get even worse in the future." For the most part, people genuinely want to do a good job.

Unfortunately, good intentions don't translate into good results. Too many leaders don't understand what it takes for them to succeed. They mean well and work hard, but they lack the proper mind-set and tools.

Consider this startling finding: a poll of 2,058 adults reported that 69% of managers are often uncomfortable communicating with employees. Isn't communication a basic part of the job? Lou Solomon, CEO of Interact (the company that conducted the survey), elaborated, noting, "Many managers are uncomfortable with becoming vulnerable, recognizing achievements, delivering the 'company line,' giving clear directions, crediting others with having good ideas, speaking face to face, and having difficult feedback conversations in general."[13]

Leading well is extremely difficult. If it were easy, more people would be doing it. Think back on your own life experience. Of the leaders you've worked with, how many would you rate as excellent? How many were middling? How many were eminently forgettable?

If you find that most of your memories fall on the negative end of the spectrum, you can take comfort in the fact that you're not alone. For most people, working in organizations with lousy leaders is just another day at the office.

But it doesn't have to be this way. There's a path out of the muddle of mediocrity. Great leaders aren't born—they're made. If you're committed, you can learn and apply specific tools to improve how you lead.

THE PURPOSE OF CRACKING THE LEADERSHIP CODE

The goal of this book is to shorten your leadership learning curve and accelerate your leadership growth. Its content is drawn from two decades of fieldwork. I've had the good fortune of getting to work with and learn from a tremendous number of leaders and teachers, and this book represents a distillation of that knowledge. My hope is that the insights and tools I offer in this book will help you reap the rewards that exceptional leadership brings.

In this book, I won't stick to the flat, two-dimensional world of leadership theory. I'll share what works and what doesn't work. At times, it's going to get messy and ugly. Above all, it's going to be real. Because leadership—authentic, conscious leadership—is hard work. But it's a journey that's worth the effort.

You'll read stories and learn concepts that are straightforward and practical. You'll have an opportunity to look in the mirror, take stock of your current skillset, and improve on it. You'll gain tools that you can apply immediately in your work for tangible results. These tools will enable you to accomplish the following:

- Improve employee engagement
- Increase productivity
- Decrease levels of employee turnover
- Expand influence
- Decrease stress
- Improve overall work-life satisfaction

KEYS TO READING THIS BOOK

Cracking the Leadership Code is divided into four sections. Part I provides context for the challenges faced by today's leaders. In Chapter 1, you'll be introduced to the framework of the master keys: connection, communication, and collaboration. Chapter 2 shares a brief history of organizational leadership, and explains how you've unknowingly inherited the bad habits of previous generations of leaders. Chapter 3 discusses the cultural and societal forces that caused that Old-School leadership to stop working, and why leaders are struggling to keep up with the speed of changing times.

In Part II, you will learn how to decrypt the first of the essential leadership principles: **connection**. Chapter 4 discusses empathy, and explains why improving this soft skill can deliver huge business benefits. Chapter 5 details the daily challenges leaders face in practicing empathy and how to overcome them. Chapter 6 unscrambles the concept of leadership credibility—what it is, why it's important, and how you can build it.

Part III takes aim at one of the most challenging parts of leadership: **communication**. Chapter 7 untangles the confusing conundrum of communication. Chapter 8 cracks the communication code, giving you six keys to improve your communication immediately.

Part IV dives deep into the third essential leadership principle: **collaboration**. Chapter 9 clarifies motivation—what it is, what it isn't, and the common traps that leaders fall into when trying to motivate others. Chapter 10 offers a new model for motivational leadership:

being a motivational choice architect. It shares the two primary needs all people have: safety and energy. Chapter 11 describes the two essential needs that need to be met to enable high performance: purpose and ownership. Chapter 12 explains the employee experience and how you can influence it to improve teamwork and collaboration. Chapter 13 addresses the question no one wants to ask: how can I implement these great ideas when I'm already too busy? This chapter shares tools, tips, and techniques on how to make things simpler. At the end of each chapter is a resources section that distills the big ideas. You can use this to begin crafting your own personal leadership development plan.

Since the new millennium, I've worked with thousands of teams, and tens of thousands of leaders in 25 countries around the world. I've coached people from frontline employees to C-Suite executives to titans of Wall Street to dog food factory workers. I've worked with teams as small as two and have led workshops for more than 2,000 participants. I've worked with every industry you can think of, as well as some industries you probably don't know exist.

In my role, I've been given an all-access pass to hundreds of companies. While working behind the scenes, I'd get confidential briefings on a team or the company's most pressing business issues. I'd meet with key players, who'd confess their deepest dysfunctions and admit what was broken and needed fixing.

After gathering all that data, I'd search for clues, on the hunt to truly understand these people and teams. I fervently wanted to find out what made them tick, because I wanted to help them to tick better. Then, I'd go back and work with the individuals, teams, and/or whole companies.

On the surface, each team's and company's situation and issues were unique. However, as I began to work with more and more clients, I started to see that they weren't so unusual after all. Because each company had people, the key to improving their performance ultimately came back to the same set of root causes: some dimension of leadership. My task was to figure out which dimension and how to help them apply it in their work environment.

THE STORY BEHIND MY STORY

My entire life, I've been gripped by the question, "Why do people do what they do?" No matter how challenging or stressful the situation, I've always wanted to make sense of it. The need to make sense of stress goes way back for me. It started in my early childhood.

To preface this, my family loved me and fed me and housed me and did the best they could. However, I grew up in an apartment filled with screaming, stressful, dysfunctional leaders—that is, the adults. Even as a kid, I knew there had to be a better way. I could see the difference when I went to visit my friends. My friends' families would talk and listen to each other. They'd do stuff as a family together. Why couldn't my family be more like them? Why couldn't my mother and grandmother lead us more effectively?

Much of the time, my home life was like a toxic work environment. There was either yelling or a complete lack of communication. As a young child, I strived to please my mother and grandmother, thinking that if I did whatever they asked, then they'd be appeased and things would get better. As I got older, I realized that no matter how well I followed their instructions, my behavior didn't change their behavior. When I was the "good employee," I still got the toxic treatment. Eventually, I checked out. I mentally and emotionally detached.

That primary stressful setting affected me greatly. I became highly attuned to other people's emotions and behaviors. I studied psychology and theater—disciplines that focus on human behavior and motivation. I learned about group dynamics and facilitation skills. And although I couldn't use all those skills to help my first "workplace," I've been putting them to good use ever since.

What I've learned is that if you dig deep enough, there's always a story behind the dysfunction. If you can find a way to bring that story out of the shadow and into the light, there's the potential to change things. You can be freed up to lead with a story and not be stuck leading from the story.

In my case, I didn't really understand what was going on with my mother and grandmother until I was an adult. They'd hidden their stories from me when I was a child—maybe in an attempt to protect me. But their stories influenced our every interaction nonetheless.

I learned that my mother and grandmother were both Holocaust survivors. They had their lives torn apart by the horrors of war. Their crime? Being Jewish and living in Nazi-occupied Belgium during World War II.

My grandmother gave my mother away to the Belgian underground resistance to hide her as best they could. At the age of seven years old, my mother had her hair dyed blond and was given a false identity and address to memorize in case of capture. She was moved from orphanages to foster homes to convents to barns every few months. This went on for three years.

Meanwhile, my grandmother was hidden separately. But eventually she was discovered, arrested, and imprisoned in a Nazi concentration camp. She was one of the lucky ones; she was liberated at the end of the war. When my mother and grandmother were finally reunited in a Red Cross displaced persons camp, they pieced together the terrible truth: nearly all the rest of their family had perished.

You can imagine how living through such experiences would change your attitude and behaviors about the world. My grandmother lived the rest of her life vacillating between shell shock and rage. She could not move beyond her past. Yet she also served as the matriarch and head of our family—the person responsible for steering the rest of us and influencing our decisions.

I view my grandmother with compassion and can entirely understand why she behaved the way she did. However, no matter how much I loved her, there's no question that she was my first exposure to toxic leadership.

Ever since, in my personal and professional life, I've been driven to understand what actions:

- Produce or destroy trust
- Improve or stifle communication
- Build bridges or walls
- Create engagement or apathy
- Create high performance or high dysfunction

Each person in an organization carries his or her own history. In working with clients and learning their stories, I've seen patterns emerge—specifically, patterns in behavior. I've seen how these behaviors are reinforced by leaders and solidify into a company's culture. This culture would then in turn influence interactions each employee would have with coworkers, colleagues, and customers. This translates into the experience of "what it's like to work here." Although these forces are invisible, they impact on everything around them.

CRACKING THE CODE

I've watched countless leaders struggle, waylaid by the same behavioral traps over and over. Try as they might, they can't get out of the story and solve these problems on their own.

But every so often, I meet a leader who, like Neo in *The Matrix*, sees through the complexity and gets what leadership is all about. Matt was such a leader.

Matt was a district manager (DM) for a global fast-food restaurant chain. He'd been with the company for 23 years, and he was not just a DM. He was *the* DM. That is, he was the number-1 top-ranked and -performing DM in the entire company for the past two years running. Out of 100 leaders, he was at the top of the chart.

That "chart," by the way, is no mere metaphor. In Matt's company, every DM knew how they ranked—*daily*—on a "hot list" (a battery of performance measures) against their peers. These metrics included the following:

- Revenue per store
- Cost of goods
- Customer satisfaction
- Drive-thru wait times
- Employee retention

Matt wasn't always number 1—or even close. For years, he ranked in the bottom half of the hot list. Something had changed in Matt, and I needed to find out what it was.

It's been said that "success leaves clues." Matt was a potential role model for his 100 peers. I wanted to make sure they'd learn what he already knew. I asked Matt, "What do you do now as a leader that helped you to become number 1? What is it that your peers in the middle and bottom of the pack aren't doing?"

That question was no accident. A key to leadership development is to focus on behavior—what you say and what you do. He replied,

> Every single DM has got a lot to do. Each one of us is managing 8 to 10 stores. With all the numbers on the hot list, it's easy to focus on what's not measuring up and be in constant fix-it task mode.
>
> That's what I did when I started, I'd hustle from store to store in task mode. I'd come in and look for what was broken and instantly try to fix it. I thought that was my job as "the big boss."
>
> What I've learned is that people don't appreciate me breathing down their necks. They don't want a fixer: they want a leader.
>
> I've been doing this for a long time now. Over the years, I've realized that the key to making the numbers is to stop focusing on the numbers. My job is to focus on the people—because it's the people who make the numbers.
>
> When I first started out, I used to walk past people on the restaurant floor, and I didn't really pay attention to them. I just saw them as worker bees. Then, when they'd up and quit, I had no idea why. I was totally clueless. They might have been really upset or unhappy, and I would have completely missed it.
>
> The key to all of it is making people your priority. If you do that, not only will your results improve, your life will get a whole lot less stressful.

Everything Matt said made sense. But it wasn't enough. It was positive, but vague, like a feel-good, self-help book. He wasn't sharing the specifics of what he said or did that made the difference. During a pause, I jumped in to probe deeper, revisiting his point about focusing on the people. "When you're focused on them," I inquired, "what is it that you say and do?"

Matt stopped for a moment and took a big breath. He replied,

When I come into the store, I spend time with my people and ask them about their lives outside of work. I really listen to what they say, because how they answer tells me what's important to them, whether that's their kids, or a sports team, or whatever. Then, the next time I come in, I can start the conversation by asking about that topic, and we bond over it. By starting there, the team knows I care about them. Then, I listen to what's been going on in the store, and together we figure out ways to solve their issues.

I'd hit pay-dirt. Matt had shared his strategy for success. It was simple, clear, and replicable. I almost had what I needed to teach the other DMs how to do what he did. We weren't quite yet done.

From experience, I knew that just giving a list of to-dos to the other DMs wouldn't be enough. They also needed to learn the pitfalls they would face as they tried their hand with these new skills. Matt's road to the top of the chart hadn't been a straight line—he'd had his share of bumps along the way. Matt was happy to share his stumbling blocks. He explained what seeing employees as "worker bees" really meant behaviorally, and he went on to share other failures that, with time and reflection, had become lessons.

LET'S GET CRACKING

If you talk to cryptologists—people who crack codes for a living—one of the first things they'll tell you is that code breaking can be frustrating work. It's filled with wrong turns and mistakes, trial and error. You've got to be in it for the long haul. Calmness and patience are highly advised.

By picking up this book and reading this far, it's clear that you don't want to settle for being in the mediocre majority. You're genuinely interested in leading people well. You want to understand human behavior and how it affects high performance. You want insights so you can know what makes people tick and tools so you can help them tick better.

Most people spend their careers working in, at most, just a handful of organizations. They tend to rely on, know, and learn what they see firsthand. My professional career has been a gift. It's rare to get to work in hundreds of organizations in the span of just one career. I've been lucky enough to gain inside access to thousands of leadership experiences, and I'm delighted to get to share these lessons with you.

Let's begin by looking back at an epic failure that taught me a tremendous amount about the basics of leadership. Though it happened in 1999, that fiasco has been etched in my memory—in great part because it was all my own doing.

CONTEXT

Every traveler knows that the trip goes a lot better if you have an excellent map. A great map provides a clear big picture while still offering the appropriate amount of specific details. It clearly demarks boundaries so you can easily identify where you are and where you want to go. The journey of leadership development works the same way. The goal of this book is to serve as such a map. The concepts and tools that you learn will help you lead more effectively. You'll be able to multiply your influence and impact. As such, you'll accomplish more things in less time.

Part I gives an overview of the journey. It prepares you for the voyage ahead. You'll learn why leading others is more challenging—and more important—than ever before. You'll hear first-person accounts as to why some leaders succeed and others fail. You'll get a brief history of leadership and how the bad habits of previous generations of leaders have been passed down to you.

In addition, you'll become acquainted with the overarching leadership framework of connection, communication, and collaboration. An entire section of the book is devoted to exploring each of these principles later. Please note: this is no academic treatise. Based on the experience of working with thousands of leaders, you're going to get the inside scoop as to what works and what doesn't. It's not always pretty. But it is always real. Let's start cracking the leadership code.

Chapter 1

BECOMING A BETTER LEADER

The Basics

We're blind to our blindness. We have very little idea of how little we know. We're not designed to know how little we know.

—Daniel Kahneman

The ballots were all counted.
Final score: 38–6.
Thirty-eight votes to six!
And it wasn't me that won the 38. It was my opponent. *How could this be?*
...I lost? For real?
Wow!
Only six votes?
I sat in a puddle of disbelief.
That can't be true!
But it was true. When all was said and all was done, I'd lost.
By a landslide.
I'd been creamed.

This all happened in 1999, but it seems like yesterday.

I was living in New York City, where I was hoping to become the new executive director of a nonprofit leadership development organization. At the annual meeting the members elected new officers.

In my mind, I was a shoo-in for the job. No one else had worked as tirelessly as I had. No one else had the "feet on the street" experience that I had. No one else was more passionate than I was.

Committed to the cause, I was a "super-volunteer." I'd put in countless hours, doing anything and everything. The outgoing executive director had called me the organization's newest rising star.

I had one competitor for the job: Gary.

Gary was a newbie: he'd just joined in the past year. Gary owned his own business in the construction industry, where he'd been quite successful. However, when it came to our nonprofit, he was still green.

Yet, somehow, Gary had trounced me. He'd captured more than 85% of the vote.

What was his secret? How had he done it?

I wouldn't find out how he managed to beat me so soundly for another month. It took me that long to set up a meeting with Gary—and not because of a busy schedule. It was my ego. I couldn't face Gary. My pride was too hurt. I needed some time to lick my wounds before I could look him in the eye.

On a blustery gray day in early December, Gary and I finally met up for lunch. We met at the Galaxy Diner, a bustling spot smack dab in the middle of Hell's Kitchen. The Galaxy is a classic New York diner, where the size of the menu is only outdone by the size of the portions. The waitresses seem like they've been working there since diners were first invented.

After some small talk and minestrone soup, I casually told Gary how surprised I was about the outcome of the election. I asked him if he was surprised as well.

"No," he answered easily.

I was taken aback. He was serious. What did he know that I didn't know?

"How did you know that you'd get all those votes?" I asked him—expecting a quick, one-sentence answer.

I couldn't have been any more wrong.

Gary's response shocked me. He had thought this whole thing out:

> I reached out to people. I invited people out to coffee and to lunch. I got to know them. I asked them how long they'd been active in leadership development and with our nonprofit. I asked them what they liked about the organization. I asked them what they would change if they could. I asked them what they hoped the future might look like.
>
> Then, I shared why I was running for executive director. I told them how important this work is to me. I told them that I wanted to build a team of people to take this organization to the next level. I asked if they'd be a part of that team.
>
> Finally, I asked them to show up on election night and vote for me, so that we could be the team to make things happen.

As Gary finished, I felt lightheaded. I propped myself up on the red cushion of the booth.

His explanation made perfect sense. In fact, it was so perfect that it hit me like a blinding flash of the obvious.

Why hadn't I done that? Why hadn't I done anything even *close* to that?

I'd been living in a fantasy world. Whether you call it inexperience or ignorance, I had just expected to be elected. In hindsight, I could see that I'd made a whole lot of assumptions:

- People in the nonprofit would know about me.
- They would have heard about all the hard work that I had done on behalf of the organization for the past few years.
- All my previous efforts would speak for themselves.
- People would know who the "best" candidate was.
- People would vote based on merit.
- I'd "earned" the job, based on my excellence and tenure.
- People would vote for me.

Given my boatload of assumptions, I never even considered taking the step of actually asking people to show up and support me. So I hadn't. And, except for five other people, they didn't.

Ask for votes? Be that explicit? It wasn't my style. It seemed so weird. So ... direct.

But Gary knew something I didn't.

Gary knew that the key to successful leadership is influence, not authority. He wasn't interested in acquiring a title and throwing the weight of the position around. Gary knew that no one wanted to work under an authoritative leader.

The whole organization ran on the backs of volunteers. We felt connected to the mission and vision of the organization. Everyone was there out of commitment, not compliance. We did things because we cared. We offered our time, talents, and efforts because we wanted to, not because we had to.

As a volunteer, working from commitment had fueled my own journey for the past three years. However, as a candidate for executive director, I'd fallen for the leadership trap of my own ego.

My fantasy of becoming the person "in charge" had intoxicated me with visions of grandeur. I'd become aloof and had neglected the principles that really mattered. I'd already envisioned how everyone else would fall in line and do what I wanted them to do. I thought I was entitled to lead. This version of reality was crystal clear in my imagination. Sadly, I was blind to the greater truth.

Gary, however, knew that leadership isn't about what goes on in the mind of a leader: it's about what goes on in the minds of people they want to lead. Understanding how things really work, Gary tapped into their energy and explicitly asked them to show up and vote for him. And show up they did. And I lost.

The experience was incredibly humbling. However, that defeat turned out to be one of the most valuable lessons of my life. Gary, through his modeling, had provided me with a map of how to become a better leader (see Figure 1.1).

The loss to Gary burst the bubble of my ignorance. I suddenly realized that there was a lot about leadership that I didn't even know that I didn't know. In preparing and executing his election victory, Gary modeled three essential leadership principles: connection, communication, and collaboration.

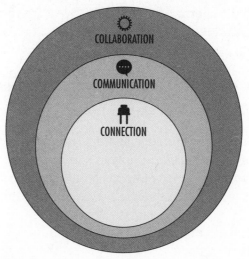

Figure 1.1   Core Components of Being
a Leader

CONNECTION

Invisible threads are the strongest ties.

—Friedrich Nietzsche

When you connect with people on a personal level, they feel that you care about them. Connection provides the spark that gets others to willingly follow your lead. It's the main ingredient in trust. Think of Gary's decision to invite members of the organization out to coffee and/or lunch. He made the members feel valued, and he sent a clear message that he wanted to get to know and understand them. Connection doesn't come cheap; you need to give of your time and attention. However, your investment pays dividends of engagement and commitment.

There's a simple yet powerful exercise I've done with dozens of groups to demonstrate the importance of connection to become a better leader.

Let's try it together right now.

Grab a pen and paper and think of the best leader you've ever worked with. It can be a work leader, school leader, sports coach, and so on. Make a list of qualities of that leader. What made them so great? Come up with at least 10 qualities.

Now review those qualities. Place each quality into one of these three categories:

1. Intelligence/smarts (understanding, reasoning, judgment)
2. Technical skills (specific ability to perform a job function well)
3. Emotional intelligence (able to identify/manage their own emotions and recognize/influence the emotions of others)

Which bucket did most of the qualities fall into?

If you're like most people, most of the qualities landed in the emotional intelligence bucket. Great leaders have a sixth sense for people. They have a knack for saying the right thing at the right time. They know that support should sometimes be nurturing and other times be challenging. Above all, they know how to connect.

COMMUNICATION

You can make more friends in two months by becoming interested in other people than you can in two years by trying to get other people interested in you.

—Dale Carnegie

Genuine, honest dialogue is one of the most powerful relationship-building tools in existence. In Gary's case, he intuitively recognized that the best leaders create candor and build trust by seeking first to understand. He didn't try to convince anyone why he was right for the job. Instead, he started by getting others to open up. He asked them to share about the things that really mattered to them. He sought to pull out their insight and experience.

Gary knew that the best way to create value in conversation was to create depth. He did this through deep listening. He asked big, broad, meaningful open-ended questions. Then, he took in what people really felt and really thought.

This ability to inquire—to draw out what matters most to people—is the basis for being an expert communicator. It's also a powerful means to build relationships.

Only after Gary made others feel understood did he seek to share his point of view. This tactic is an essential key to increasing influence. After all, at that point in the conversation, Gary knew exactly what was most important to the person he was speaking to; they had just told him.

For example, after hearing a member share their desire to attract more socioeconomically diverse members, Gary responded by sharing an idea on how to offer more scholarships for leadership trainings. This naturally created common understanding.

Gary's ability to create commonality is what psychologists call *the similarity attraction effect*. This is the phenomenon in which people are attracted more strongly to others who are similar to them ("like attracts like"). Gary's skill at creating Shared Understanding took a solid connection and made it even stronger. Then he could build a platform for working together.

COLLABORATION

> The fun for me in collaboration is, one, working with other people just makes you smarter; that's proven.
>
> —Lin-Manuel Miranda

Gary wasn't interested in leading in a vacuum. He knew that to achieve success, it would take a team. He didn't just ask for votes; he asked for help. He asked others to join him on this mission of building the organization.

In making this request, Gary tapped into one of the strongest motivators of human behavior: the desire to be part of something that is greater than oneself. When you work toward a greater good, it brings a tremendous sense of purpose and meaning.

Moreover, when something really matters to you, you naturally bring more passion and energy to it. You also feel the satisfaction that comes from making progress toward a meaningful goal.

Gary created a vision in which people could already see themselves as part of the bigger picture. He got them excited about turning that vision into a reality. The next logical step was to act: to elect Gary so that they could get started making their vision come to life.

Finding ways to inspire and motivate those whom you lead brings your influence to a whole new level. When you harness the power of collaboration, you will achieve so much more than you could otherwise.

LOOKING IN THE MIRROR

You don't need to change the world; you need to change yourself.

—Miguel Ruiz

Connection + Communication + Collaboration

= Your Leadership Effectiveness

Ultimately, your leadership will be judged by your behavior: what you say and what you do. How you show up as a person is how you show up as a leader. You can't separate the two.

This idea isn't new. About 2,500 years ago, Socrates wrote, "To know thyself is the beginning of wisdom." "Knowing thyself" has been rebranded as "self-awareness" in our present-day society.

Self-awareness is the foundation of emotional intelligence (EI). It's the basis of creating effective working relationships. After all, if you don't recognize your own drives and actions, how can you begin to understand the drives and actions of others?

Not only is EI essential to lead in today's organizations but also it's the competitive advantage of anyone who aspires to lead. In fact, when IQ and technical skills are roughly similar, EI accounts for nearly 90% of what moves people up the organizational ladder.[1]

Marshall Goldsmith, considered by many to be the world's preeminent executive coach, wrote a best-selling book called *What Got You*

Here Won't Get You There. If leaders want to continue to develop, he argues, they must grow and change—and the first step of change is self-awareness. You need to hold up the mirror and pay attention. After all, you can't change what you don't see. Self-awareness is the skill that enables you to transform unconscious incompetence or competence into conscious competence. You can't become excellent at anything if you're oblivious as to why and how you do it.

Know thyself. It sounds so easy.

But it's easier said than done. Looking in the mirror is a lot harder than it seems. It takes humility to recognize that what's staring back at you is less than perfect.

We humans have a cognitive bias called *illusory superiority*. It's the reason that 90% of drivers think their driving skills are above average.[2] It's common to overestimate our own abilities relative to others. Looking at our own flaws is hard. Some people find the process of self-examination so uncomfortable that they will repress, hide, or deny the facts. I certainly hid from the truth in the run-up to the election with Gary. However, as ostriches demonstrate so well, putting your head in the sand doesn't make reality go away.

If the idea of change makes you uncomfortable, you're on the right track. Leaders who are committed to developing themselves keep putting themselves in situations outside of their comfort zone. They know it's the only place they will grow.

FOCUS ON THE FUNDAMENTALS

Success is neither magical nor mysterious. Success is the natural consequence of consistently applying the basic fundamentals.

—Jim Rohn

When Gary shared his winning strategy with me, I was thunderstruck—and not just because it was a great strategy. I was astonished by how simple it was. Connection, communication, collaboration. In hindsight, it all just seemed obvious—common sense, even. So why hadn't I done something similar?

It's one thing to understand something conceptually. It's quite another to put it into practice. I thought I'd "got it." But all I had gotten was the idea of leading. I hadn't followed through with action. I thought leading meant being all sophisticated. These basics? They were beneath me.

Yet, those fundamentals are the foundation for success. No, they don't require a great deal of sophistication. But they do require unusual amounts of focus, effort, and tenacity.

As an example, imagine that you're a star high school basketball player. In fact, you're so good that you're voted an All-American. Division 1 colleges fall all over themselves to give you a scholarship to their school. You could go anywhere you want.

You decide to go to UCLA. UCLA has built an amazing program and has won the last seven men's NCAA championships. No other school has won more than two in a row.

You're excited. It's now the first day of practice. You've come to play for Coach John Wooden, the winningest coach in basketball history. Coach Wooden is known as "The Wizard of Westwood." What wisdom will he impart on the first day?

Coach Wooden begins the first lesson in the locker-room. He starts by telling you to take everything off of your feet. He then says,

> The most important part of your equipment is your shoes and socks. You play on a hard floor. So you must have shoes that fit right. And you must not permit your socks to have wrinkles around the little toe—where you generally get blisters—or around the heels.[3]

You might think, "Has coach lost his mind? Doesn't he know I'm an All-American athlete? Is he for real?"

Coach Wooden doesn't stop there. He details *how* to put on your socks and shoes—holding the sock up while you put on the shoe, how to tie it and double-tie it. "I don't want shoes coming untied during practice or during the game," he argues.[4]

What?!

You came all the way to UCLA to learn how to pull up your socks and tie your shoes!?

Coach Wooden then turns around and closes his practice by saying,

> If there are wrinkles in your socks or your shoes aren't tied properly, you will develop blisters. With blisters, you'll miss practice. If you miss practice, you don't play. And if you don't play, we cannot win. If you want to win Championships, you must take care of the smallest of details.[5]

Coach Wooden was a master of the details. In fact, over his career, he developed a philosophy of coaching and leadership that he called the "Pyramid of Success." Bigger things only came as a result of smaller things, and smaller things were based on fundamentals.

Whether it's basketball or leadership, success is based on fundamentals: learning them, mastering them, applying them, and teaching them to others.

These small details aren't hard to understand. The challenge is to consistently apply the fundamentals on a daily basis. That's what separates the amateurs from the pros and the average from the excellent.

Years ago, I had the opportunity to have dinner with a colleague and her father. Her father had started working more than 30 years before as a salesman for a food processing company, and, in the course of his career, he rose up the ranks and became CEO of what was a multibillion-dollar organization.

I asked him, "At what point in your career did you feel like you arrived? That you could relax and not work so hard to prove yourself? Was it when you became CEO?"

He beamed and broke into a hearty laugh. "Relax? Not prove myself? That's easy. I remember that day vividly. It was the day I retired."

He continued, "When you lead, you keep coming back to the fundamentals: being a role model, communicating clearly, managing your time, providing vision, making informed decisions. That never ends. The day you stop doing that is the day you get into trouble."

Connection, communication, and collaboration: you'll spot their fingerprints all over the handiwork of outstanding leaders. By the end of this book, you'll have a thorough understanding of these principles. You'll be armed with dozens of specific tools of how to apply them back at work. You'll be well equipped to make extraordinary leadership an everyday occurrence.

In doing so, you'll separate yourself from the pack. For as simple as the basics seem to be, they're not practiced consistently. These leadership fundamentals are sorely lacking in today's 21st-century organizations.

As we've already seen, most of today's leaders are mired in mediocrity. But it's not for lack of desire or effort. There are a lot of invisible forces working to get you stuck in a rut. The forces at play are much bigger than interactions at a personal level. As the acclaimed management consultant W. Edwards Deming stated, "A bad system will beat a good person every time."[6]

These undercurrents are cultural, institutional, and societal in origin. They've been around for a long time and affect us in ways we don't even realize. It's important to know how these dynamics shape the way you see, think, and act as a leader. Understanding them enables you to step back and look at leadership through a long lens and see the big picture.

When you have this context, the basics will be illuminated with a rationale you wouldn't have otherwise. You'll see how what you do fits into the larger whole. Then, when you apply the basics, you won't be mindlessly following a leadership checklist that someone else wrote out for you. So, before diving deep into these three fundamental principles, let's look at these influences and how we got into this mess in the first place.

Chapter Resources

Become a Better Leader

- I know that the key to successful leadership is influence, not authority.
- I recognize that leadership positions are privileges, not entitlements.
- I reach out and build relationships with others.
- I focus on building my emotional intelligence as much as my smarts and technical skills.
- I look for commonalities with others.
- I'm willing to look in the mirror and pay attention to what's really there.
- I work daily at practicing the fundamentals of leadership.

Chapter 2

YOUR INHERITED LEADERSHIP LEGACY

Progress, far from consisting [of] change, depends on retentiveness...
Those who cannot remember the past are condemned to repeat it.
—George Santayana

How did we get here?

How did we get to the point that employees have such low confidence in their leaders? How is it that more than half of employees don't trust their colleagues, leaders, and companies? Why do we have such a failure of credibility? How did we wind up with such a crisis of leadership? Consider the following story:

A young woman decides to host a holiday dinner party in her own apartment for the very first time.

She's planning to cook her family's traditional meal: a holiday roast. The recipe has been passed down from mother to daughter for generations.

She buys all the ingredients and looks over the recipe. She notices something a bit odd. The last step of the recipe says, "Cut the end off the roast before you put it in the oven."

This makes no sense to her. So, she calls up her mother.

29

"Mom, I'm cooking the family holiday roast, and the recipe says to cut the end off the roast before you put it in the oven. I didn't know you're supposed to do that. Why do you do that?"

Her mother replies, "That's a great question. You know, I don't really know. That's the way my mom taught it to me. Why don't you ask grandma?"

So the young woman calls her grandmother and asks the same question about the roast. Her grandma answers, "I don't know. That's the way my mom taught me. Why don't you ask her why?"

The young woman's great-grandmother is 94 years old but still has all her faculties about her. The young woman calls her up.

"Great-grandma, I'm making the family traditional holiday roast for the first time. The recipe says that you should cut the end off the roast before you put it in the oven. I asked my mother why you do that, and she didn't know, so I asked grandma, and she didn't know, so that's why I'm calling you. Why do you cut the end off the roast?"

After a long pause, there's a sigh on the far end of the phone line.

"We had a small oven."

I've shared this story with countless groups over the years. It always gets a huge laugh, because the absurdity is all too familiar. People know what it's like to work at organizations suffering from "small-oven thinking." So many aspects of their workplace don't make sense, and yet, just like the mom and the grandma in the story, they keep doing things the same way. Questioning the past is too risky. It's safer to keep doing things the way they've always been done.

Ultimately, the reason companies behave in a small-oven manner is that their leaders have a small-oven mind-set. They have a built-in immunity to change. As Lisa Bodell, CEO of Futurethink, an innovation consultancy, says, "The only thing more resistant to change than a human being is a company."

Caught up in the pressure to constantly produce, many of today's leaders don't take time to stop and question their own methods. It's all action, no reflection. When it comes to how they lead, they do what they do because that's the way it was always done. Yet, isn't doing the same thing repeatedly and expecting a different result the definition of insanity?

The nature of the workplace has radically transformed over the past 30 years. These changes didn't happen overnight. There was no blaring of trumpets or great dramatic flourishes pronouncing that a new era of work had arrived. It crept in slowly, one day at a time. And as the weeks and months and years passed, our work world has been irrevocably altered.

Consider, for example, the number of business communication interactions the average executive takes part in. In the 1970s, it was about 1,000 a year. Today, it's more than 30,000 a year.[1] This tidal wave of information has dramatically changed the skills leaders need to function effectively today.

Maria, an executive vice president for a luxury retailer, describes it this way:

> I was hired to head up marketing for this company. But do you know what my real job title is? I'm an email-processing machine. On an average day, I get 300 emails in my inbox. I'm not talking spam or junk or company-wide CCs. Three hundred items that clamor for my attention.
>
> And of course I can't really give my full attention to these items because I'm booked into back-to-back meetings all day long. Most days, I get excited for 6:00 p.m. to come, because then I can get some of my actual work done. Look, if I'm really honest, in the constant hustle, things are slipping through the cracks. There's just too much to do on the to-do list. For one thing, I'm not spending enough time developing my team. Something's going to give. I'm just not sure what it is.

In addition to having to process more information, the boundaries between work and "life" are disappearing. People are working longer and harder than ever. A recent study found that although the 40-hour week is generally accepted as "normal," adults employed full-time have reported working an average of 47 hours each week.[2] They're also expected to check in more frequently: nights, weekends, and vacations. A survey of employed email users finds that 22% are expected to respond to work emails when they're not at work.[3]

Jasmine, a middle manager at a technology company, explains the stress this way:

> When I wake up in the morning, the first thing I think about is my to-do list. It's never ending and seems to get longer every month. When I think about it, I get anxious, because I know I won't have enough time to do what I need to do. Then the day goes by, and I do what I can, but most nights, when I'm trying to wind down and get to sleep, my last thought of the day is "I didn't get enough done."

Leaders like Jasmine, caught on the hamster wheel of activity, are too busy to deal with the complexities of leading in today's workplace. What's more, they're too overloaded to recognize or admit that the way they're working isn't working.

Although information technology has advanced, our leadership practices have not. Most of today's leaders are painfully unaware of how all the changes in the workplace have made it so much more difficult to lead effectively. They don't realize that they're attempting to lead in the early 21st century using early 20th-century practices. The practices they're using were designed for a very different world. Continuing to use them perpetuates small-oven thinking.

So what's a 21st-century leader to do? What's the best way for leaders to change their approach to leading? The way to go forward is to look backward. After all, to get a handle on the future, you must understand the past.

Like the young woman and her family recipe, you can't take what's given to you for granted. Becoming aware of your inherited leadership legacy is crucial, because you won't be able to change what you don't notice.

A BRIEF HISTORY OF LEADERSHIP IN ORGANIZATIONS

New parents often experience a moment that shocks and amazes them: the first time they catch themselves doing or saying the exact thing that their own parents did or said to them. Without even trying, they've internalized the behaviors of the previous generation.

Most people who go to work as managers and leaders in organizations don't study the history of organizational management and leadership. They're too busy doing their day jobs. They're not aware that their leadership philosophy (with all its assumptions and beliefs) is based on a worldview that has long outlived its shelf life.

Before the dawn of the industrial revolution, commerce was manufactured in people's homes and on small-scale farms. Work was done using basic hand tools and machines. For example, textiles were made on hand looms and then sold at local markets. The homemade nature of this work meant that production was limited.

However, all that changed with the arrival of industrial-era machines and tools. In the textile industry, the spinning Jenny (a form of power loom) changed the game. Before its invention, a worker could only work one spool of yarn at a time. The first spinning Jenny could work *eight* spools. As the technology improved, the number of spools on the power loom grew to 120.

With the advent of these new machines, a seismic shift occurred. The center of work moved from homes to factories. Mass production bloomed, and factory workers were in high demand.

For the first time in the history of human commerce, the birth of the factory era created a new necessity: the need for a large-scale labor force. Factory owners had sunk considerable investment into factories and equipment. They were keen to harness the newfound power of steam and electricity. To make their resources profitable, they recognized that they'd also need to find ways to harness the power of the *human* resource.

With this insight came a series of new questions. How would these employees be hired? Trained? Organized? Led? Which ways of leading were better than others? The attempts to answer these questions led to the discipline now known as management.

Organizational management was started by mechanical engineers: people who were trained to see the world as engineering problems to solve. The aim of scientific management (as it came to be called) was to improve efficiency, especially labor productivity. The goal of leadership was to get labor to do more work in less time.

For the manager, people were not the competitive advantage: the factory was. Having the latest and greatest machine was of primary importance. Employees were subordinate cogs in this mechanical worldview.

The man considered to be the father of scientific management was an engineer named Frederick Winslow Taylor. Taylor had a deep-seated belief: he thought employees were only out to take advantage of their employers and therefore must be controlled. Taylor was certain that most of the employees on the shop floor spent a lot of their time on the job goofing off and working slower than they could.

Left to their own devices, Taylor believed, workers would work at the slowest rate possible, a behavior commonly known as *soldiering*. From Taylor's perspective, soldiering wasn't just bad business; it was morally reprehensible. He wrote of soldiering as "the greatest evil with which the working-people ... are now afflicted."[4]

Therefore, employees were not to be trusted. Taylor felt employees spent every possible moment conniving new schemes to take advantage of their employer:

> Hardly a competent workman can be found who does not devote a considerable amount of time to studying just how slowly he can work and still convince his employer that he is going at a good pace.[5]

For Taylor, the perfect worker was the one who questioned nothing, understood everything, and did anything he was told to do. Taylor wrote that the ideal worker should be "so stupid ... that he more nearly resemble[d] in his mental make-up the ox than any other type."[6]

With the publication of *Principles of Scientific Management* in 1911, Taylor's ideas spread like wildfire. His ideas became the dominant mode of business thinking for the first half of the 20th century.

Taylor's beliefs set the norms of how a workplace should work. In a very short time, the prototypical relationship between leader and employee was born. It was a relationship forged in the cauldron of power, fear, and control.

THE TAYLOR APPROACH TO LEADERSHIP

In Taylor's system, work was firmly divided between management and labor. Management did all the "thinking" and laborers did all the "labor." If you were a manager, communication meant telling people what to do.

Moreover, that communication was top-down: no questions asked. After all, in a giant machine, what "parts" ask questions? Telling people what to do became the norm of factory floor communication. The job of the leader was to give orders and maintain order.

Think for yourself? Speak up? Challenge authority? If you were a worker, raising your hand and speaking out might get you killed. Not metaphorically, but literally.

Labor-related violence usually began with workers speaking up and wanting better working conditions. In fact, between 1850 and 1920, in the United States alone, there were at least 74 separate incidents when workers calling for safer conditions were killed by law enforcement officials, members of the company militia, armed detectives, and guards.

In the industrial era, workers were expected to do, not think. They were meant to show up, shut up, and do as they were told. For the jobs at hand, there wasn't much need for analysis and complex problem-solving.

Henry Ford, founder of the Ford Motor Company (and one of Taylor's best-known disciples), pioneered the use of the assembly line in the auto industry. His disdain for the aptitude of his workers was quite well known, famously quipping, "Why is it every time I ask for a pair of hands, they come with a brain attached?"

Taylor and his engineering disciples (known as *Taylorites*) were obsessed with getting workers to do more work in less time. Using stopwatches and some very fuzzy math, they originated what became known as time-motion studies. They believed there was one best way to do things, and management's job was to find it. Once "the way" was found, management's job was simple: command-and-control.

WHY COMMAND AND CONTROL ENDURED

Command-and-control was the dominant mode of leadership for most of the 20th century. In hindsight, it's hard to believe that so many employees would put up with practices and conditions that we'd now find intolerable. But there were quite a few factors that existed that allowed leaders to successfully employ command-and-control for so long.

Jobs and Education Were Scarce

At the turn of the 20th century, the standard of living was much lower than it is today. Disposable income was the privilege of only a wealthy few.

There was no middle class to speak of. In 1900, the average family had an annual income of $3,000 (in today's dollars). Most people had no indoor plumbing, no phone, and no car. About half of all American children lived in poverty. Most teens didn't attend school; instead, they labored in factories or fields.[7]

Working to put food on the table was no metaphor. It was literal. Opportunities for steady employment were few and far between. People who landed a factory floor job with a regular paycheck were primed for obedience; questioning authority would put their golden egg at risk. As such, they'd put up with a lot of lousy behavior.

Factory Work Paid Well

On a cold day in January 1914, an estimated 10,000 people lined up outside of Ford Motor Company's employment office desperate to be hired.[8] Henry Ford had announced an extraordinary offer to job candidates: he was willing to pay $5/day. That was more than twice the average factory wage at the time. Ford set a precedent that was followed by other companies over time: pay your workers well, and turnover and absenteeism will go down. After this wage increase, the Ford Motor Company doubled its profits in less than two years.

Ford's move to raise wages also gave birth to the U.S. industrial middle class. A salary of five dollars a day allowed workers to enjoy a standard of living the likes of which had never been seen by working-class people. There's a sign outside the abandoned Model-T plant in Highland Park, Michigan, that says, "Mass production soon moved from here to all phases of American industry, and set a pattern of abundance for 20th-century living."[9]

Workers knew (and were often reminded by managers on the floor) that if they didn't want to do the work, there were five other people outside who'd be ready to jump at a moment's notice. The golden handcuffs of high wages kept most people obedient in the command-and-control system.

Work Was Static

For most employees, factory work didn't involve a great deal of technical skill. The basic job functions of what needed to be done on the assembly line could be learned relatively quickly. The skill that was in demand was perseverance. Workers would have to stand in one place on the line and do the same thing over and over again. All day. Every day.

Because the work process was so repetitive, managers were not interested in things being done differently. Traits such as innovation or creativity were off limits for employees. "Just do your job" was a key operating principle.

After all, there were production quotas to hit. Managers didn't want anything to stand in the way of that assembly line. Thus, a "do as I tell you to do" ethic became the norm.

Business Cycles Were Slow

Managers focused on command and control of the labor force because on a day-to-day basis, things stayed pretty much the same. For example, the Ford Motor Company started manufacturing the Model T automobile in 1908. They kept manufacturing that same make and model of car until 1927. For 20 years, the Model T didn't change. As Henry Ford famously said, "Customers could get it in any color they wanted, as long as it was black."

Because the speed of market changes was so slow, leaders weren't worrying about external threats to their business model. What they did last month they'd do next month. This plodding pace enabled leaders to spend their time and energy on controlling the workforce to preserve the status quo.

Less Access to Information

At the start of the 20th century, employees had no way of knowing and no way of finding out if the grass was greener at some other company. There was no LinkedIn to network for new job opportunities, no monster.com to read up on new job postings, and no glassdoor.com to find out if the company you're interviewing with is a place that you'd actually want to work.

Living in this information vacuum, workers were stuck in their circumstances. However, because the lack of information was such a cultural norm, no one expected anything else. They just put up with their situation.

Through its first few decades, command-and-control achieved tremendous results. In this new industrial era, it was considered an essential part of business success. Its philosophy expanded from factories to many other sectors of the economy. As it grew, it also migrated to business school classrooms, where it became standard dogma for much of the 20th century.

SCIENTIFIC MANAGEMENT'S INFLUENCE ON BUSINESS SCHOOLS

Did you ever wonder where business schools came from? They haven't been around forever. Harvard University was the first American university to offer a Master's in business administration. Founded in 1908, it based its first-year curriculum on Frederick Taylor's principles of scientific management. The program was built on analysis, synthesis, logic, rationality, and efficiency.

The MBA approach to managing a business was built on the belief that an organization (and its people) functioned like a machine. With proper tinkering on the part of management, the machine could be engineered for the ultimate prize: continuous peak efficiency. Every challenge the organization faced was an engineering problem to be solved. Sound familiar?

If you listen closely to the language of business, you can still clearly hear the language of engineering. Its mechanistic, dehumanizing influence has affected beliefs, words, and behaviors in the workplace for more than a century. Some common examples of this include these concepts:

- Your job fits in a *box* on the *bottom* of the org chart.
- You report to your *superior*. You are his or her *subordinate*. You report *up* to that person.
- You are a *rank- and-file* employee.
- If we don't have direct reports, we may have *dotted-line responsibilities*.
- Salaries are one of the *biggest costs we incur* around here.
- We don't have enough *human resources*.
- Let's *deploy* for this new product launch.
- I'm going to send this up the *food chain* for approval.
- Let's *interface* before the 3 p.m. meeting.
- Get the proposal ready *double-time!*
- It's important that we *drill this down* to the *front lines*.
- We'll get this out to the *masses*.

How would it make you feel to know that there are leaders who are meeting together, trying to find the best way to drill stuff into you, along with the rest of the frontline masses?

In large organizations, personnel networks were modeled on the military, with layer on layer nested into the chain of command. Control was established through rigid hierarchy, structures, and processes. Rules were designed to maintain order and the status quo. Going outside the lines was considered a rebellious act and insubordination.

In this system, newly minted MBA graduates would join "high-potential" programs in large companies. Once on board, they would rely on the strengths that got them jobs in the first place: analysis and problem-solving. They'd in turn become the next generation of business leaders, continuing this cycle of mechanical thinking they'd known for their whole professional lives.

The rule of thumb was that employees were expected to be loyal and obedient. Junior employees knew their place: wait your turn, pay your dues, put in your time, and you'll be rewarded with a chance to climb the ranks. Then, you'd gain more money, prestige, power, a better parking space, and the corner office.

THE LEGACY STOPS PAYING DIVIDENDS

For much of the 20th century, the value proposition of the corporation was that if you were a dutiful employee, you'd have a job for life, a gold watch after 20 years of work, and a comfortable pension waiting for you in retirement. Things hummed along like this for decades, and traditional leaders kept managing using their rulebooks and regulation manuals.

This was the legacy that was passed down from one generation of leader to the next. Maybe this is the leadership recipe that you inherited: keep things orderly, and all will be well.

There's just one problem: it doesn't work anymore.

Twenty years with the same company? Not likely. Comfortable pension? Even less likely. Things humming along smoothly? Not a chance. The man in the grey flannel suit is long gone. He's been replaced by members of the free agent nation.

Command-and-control is no longer a viable leadership strategy. Society has transformed, and amid these changes, the rules of business have been rewritten. The relationship of employee to employer is radically different. In this new world of work, Old-School leadership didn't really stand a chance. The next chapter explains why Old-School leadership stopped working.

Chapter Resources

Break Free of Old Leadership Paradigms

- I question my inherited leadership habits.
- I start with a leadership paradigm of trust, not fear.
- I use a leadership language that describes people, not machines.
- I understand where the command-and-control style came from, and why it lasted for so long.

Chapter 3

WHY OLD-SCHOOL LEADERSHIP STOPPED WORKING

In the future, there will be no female leaders. There will be just leaders.
—Sheryl Sandberg

On February 19, 2017, Susan Fowler published a blog post on her personal website. The software engineer, by her own account a "really introverted and really shy"[1] person, had previously blogged on various subjects, including computer science, myrmecology (the study of ants), philosophy, physics, and software engineering. However, on this day in February, she decided to tell a "strange, fascinating, and slightly horrifying story that deserves to be told while it is still fresh in my mind, so here we go."[2]

Fowler's post, titled "Reflecting on One Very, Very Strange Year at Uber," detailed her personal account of the rampant sexism and systematic culture of sexual harassment at Uber, the multibillion-dollar ride-hailing company and her former employer. Clocking in at 2,910 words, her essay quickly went viral.

Fowler's post was the catalyst that sparked a chain of events that led to the termination of more than 20 Uber employees, including cofounder

43

and CEO Travis Kalanick. Further investigation into the company's business practices revealed even more wrongdoings. These revelations hurt Uber's business. It lost significant market share to Lyft, a smaller player in the ride-sharing industry.[3]

The influence that Susan Fowler and her story carries represents a giant swing in the power dynamics of the workplace. Fowler, a single employee in a large organization, had the information and the platform to broadcast her insider experience to the world. She affected public sentiment in a way that wasn't possible in the early days of the industrial revolution.

Clearly, this was not the work of a person who "resembled in his [or in this case, her] mental make-up the ox more than any other type." The world that Frederick Winslow Taylor knew has vanished. In its place, we have a workplace that moves lightning fast and is perpetually in flux. The skills needed—by both leaders and employees—to navigate this sea of uncertainty is profoundly different. To succeed, today's leader needs to know how to create an optimal work climate suited to our era.

In a recent study, the consulting firms Towers Watson and Oxford Economics asked employers what skills managers and employees will need most in the next 5 to 10 years. The top skills noted were as follows:

- Relationship building
- Teaming
- Co-creativity
- Brainstorming
- Cultural sensitivity
- Ability to manage diverse employees[4]

In another study (conducted by IBM), 1,700 CEOs from 64 countries in 18 industries were asked, "Which are the most important leadership qualities to possess?"

The top four responses:

1. Collaborative
2. Communicative
3. Creative
4. Flexible[5]

These two studies share a common denominator. The leadership skills now most in demand are what are commonly known as the "soft" (or people) skills. Positive attitude, working well with a team, and being adaptable are all examples of these soft skills.

It wasn't always this way. The fact that these soft skills are now the top priority is a drastic change from the days when the skills considered most valuable were the "hard" (or technical) skills. Examples of hard skills include business acumen, data analysis, and quantitative decision-making.

You need go back no further than the late 1970s to find the difference. Back then, if a child was a good student and wanted to advance to the top rung of the professional ladder, then the student was expected to become either a doctor or lawyer. Back in the day, medicine and law sat on the top of the academic and professional hierarchy. Follow the linear track and do well, and you'd be rewarded with a highly compensated, successful career. To be a doctor or a lawyer was the epitome of what the management author Peter Drucker called *knowledge work*.

According to Drucker, knowledge workers differentiated themselves through their "ability to acquire and to apply theoretical and analytic knowledge."[6] In the industrial age, workers were prized for their brawn. It was the managers and leaders who were prized for their brains, more specifically, their analytical brains. In particular, the analytical types—the engineers, the lawyers, the doctors—ruled the roost at work.

But then things changed. In the information age (1980s to the present) knowledge work isn't the province of a rare few occupations. Now, it's the de facto way of working in every industry. The ability to think critically and creatively has been pushed down through the organizational pyramid right out into the front lines. Responding to customer needs quickly and competently is no longer exceptional; it's the ticket to entry to play in the game of business.

In this new world, leaders can no longer be narrow, linear directors. When Old-School leadership rubs up against New-School knowledge work, the results can be disastrous. Susan Fowler's blog about her experience at Uber is a case in point.

The nature of what leaders need to do has transformed. Leaders now need to coordinate and facilitate complex interactions with a variety of different people. As such, their need to connect, communicate, and collaborate is more important than ever. This change of focus is captured perfectly by the title of Daniel H. Pink's seminal book, *A Whole New Mind: Why Right Brainers Will Rule the Future*.

This change didn't just happen out of the blue. Building on Pink's argument, the end of the 20th century brought with it three megatrends—massive societal shifts—that altered the world in which we live and work. For anyone who wants to be able to understand and influence others, knowing how these megatrends have shaped our beliefs and behaviors is essential.

MEGATREND 1: GLOBAL AFFLUENCE AND CHOICE

Since the start of the industrial revolution, the world has gotten wealthier and wealthier. In the United States alone, in the period between 1820 and 1998, real GDP (gross domestic product) per capita increased 21.7-fold, or an average of 1.73% per year. Measured in constant 1990 dollars, the GDP per capita in 1820 was $1,257. In 1998, it was $27,331.[7]

Increasing affluence isn't just a U.S. phenomenon. According to the World Bank, global GDP has increased from $3,692 in 1960 to $10,284.[8] And this boom in affluence hasn't been limited to wealth; people have gotten healthier as well. Just since 1960, average world life expectancy has soared from 52.58 years to 71.89 years in 2015.[9] As Richard Easterlin puts it,

> Most people today are better fed, clothed, and housed than their predecessors two centuries ago. They are healthier, live longer, and are better educated … Although the picture is not one of universal progress, it is the greatest advance in the condition of the world's population ever achieved in such a brief span of time.[10]

This higher standard of living has created an ever-increasing global marketplace. More people have more money to buy more things. Combine more money with decreased transportation costs and improved manufacturing technology, and you've got the ideal environment to create a mass proliferation of stuff. We are truly living in a material world.

Plenty has become a fact of life for most Americans. In the United States, there are more automobiles than there are licensed drivers to drive them. The average U.S. home has only 2.5 people but 2.86 TV sets.[11] All this stuff has led to the boom of a whole industry: self-storage. The self-storage industry is now a $32.7 billion industry in the United States[12]: three times larger than the motion picture business's revenue.

As a society, we've been living with so much stuff for so long that we now take it for granted. This affluence has not only invaded our closets and garages but also it's taken up residence in our psyches. It's changed our entire relationship to the idea of choice.

Consider that a century ago, if you wanted to eat cereal for breakfast, you'd go to the market and buy some type of uncooked grain: wheat, rye, oats. You'd bring it home and cook it yourself.

Today, if you wanted to buy hot cereal, you could go to the store and buy bulk oats. But would you choose organic or conventional? Slow-cook or quick or instant? Steel-cut or rolled? Or would you prefer to buy pre-packaged oats? Single-serve pouches? Plain? Maple and brown sugar? Apples and cinnamon? Peaches and cream? Raisin, date, and walnut? Apple and cranberries? (I'll stop … you get the idea.)

Choice after choice after choice. And we're only talking oatmeal. If you wanted cold cereal, you have an entire aisle filled with shelves of boxes of different shapes, grains, colors, and flavors.

The mind-set of "have it your way" goes way beyond the cereal aisle. It's permeated most of our day-to-day lives. We expect choice in our cereal, our sneakers, our handbags, in practically everything. With so much more supply than demand, the abundance of choices has shifted the balance of power from producers to consumers.

As consumers, our very beliefs about what it means to consume have also changed. With one-click ordering and drone delivery, our expectations have risen dramatically. We relate to the very concepts of "needing," "wanting," and "having" in a very different way than people did 100 years ago. What's now perceived as a "necessity" is very different. Someone might casually say, "I need to get the latest model of iPhone," and not even realize that they don't actually *need* it: they *want* it.

Why should leaders care about these dynamics of choice and affluence? In this age of abundance, it's obvious that we have higher expectations as consumers. Less obvious, but equally important, is that our expectations as employees have also increased.

For many people, work is far more than just a job. It's where we go for inspiration and motivation. It's the place we forge our identities. It's what we answer with when someone says, "What do you do?"

In their book *The Human Capital Edge*, Ira Kay and Bruce Pfau share research on what employees want from work. It turns out that regardless of race, gender, or age, there are four key questions that employees ask when they consider joining, engaging, or staying with a company:

- Is this a winning organization that I can be proud of?
- Can I maximize my performance on the job?
- Are people treated well economically and interpersonally?
- Is the work itself fulfilling and enjoyable?[13]

It's clear from these questions that today's employees aren't going to work only to take home a paycheck. They also want to take home meaning and purpose.

This is what Susan Fowler was looking for at Uber. Similar to every employee, Fowler asked herself these four key questions. To discover the answers, she looked first to the same place that all employees look: to the behavior of the company leaders. Through their actions, they set the foundation for the company culture. Their actions say, "This is how things get done around here." Fowler was horrified by the response from upper management after she shared her incident of sexual harassment. She quickly hit a personal tipping point at which she could no longer reconcile the disconnect between the Uber culture and her personal values.

A hundred years ago, if a factory worker didn't feel aligned with the values of the organization, that person, like Fowler, had the option to resign. But Susan Fowler could do much more than just quit her job.

MEGATREND 2: COMPUTERIZATION

Fowler's blog post wouldn't have wielded such force if hundreds of thousands of people hadn't read it. Given the ubiquity of our digital devices today, it's easy to take for granted the technology that enabled so many people to read her post in the first place.

Older readers will recognize that just a generation ago, what a big deal (and cost) it was to make a "long-distance" call. Today, with Skype and other web-based services, you can video chat for hours for free. We are all the sons and daughters of the fiber-optic revolution, which enables data, ideas, and even 3-D objects to be shared as easily with someone on another continent as with someone in another room down the hall. Moreover, sharing and applying information is the primary driver in most modern workplaces.

The explosion of cheap computing power pushed us out of the industrial age and into the information age. Computerization has transformed the nature of work. Repetitive, algorithmic parts of jobs have been automated, outsourced, and offshored.

What remains for the worker is knowledge work. This type of work is heuristic, meaning that it's not predictable, and there's no clear-cut predefined answer. It relies on having ideas, creating strategies and hypotheses, testing, and observing what works or doesn't work.

Knowledge work is filled with challenge and variety. Not only do knowledge workers need to "come with a brain attached" but also they need to continuously use it. They're asked to creatively problem-solve, which involves these skills:

- Correctly framing the problem/challenge
- Generating multiple ideas to solve the problem
- Choosing the best idea(s) to implement
- Implementing a solution
- Noticing the outcome and adjusting solutions as necessary

Knowledge work is on the rise, and non-knowledge work is on the wane. Today, it's commonplace to buy groceries in a supermarket and never deal with a live person. It's the norm to bank via computer. Driverless cars are on the horizon. A study by the McKinsey Global

Institute found that from 2001 to 2009, the number of routine transaction jobs such as bank tellers and checkout clerks decreased by 700,000 in the United States. Manufacturing jobs over that same period decreased by 2.7 million.[14]

Although routine transaction and manufacturing jobs have decreased, jobs dependent on human interaction—doctors and teachers, for example—have increased by 4.8 million. Interaction jobs have become "the fastest growing category of employment in advanced economies."[15]

Leading knowledge workers requires a more complete approach than leading in past generations. No longer are employees seen as mindless worker bees. Now, leaders need to be more involved and nurture and develop the whole person that comes attached to the pair of hands.

Some organizations have progressed with the times, and their leadership philosophies reflect this new world of work. Sadly, others haven't. They remain trapped in their inherited history and the archaic thinking of Frederick Winslow Taylor. The command-and-control paradigm of leadership is still alive and well. It's why the data say there are such low levels of leadership effectiveness and trust. Leading through fear and threats suffocates good decision-making and keeps teams mired in mediocrity.

Esther, a relatively new CEO of a regional bank, shared an example of her top-down culture this way:

One of the first things I noticed around here is that our people don't feel empowered to speak up. When I first came on board, I sat down with the executive team (my direct reports) and asked them to show me the project plans for their top priorities. As they reviewed their plans, they shared the plan deadlines with me. I asked them, "How did you choose these dates for these projects?"

They said, "We tell the teams when things are due."

"Did you get any input from the teams on the deadlines?" I asked. "Did you think to ask the people doing the work when they could get things done?"

There was a long silence. "No. That's how we've always set deadlines. We tell them what to do. No one ever pushes back on the deadlines."

The kicker of the whole thing? The deadlines are consistently missed.

At Esther's company, this top-down style neglects a key ingredient to lead knowledge workers: trust. When knowledge workers are trusted, they feel empowered to be creative, solve problems, and perform better. For sustainable success in the long term, trust is a must.

MEGATREND 3: TRANSPARENCY

In *To Sell Is Human*, Daniel H. Pink shares a huge idea that has radically altered our information economy: the switch from information asymmetry to information symmetry.[16] For example, as Pink illustrates, until quite recently, if you wanted to buy a car, you were at a distinct disadvantage. The car dealer had access to more information than you did. This information asymmetry meant that sellers had the power to withhold information about product quality. Were you buying a decent car or a lemon?

You'd see the sticker price, but it'd be difficult to learn the average price of that make and model. Were you paying a fair price or being gouged? You could try to haggle the price down, and then, if you still weren't sure, you could walk off the lot and travel from dealer to dealer to create a hypothesis of a best educated guess. This approach would take a lot of time. It'd also create a lot of stress by having to negotiate with every single dealer.

Information asymmetry meant that the buyer had to be cautious. Not having adequate information meant that customers had low trust in merchants. Thus, transactions would move rather slowly.

That all changed with the internet. Suddenly, there were web-based companies whose sole purpose was creating information symmetry. They wanted to make sure that customers had access to as much accurate information as possible. Information symmetry facilitates trust between buyers and sellers and levels the playing field.

Avis Steinlauf, the CEO of the automotive information company Edmunds, explains, "It's remarkable how simply providing a fair, upfront price can get deals off on the right foot. Our focus moving forward is to continue identifying these pain points and figure out how Edmunds.com can play a role in building a bridge of trust between car shoppers and dealers."[17]

The auto industry isn't the only sector in which the rules of the information asymmetry game have changed. In real estate, websites such as Redfin, Trulia, and Zillow share important information with eager house hunters.

Like it or not, transparency is the new normal for leaders in every industry. On the internal side, websites such as Glassdoor allow employees to post confidential career information. It gives job candidates insight on how the company is managed, what it's like to work there, and average salaries. Pre-internet, it was nearly impossible to gain this kind of insider knowledge.

In addition, social media gives every employee a platform to broadcast his or her views. Fowler's post went viral because it was shared on Facebook, LinkedIn, and Twitter. The #metoo movement (which gained momentum in the wake of Fowler's post) calling out sexual harassment and assault has toppled leaders in multiple industries, including Hollywood, politics, journalism, music, science, and academia.

Leaders need to be aware that not only can every employee broadcast his or her views but also so can every customer. With a cellphone camera in everyone's pocket, anyone can become a frontline journalist.

Consider the fiasco that United Airlines went through in April 2017 when one passenger filmed another passenger being forcibly dragged from an airplane. The shocking video was posted on YouTube and received over four million views. United Airlines was caught in a public relations nightmare, and their company stock dropped $1.4 billion due to the incident.[18]

In the age of transparency, command-and-control leadership loses its iron grip. People have options. If they're dissatisfied, knowledge workers can take their valuable skills and easily go work somewhere else. They know that with a few clicks on LinkedIn, they can search out greener pastures. They don't have to put up with lousy leadership that was the norm a couple of generations ago.

Smart leaders understand the accountability that comes with increased transparency. They know that organizational missteps can bring huge consequences. Every unhappy customer or employee can blog, share, or tweet his or her frustration to the world.

On the flipside, smart leaders also recognize the huge opportunity that increased transparency brings. Employees and customers can become raving fans and brand ambassadors if you exceed their expectations. Some leaders have built their entire business on building trusting relationships.

For example, the retailer Nordstrom has made its name synonymous with exceptional customer service. Stories of Nordstrom's employees going above and beyond are legendary. In one such story, a woman in North Carolina lost the diamond from her wedding ring while trying on clothes at a Nordstrom store. *The Seattle Times* explains:

> A store security worker saw her crawling on the sales floor under the racks. He asked what was going on, then joined the search. After they came up empty, the employee asked two building-services workers to join the search. They opened up the bags of the store's vacuum cleaners, where they found the shiny diamond.[19]

Nordstrom's leadership doesn't create a culture of such dedicated employees by accident. They see their employees as vital partners in the success of the company. Whereas other retailers may have long and elaborate employee handbooks, Nordstrom's handbook has only one rule. It reads: "Use good judgment in all situations."[20]

Using good judgment. It's a fundamentally human skill that can't be replaced by an algorithm or a robot. It's the essence of heuristic work. It's also the essence of ethical leadership.

THE LEADER OF THE FUTURE

The world has changed, and it's not going back. Leadership needs to keep up with the times. The megatrends of affluence, computerization, and transparency have made our world flatter and faster. Understanding the implications of these trends (for better and worse) is essential.

When you know the macrocosm, you can better lead in your organizational microcosm.

Organizations need to continually evolve or risk becoming obsolete. Business models that used to last for decades or centuries are being disrupted. What do hulu, Fitbit, Spotify, Dropbox, Airbnb, Kickstarter, and Quora all have in common? They're all billion-dollar businesses that didn't exist 15 years ago. And that's just a few.

Consider this statement from a COO of a Fortune 25 company that I heard at his company's annual leadership conference:

> The way we do business has fundamentally transformed. With the advent of new technology and the ever-increasing rate of change and innovation, we can no longer afford to find ourselves on a burning platform. The companies that wind up on a burning platform are done. The challenge in this competitive landscape is to predict where the potential burning platform will be six months or a year from now, and course-correct *now*, so we never wind up on the platform in the first place.

In this flatter, faster world, there's no way one person can corner the market on knowledge. You're dependent on the eyes and ears of your people—and their willingness to share what they see and hear. Thus, being connected becomes more important than ever.

To compete, smart companies have reorganized to share knowledge and decision-making with the front lines and the customer. This structure is much more complex than the linear, hierarchical systems of the past. The only way such a restructuring works is if there's effective communication in every direction.

In addition, many companies are abandoning top-down planning models. To meet the increased demands of customers, they're implementing agile methods to drive rapid innovation and a better customer experience. Collaboration is key to making this nimbler approach to doing business flourish.

The successful organizations of tomorrow will be led by "New-School" leaders. They're the ones who will know how to catalyze a new generation of talent. They'll be equipped to solve complex problems and create innovative solutions for pressing problems. Their leadership will create value for their employees, organizations, and customers. They'll do this by harnessing the power of these basic skills—connection, communication, and collaboration—so that in this brave new world of work, their teams and companies don't just survive but thrive.

Chapter Resources

Lead into Tomorrow

- I see how soft skills are vital to effective leadership.
- I know that employees have high expectations. They want more than a job: they want inspiration, motivation, and purpose.
- I work to make my organization a place that people can be proud of.
- I recognize that every employee and customer has a platform to share what they really think about me and my organization with the world.
- I see how increased transparency creates a need for greater accountability.
- My first rule of leadership is use good judgment in all situations.

Part II

CONNECTION

World-renowned experts James Kouzes and Barry Posner define leadership as "the art of mobilizing others to want to struggle for shared aspirations."[1] You can't mobilize people unless you have a relationship with them. You can't get them to want to do anything (let alone want to struggle) unless they feel positively about that relationship. And you can't have shared aspirations without common bonds. People in organizations who are connected are more engaged, more satisfied, and higher performers than their disconnected peers.

Leaders achieve their results through the results of others. Leaders who excel at connection multiply their impacts. Expectations are clearer and goals are aligned. Better input is shared before decisions are made. More ideas lead to more innovation.

Connection leads to candor. Connection builds confidence. Connection creates community.

In Part II, you'll learn how to create connection with those you lead. You'll discover the vital role that empathy plays as the basis of connection. You'll see what actions build and enhance your credibility, and what can tear it apart.

It's been said that the best way to test your leadership is to turn around and see who's following you. As you begin to practice and develop the principle of connection, you won't need to turn around and check. You'll already know.

Chapter 4

EMPATHY

The Basis of Connection

You can only understand people if you feel them in yourself.
—John Steinbeck

People with a finely tuned sense of empathy are better at building relationships, trust, and collaborating more effectively than others. They're the ones who colleagues refer to as having a "knack with people." And because every business is a people business, this is a knack worth having.

Empathic leaders are skilled connectors. Development Dimensions International (DDI), one of the world's largest leadership development consultancies, studied more than 15,000 leaders across 300 companies in 18 countries. They found that leaders who master listening and respond with empathy will perform more than 40% higher than their peers in overall performance, coaching, engaging others, planning and organizing, and decision-making.[1]

Richard S. Wellins, senior vice president, states, "Being able to listen and respond with empathy is overwhelmingly the one interaction skill that outshines all other skills leaders need to be successful."

This chapter explores the complex dimensions of empathy. You'll get to know what it is and what it isn't. Empathy is much more than a touchy-feely concept, and you'll get a firm grounding in the business benefits that empathy brings. You'll walk away with a clear understanding as to why it's so essential to your leadership.

Before we begin, I want to share a personal experience of the connection between empathy and leadership. It all started with an ordinary trip to a grocery store.

It was a crisp October day, both sunny and breezy, the kind of brilliant autumn day that New England is famous for. The entire afternoon was blocked off for errands. I'd grabbed Miranda, my then three-year-old daughter, and strapped her into the car seat behind me. We'd already gone to the library to drop off some books, to the dry cleaners to get some shirts laundered, and picked up her six-year-old brother, Alexander, from kindergarten. All this while listening to *Raffi Live in Concert* on repeat.

We headed south to our last stop of the day: shopping at Trader Joe's. The nearest Trader Joe's from my house is a bit of a trip. To get there, you have to cross the bridge over the Connecticut River, and with traffic, this can take up to 40 minutes.

On this October day, traffic was surprisingly light, and all was proceeding according to plan. The minivan was filled with music, singing, and laughter. That is, until we got to the Trader Joe's parking lot.

As I got out of the car, I patted down every pocket I had. My wallet was missing! Where had I left it? I replayed the afternoon over again in my mind and realized that I hadn't used my wallet for any purchases thus far. Knowing me, I probably just left it at home.

A quick phone call to my wife confirmed my suspicion. My wallet was sitting on the table at home where I'd left it. Now I had another problem to deal with: I had no money or credit cards to go shopping.

A potential solution popped into my head. Because I traveled so much for work, I happened to know my credit card numbers, expiration dates, and security codes from memory. I thought that maybe the store could call in my card number (the way you'd do it if you were purchasing something over the phone) and get my purchase approved.

I hoisted a squirming Miranda to the rear of a shopping cart and struggled to get her large toddler feet through the square openings of the child seat. After finally succeeding in getting her situated, I realized that Alex was nowhere in sight. He'd wandered off on his own through the store. After finding him in the freezer aisle ogling the ice cream, I grabbed his hand and led my dynamic duo to the manager's station. There I met Carlotta, a tall woman with a Hawaiian shirt on. I told Carlotta what had happened and proposed my solution of calling in the credit card.

"I'm really sorry," she told me. "I wish we could, but unfortunately, we need to have the physical card to process the transaction."

My heart sank into my stomach. So much for a good idea. This whole trip to the store had been a waste. I was really upset with myself. I still couldn't believe I'd left my wallet at home. There was nothing left to do but put my tail between my legs and head back to the minivan.

I exhaled a huge sigh of disappointment. Just then, I noticed someone else's presence in the manager's booth. A balding man with glasses was looking intently at me. He was also wearing a staff Hawaiian shirt. His nametag read "Peter: Assistant Manager."

Peter said, "Hey." Then he just paused and looked at me directly. Our eyes met.

He then said, "You live in Northampton, is that right?"

"Yes," I replied.

Peter nodded at me. "I do that drive a lot. It's not so easy to get here. Especially with the construction going on right now over the bridge."

I suddenly felt a lot more relaxed. Peter really got me.

He continued, "Sorry about your wallet. You know, stuff happens. Why don't you just go ahead and do your shopping. When you're done, have the cashier call me over. I'll put it on my credit card and you can pay me back."

It took me a second. "What?" I asked, dumbfounded.

"Do your shopping, and I'll put the purchase on my credit card."

"Is that a store credit card?"

"No. It's my personal credit card," Peter said nonchalantly, as though he did this every day.

"You would DO that?!"

"Yeah, no trouble. Next time you're in the store you can pay me back."

"I don't come over here often. I'm heading out of town for work—
I wasn't planning to come back for a few weeks."

"No trouble. Pay me when you come back," Peter smiled. "You'd be
surprised. It happens more often than you'd think."

I was completely floored. Here was a guy who I'd just met, about to
make an unsecured loan to a complete stranger.

"Thanks," was the best I could muster.

We did our shopping. The total was $73.42.

I left on a business trip the next day, but there was no way I could
let weeks go by without repaying Peter. I made sure to ask my wife to
make a special trip over the river, along with a check and a handwritten
thank-you note.

On that afternoon, Peter did more than give me financial support; he
gave me emotional support. Our interchange wasn't just transactional;
it was personal. Peter connected to what I was going through—my
circumstances, my story, and my feelings. With that knowledge, he
quickly acted to help me out.

Peter's action left quite an impression on me. Not only do I shop at
Trader Joe's more regularly since that day, but when I go in, I make a
point to say hello and connect with the staff members. I've gotten to
know them as people. I feel like part of their community. Empathy can
be contagious.

Not only do I feel gratitude toward Peter and my local store but also
I now have a soft spot for the brand of Trader Joe's. I guess you could
call me one of their raving fans. I've been inspired to share this story
with hundreds of people when leading seminars. Remarkably, quite
a few members of these audiences have approached me afterward to
tell me their own Trader Joe's story. They too have had a connection
with a Trader Joe's employee who went completely above and beyond
for them.

As a company, Trader Joe's has found ways to codify and demonstrate
empathy for their customers. Not only do these connections feel good
but also they're good for the bottom line. A recent report found Trader
Joe's sells $1,734 per square foot of store space (the profitability metric
in the grocery sector). To give you a sense of how much this dominates
the competition, Whole Foods sells $930 per square foot, and Kroger
sells $496 per square foot.[2]

WHAT IS EMPATHY?

I think we all have empathy. We may not have enough courage to display it.

— Maya Angelou

There are two main aspects of empathy. The first is **cognitive empathy**. This is the ability to see things from other people's perspectives. This skill enables you to step into their shoes and understand not only their point of view but also the various forces that informed how they arrived at that point of view.

The second aspect of empathy is called **affective empathy**. It's the ability to notice someone else's emotional state and respond appropriately. Being empathic in this way takes nuance. It takes a high degree of attunement to listen beyond what people say to what they mean.

Empathy is programmed into us. As humans, we're hardwired to emotionally attune with those around us. Our brains have cells called mirror neurons, which are designed to reflect the actions and emotions of others.

Mirror neurons fire when you do an action, as well as when you simply watch someone else doing the same action. These neural-emotional circuits are open-looped, which is what connects us to those around us. For example, your mirror neurons activate when you hear a baby cry out in distress and you feel moved to go and help the child.

You see massive displays of empathy in the wake of natural disasters or large-scale crises. For example, I was living in New York City during the 9/11 attacks. In the aftermath, I was compelled to do something—anything—to help. I called up five hospitals to see if I could be of support in any way. In each case, my request was turned down. Why? The hospitals had been flooded with volunteer requests and were completely at capacity.

Empathy is the catalyst for cooperation within groups. Working together is what allowed small tribes of our paleolithic ancestors to survive and ultimately thrive. Though they were smaller, weaker, and slower than the predators around them, their capacity to team up gave them a competitive edge.

As good as it all sounds, our species' relationship with empathy is not all rainbows, peaches, and cream. It turns out we're not all empathy, all the time. What gets in the way?

Although we are hardwired to empathize with others, we don't express it with *all* others. Some people are in our empathy circle, others are excluded. What makes the difference? Whether we already feel acquainted with them. Family members and friends make the cut. Strangers don't. That's why tribal warfare has continued from the days of hunter-gatherers to the present day.

But there doesn't have to be a war or a tribal feud to see the effects of our ancestral wiring. In a recent experiment at the University of Virginia, psychologists placed the subjects in a functional magnetic imaging (fMRI) scanner so they could observe brain activity.

There, the subjects learned of the potential threat of an electric shock. They were told that the shock would be given to either the subject, a friend of the subject, or a stranger.

When the subject thought they'd receive the shock, the regions of the brain that respond to danger lit up. When they learned that a stranger would get a shock, these same parts of the brain remained quiet. Most surprisingly, however, when they learned a friend would receive a shock, the same danger parts of the brain lit up to the same extent they did when they thought they'd get the shock themselves.

"The correlation between self and friend was remarkably similar," lead researcher James Coan said. "The finding shows the brain's remarkable capacity to model self to others, that people close to us become a part of ourselves, and that is not just metaphor or poetry, it's very real."[3]

This research shows why it's so important for leaders to be inclusive. Inclusivity brings people into your empathy circle. You'll not only better look out for your "tribe" but you'll reap the benefits as well.

LEADERSHIP BENEFITS OF EMPATHY

Demonstrating empathy—showing that you care—forms the basis for building effective working relationships. When you give others empathy, they will reciprocate with gifts in kind. These gifts include trust, insights, and innovation.

Empathy Builds Trust. Trust Gets Results.

Trust is the new currency of work. In our high-tech, mobile age, it's easier than ever for employees to jump ship and for other employers to poach your people. Loyalty and engagement cannot be mandated. Commitment is built from the ground up, one relationship at a time.

If trust is high, both people and results prosper. A Watson Wyatt study found that high-trust organizations outperform low-trust organizations in total return to shareholders by 286%.[4]

Low-trust workplaces are energy drains. In such environments, people don't feel comfortable being genuine. They're afraid they won't be accepted. Instead, they resign themselves to wearing a corporate mask. Empathizing allows the walls to come down. Instead of spending valuable energy operating on the defensive, employees can focus on working toward the mission of your organization. At the same time, you'll increase your influence.

CHIEF EMPATHY OFFICER

In 2014, Angela Ahrendt stepped into a leadership void. The position she filled, VP of retail and online stores, had been vacant for over a year. She had to start fresh: the previous VP had only lasted six months in the job. A horrible cultural fit, he'd incensed the retail staff of nearly 60,000 employees by reducing hours and cutting benefits. If that wasn't pressure enough, Ahrendt's new company also just happened to be the most valuable company in the world: Apple.

Ahrendt was no leadership novice. She'd just left her role as CEO of Burberry, where she'd reinvigorated the classic fashion brand, growing Burberry's value from 2.1 billion pounds to over 7 billion pounds in the six years she'd served.

So when Ahrendt started at Apple, what would she do? How would she lead as head of retail for the world's biggest company? What bold steps would she take?

For the first six months in her role, she led by listening. As Ahrendts describes it, "I didn't dare say anything prior to six months. My dad used to tell me, growing up [citing Abraham Lincoln], 'It is better to remain silent and be thought a fool than to open your mouth and relieve them of all doubt.'"[5] With her ability to quickly build rapport, she served as Apple's de facto CEO—chief empathy officer.

Ahrendts went out in the field and visited more than 100 stores, call centers, and back offices. She empathized with employees. She spent time with frontline workers, answering their questions and listening to their criticisms. She got to see Apple from their perspective. She learned that they felt disconnected. The culture (and employee engagement) were suffering.

After her retail road tour, Ahrendts initiated a weekly video communication sent out to all stores. It's described as "part strategy and part pep rally," and is when Ahrendts lays out the weekly game plan. She also created an internal app where employees can give feedback or share ideas. Ahrendts reads every single comment that's submitted. How has Ahrendts's empathy influenced this $21.5 billion unit of the company? In 2015, Apple's retail annual employee retention rate hit a record high 81%. This is in the retail industry—a sector that averages an annual retention rate of about 40%.[6]

Repeated acts of empathy send a clear message: *I'm on your side*. When you show people you care, they become trusting (and trusted) team members. From this place, they're willing to give you their loyalty and commitment.

Empathy Creates Insight. Insight Creates Results.

What is insight? Insight is deep understanding into all parts of an issue. Gaining insight is a process in which gaining facts is just the first step. Next, we need to figure out what those facts mean.

The problem is that we don't all get the same meaning out of facts. My meaning is based on my past, my preferences, and my culture, all of which are different from yours. Merely having information isn't enough. We need to transform data into insight. This isn't easy, especially in an era of data overload. Futurist John Naisbitt predicted this phenomenon over 35 years ago, when he wrote in his bestselling book *Megatrends,* "We are drowning in information but starved for knowledge."[7]

After we create this meaning, we next fill in any gaps of understanding with our own assumptions and biases. These will differ, based on our individual history, hopes, desires, and fears. Finally, we arrive at our version of "reality." From here, we make decisions, act, and get our results.

Results come from the choices we make. Poor decisions lead to poor outcomes; great choices yield great results. The choices we make are only as good as the knowledge we have when we make them. Thus, knowledge is the key to informed decision-making.

One of the biggest challenges with getting genuine insight is the tendency to skim through these steps. For most people, this entire insight-gaining process happens in the blink of an eye—and completely unconsciously. People with a low degree of empathy don't question their own assumptions and quickly jump to their own conclusions.

However, people with a high degree of empathy are inquisitive. They actively seek out differing points of view. They crave depth and breadth. Before they make decisions, they want to understand as much as possible.

Empathic leaders pick up on subtle cues that tip the balance of insight in their favor. Consider the case of Joanne. Joanne is currently the director of brand strategy for a high-end retail chain. Early in her career, she managed the cosmetics department in one of the chain's stores.

One of her frontline employees, Emma, had been working the cosmetics counter for about four months. Emma was about 18 years old. Emma was terrific with customers, but as Joanne described her, "a little rough around the edges."

Part of Emma's job was to do makeovers on customers. She was an excellent make-up artist and was also extremely personable, building rapport with the women at the counter.

However, some aspects of her performance were not up to par. By the time the makeover was done, Emma's counter would be a total mess. She wasn't able to get it fully clean for future customers. Also, whenever Joanne stopped by, she noticed that Emma's uniform would look dirty, with bits of makeup on it.

Appearances were a huge company value and selling point, and they had clear policies around appearance that could not be violated. Maintaining a neat appearance was not a nice-to-do: it was a must-do. Joanne coached Emma on her performance gaps. Her counter cleanliness immediately improved, but her uniform continued to look dirty during the weekend shifts.

Joanne was torn. As much as she liked Emma, and as much as she had potential, this appearance issue was not okay. Joanne started thinking about letting Emma go.

Joanne told me,

I remember the day vividly. I went to meet Emma at the start of a shift in the employee break room. I'd thought through what I was going to say. I was going to tell her that she should pack her things and leave. However, when I looked in her eyes, something told me that there was something else going on. I needed to get more information.

Taking that extra moment to ask her about her side of the story was the best thing I ever did as a manager.

What I learned was that Emma had been living on her own since she was fifteen years old. Her parents had basically abandoned her. She had next to no money and was living in a tiny single room, with no stove, no bath, nothing. She was also responsible for her younger brother.

She had to wash herself in her sink, and do her laundry in the sink as well. Given her hours and her commute, she couldn't figure out a way to wash her work uniform and find a way to get it to dry unless she had a day off in between shifts, so her uniform would always end up dirty towards the end of her workweek.

When she shared that with me, I realized that, yes, it was only toward the end of the week that her uniform was dirty. It was always fine on Tuesday, after her day off.

Here I was, thinking I had this lazy or irresponsible girl on my hands. Nothing could be further from the truth! Instead, Emma was busting her tail trying to do anything she could to make her job work. To make her life work. I never looked at her in the same way again.

I asked her if it would help if she had an extra uniform or two, so she wouldn't have to worry about cleaning it every night. It was against policy, but in this case, I was happy to bend the rules for her situation. When I mentioned that I'd like to help her with two extra uniforms, she started to cry right there in front of me. The lesson I learned from Emma is that there's always a story behind the story. It's my job as a leader to find out what that backstory is.

Empathy is what prompted Joanne to dig deeper and ask Emma further questions. It's what allowed her to create a connection so that Emma felt safe to tell the truth. Without empathy, Joanne would have lost an outstanding employee who delivered great results with excellent customer service. Demonstrating empathy can illuminate problems you might not notice otherwise and help you create solutions.

Empathy Fosters Innovation. Innovation Gets Results.

Executives know that their company's competitive advantage lies in their ability to create new and better products, services, or processes that internal and external customers find valuable.

Unfortunately, there's a crime being committed right now in corporate meeting rooms all over world. New ideas are being assassinated. Employees are putting forth novel approaches to doing things, and their thoughts are being shot down. The driving force behind this crime is fear: fear of the new, fear of change, and fear of failure.

A weird thing happens when leadership kills ideas: the pipeline for other potential ideas suddenly dries up. If someone witnesses an idea assassination, there's no way they're going to put their own suggestions out there to be shot down. It feels too risky. So, idea generation slows to a trickle.

Empathic leaders recognize that you can't create a culture of innovation without fostering a climate that supports it. They know that new ideas, like young seedlings, are not fully formed yet, and they need support and nurturance to take root and grow. When people know that you support their ideas, they feel comfortable to speak up and share what they think and feel.

Let's return to the example of Apple. For years, Apple (similar to many companies) tried to solicit suggestions from their retail employees. However, their efforts were sporadic, and without further resources and attention, it never went anywhere.

Fast forward to when Angela Ahrendts joined the company. We've already learned how she created connection with thousands of retail employees by traveling around and visiting more than 100 stores. It was only after she'd built these relationships, and started the ongoing weekly video communications that she introduced the internal app for ideas and feedback. Without that real-time, face-to-face trust-building process that Ahrendts led the company through, the app concept could have bombed. Employees would have seen it as one more drilled-down management flavor-of-the-month thing to get through until it disappeared.

But because the climate was tended to first, the app worked remarkably well. It was through the app portal that Ahrendts and her team got the idea for the Genius Bar's concierge service. This allows customers to make a reservation for their appointment, rather than just walking up and having to wait their turn. The idea for the concierge service came from a Texas associate who saw the process used while she was waiting at her local Dallas department of motor vehicles.[8]

The best innovations come from the best ideas, and it turns out the best ideas are more likely to emerge when you have a large quantity of ideas to choose from. Using empathy can help foster a climate where people will feel good about sharing their ideas with you.

If empathy brings all these benefits—trust, insight, innovation— then why isn't it practiced more often? Shouldn't it be standard operating procedure everywhere? Sadly, it's not. Leaders face many challenges to leading with empathy. You'll learn about these challenges and gain tools to conquer them next.

Chapter Resources

Create Empathy

- I choose to be empathetic: doing so improves my leadership performance.
- Empathy is my key to transforming transactional relationships into personal relationships.
- I seek to see things from others' perspectives.
- I notice others' emotional states and respond appropriately.
- I work to include people in my empathy circle.
- I create commitment one relationship at a time.
- I spend time listening to feedback and answering questions.

Chapter 5

EMPATHY

Connection in Action

Leadership is about empathy.

—Oprah Winfrey

Demonstrating empathy—showing people that you understand them and that you care how they feel—is a key to real connection. And it can be so much more. It can inspire and transform.

Consider the story of Glenn. Glenn is a senior leader for a global hospitality company. I was training Glenn and about 20 of his peers. The group was discussing the subject of beliefs, specifically, how our beliefs transform facts into stories that reflect our points of view. One thing about beliefs is that although they may feel rock-solid certain, they can change.

I asked the group this question: "Can you think of something you once believed that you no longer believe?"

I've asked this question many times to multiple groups. The most common answers I usually hear are Santa Claus and the tooth fairy. I'd expected to hear one of these common answers. But Glenn surprised me.

"Yeah, I never really liked people a whole lot."

I thought to myself, "Where's this going?"

Glenn continued. "Yeah, I guess you could've called me a curmudgeon. And as a manager, I was a real SOB. All I cared about was my own family, and at work I only cared that people made their numbers."

Now I was concerned the whole session was going off the rails.

But then Glenn shifted.

But all that changed two years ago. You see, my wife was diagnosed with stage 4 breast cancer. People out of the woodwork, people I didn't even know, neighbors, people from the kids' school, just started showing up. Helping. Making meals, arranging play dates for the kids, doing drop-offs and pickups. It completely restored my faith in humanity.

And at work? I started realizing that the people on my team—they had families, too. They had challenges, too. I started asking them what was going on outside of work. Talking with them. I'd like to think I'm not the same SOB I used to be.

When Glenn finished, I looked around. Several people had misty eyes. I had a lump in my throat. The empathy that Glenn had experienced had changed him.

Understanding people and showing them that you care seems like it should be simple. However, when you put people into fast-paced, high-pressure situations, simple gets buried by complex. With looming deadlines, changing priorities, and information overload, empathy can get lost in the shuffle. Leaders face numerous challenges to leading with empathy. In this chapter, you'll discover six of the biggest of these challenges. Then, you'll learn six key practices to overcome these challenges and grow your empathic skills.

CHALLENGES TO LEADING WITH EMPATHY

In an ideal world, where you have infinite time and infinite resources, being empathic would be easy. However, in the real world you're going to come face-to-face with one or more of the barriers that will hinder your abilities. There are six primary challenges to leading with empathy:

- Lack of practice
- Right–wrong mind-set
- Fear mentality
- Impatience
- The hot–cold empathy gap
- Power

Let's unravel these challenges to see how they work.

Lack of Practice

At its core, empathy is a behavior—something you say and/or do. Similar to any other behavior, if it isn't natural to you, your skill at it will only improve with deliberate practice. Think of empathy as a muscle—it needs to be exercised regularly to get stronger. If you don't use it, it atrophies.

Historically, in the hard-charging traditional business world, empathy has been undervalued or even ignored. Empathy can be hard to measure, and it is usually left out of the cluster of key performance indicators, which include metrics such as revenue, profit, and quality.

Though empathy is difficult to measure, it affects everything around us. How we feel at work might seem superficial, but it's not. How we feel greatly influences how we perform.

As researchers Tony Schwartz and Christine Porath have found, "Feeling cared for by one's supervisor has a more significant impact on people's sense of trust and safety than any other behavior by a leader. Employees who say they have more supportive supervisors are 1.3 times as likely to stay with the organization and are 67% more engaged."[1]

Caring—or a lack thereof—explains why empathy is the most critical driver of overall performance. Leaders who don't practice empathy fuel their teams with the emotional equivalent of low-octane fuel. The journey is full of knocks and more prone to breakdowns. No wonder people who aren't cared for leave. After all, no one has quit their job after having the thought, "My boss was too empathetic."

Right–Wrong Mind-set

Another challenge to empathy is rigid thinking. For most of us, education (both formally in school and informally at home) was built on finding the one, singular right answer. In fact, we got rewarded with gold stars and high grades for showing that we had learned what was right. And when we strayed from the right path, we'd get punished with low grades, red pens, and detention. As a result, we deeply internalized this right–wrong way of thinking.

Fast forward to adulthood and working in an organizational environment. In your workplace, decisions are made all day, every day. No one works on an island—there are lots of times when you'll need to get input from others before choosing which way to go next. When someone disagrees with you, do you cling harder to being "right" than you do to maintaining a connection with them? Do you dig in to your position even more?

Clinging to a need to be right closes you off to the perspective and experience of others. You don't listen—you fake listen. You only care about others to the level that they agree with you. Only the expression of certain thoughts and feelings is okay. Everything else is out of bounds.

With their high need for control, leaders with a right–wrong mind-set are stuck in their own way of doing things. They really don't want to hear what others have to say. They just don't care. This lack of caring keeps them from creating genuine empathic connections. And you can bet their team members pick up on that and adjust their own behaviors accordingly.

Fear Mentality

Many leaders I've worked with are afraid of all of this "feelings stuff." They think it's going to overwhelm everyone and bring progress to a screeching halt. They don't really want to get to know their people. Bob, a managing partner at a consulting firm told me, "If I get to know them, what am I going to find out? I don't know if I want that much information!" For leaders like Bob, explicit feelings are off limits. They believe emotions are too messy. Or maybe they've taken a personality assessment and they've labeled themselves as a type who prefers logic and analysis over feeling and intuition.

Other leaders fear that if they open up to their people, they will be seen as "soft." Their vulnerability could be something to be taken advantage of. Maybe they experienced a situation like this in the past, and they don't want to experience it again.

Then there are the leaders who think that work is no place for empathy. They've honed their leadership sensibility in the Michael Corleone school of business. Michael Corleone, the fictional mafia kingpin, was played by Al Pacino in the three *Godfather* movies. In the first film, he famously tells his brother Sonny, "It's not personal; it's strictly business."

At Godfather, Inc., the corporate culture is extremely low trust. Everyone (including the senior executives) is motivated by fear. Namely, they're scared that someone's out to kill them. Granted, this fear is well founded, because in their mobster world, knocking each other off is business as usual. Such behavior has been going on for generations.

Although *The Godfather* is an extreme, and fictional, example, the "it's strictly business" mind-set is far too real. I've worked in dozens of companies where the unspoken norm is, "You want to share your feelings here? Fuhgeddaboudit."

In addition, the way many organizations run promotes a fear-based mentality. Continuous waves of downsizing leaves people feeling like "headcount"—mere fungible commodities. This creates a low-trust environment. In order to cope with the stress, people emotionally disconnect from their remaining colleagues and reports. When we're disconnected from others, we don't empathize with them.

Impatience

Empathy, truly understanding someone, doesn't happen in an instant. In the digital age, information travels at the speed of light, but human interactions move much more slowly. To get the complete picture—cognitively and emotionally—takes some time. Demonstrating empathy means being patient.

Patience is in short supply in today's business environment. In fact, many of the companies I've worked with have codified impatience as a core competency, reframing it as "bias for action."

It's understandable that a bias for action would be valued in organizations. It takes action to deliver results. However, bias can create a series of downward performance events (see Figure 5.1).

Leaders with a bias for action may be operating with the unconscious belief that they don't have the time to offer empathy. After all, they're busy people with lots to do. But this belief has an unintended impact: making those around them feel less valued and understood. When people feel devalued, their motivation plummets. These lead to declines in performance. Ultimately, results suffer.

To be effective, today's leader needs to embrace a paradox. On the one hand, they need to know when it's time to slow down and move

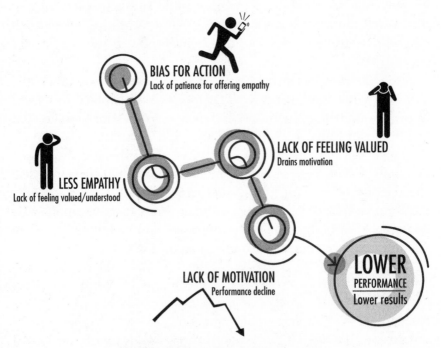

Figure 5.1   Effects of Impatience

at the speed of cultivating relationships with empathy. On the other hand, they need to know when to accelerate into action mode to get things done. To harness the power of human performance, sometimes the best way to move fast is to go slow.

The Hot–Cold Empathy Gap

There's a running dialogue that I often have with my wife, Mary. It's gone on for years now. It sounds something like this:

Mary: It's really cold in here.
Me: You're cold? It's not cold. I'm warm.
Mary: How can you be warm? I'm freezing. It's cold.
Me: No, it's not.

(And so on and so forth.)

In our back-and-forth, Mary and I demonstrate how easy it is to unwittingly fall into the trap that psychologists call the hot–cold empathy gap. It's the cognitive bias where we fail to recognize how much our own experience influences what we think of as reality.

The hot–cold empathy bias applies to much more than the literal temperature. It also refers to our own emotional states. For example, *hot* states include rage, terror, and hunger. *Cold* states include emotions such as calm, boredom, and concern. When people are in a cold state, they find it difficult to relate to what someone in a hot state is going through and vice versa.

At the same time, people also don't recognize how much the way their present emotional state influences their opinions. For example, if you ask someone "How happy are you with your job overall?" that answer will depend on how happy they feel at the moment you ask them.

Assuming that others see, feel, and think about things the same way you do will keep you stuck. Leaders suffering from the hot–cold empathy gap find it challenging to relate to what their employees are going through.

Bernice, a participant in a leadership workshop, shared a story of a leader with an extreme case of the hot–cold empathy gap. Bernice's aunt had passed away, and she asked her boss for an afternoon off to attend the funeral. The boss looked slightly befuddled, and said, "Do you really have to? I think we need you here at the office more than your aunt needs you today."

Power

The higher a leader climbs in an organization, the more disconnected he or she can become.

Over two decades of research, Dacher Keltner, a psychology professor at UC Berkeley, concluded that people under the effect of power act as though they had a traumatic brain injury. They become "more impulsive, less risk-aware, and, crucially, less adept at seeing things from other people's point of view."[2]

In further research, psychologists Michael Inzlicht and Sukhvinder Obhi found that when people experience power, it changes how sensitive their brains become to the actions of others. In other words, they specifically studied how power influences empathy.

Inzlicht and Obhi began their experiment by asking subjects to recall and write about a time where they remembered feeling either powerless or powerful. This was to prime them to a powerful or powerless state. Next, the subjects were shown a video of a human hand squeezing a ball.

Just watching a hand squeezing a ball activates mirror neurons in the brain. While watching the video, participants' brain activity was measured using transcranial magnetic stimulation (TMS). TMS was used to measure the degree to which these mirror neurons were firing, which is considered a standard scientific metric for determining empathy.

The results found an inverse correlation between feelings of power and mirror neural activity. The more powerful subjects felt, the less empathy they had. The less powerful, the more empathic. As the authors of the study put it, "Power, it appears, changes how the brain itself responds to others."[3]

Just because power influences a leader's level of empathy doesn't mean he or she is destined for a lifetime of cruel and callous behavior.

There are plenty of leaders who are incredibly empathic. They do this by staying vigilant. They stay on guard against the pitfalls of power that can lull them into a place of not caring about others.

Smart empathic leaders seek out new ways to build bridges between themselves and people at all levels in the organization. They look for ways to close the power–empathy gap. As an example, Charles Phillips, the CEO of Infor, a software company, shares his cellphone number with all company employees.[4] He invites them to reach out via voice or text whenever they want. It's a way for him stay open and keep information flowing.

These challenges—lack of practice, right–wrong mind-set, fear mentality, impatience, the hot–cold empathy gap, and power—keep leaders and organizations stuck in the past. To succeed moving forward, authority must give way to inclusion. High-performing teams and companies will be people-centric. Empathy is a critical part of this equation.

FACING THE CHALLENGES TO BUILD EMPATHY

Seeing all these challenges to empathy might leave you a bit discouraged. But fear not—there's some good news. There are just a handful of simple-to-learn, easy-to-apply practices that you can do to strengthen your empathy muscles.

Thankfully, you aren't starting from scratch. You've already seen that humans are neurologically wired for empathy, so the capacity for developing this skill is in your DNA. The key is making these behaviors a priority. Commit to practicing empathy, and focus on taking small steps forward with one or more of these six actions:

- Listen with purpose
- Practice being open
- Cultivate curiosity
- Engage with strangers
- Break your habit patterns
- Spend time in another person's shoes

Each of those approaches deserves closer examination.

Listen with Purpose

It's one thing to let others talk. It's quite another to listen with purpose. You may have found that listening seems like the most boring thing in the world. If that's true for you, you haven't given listening a fair shot.

Kyle is a senior executive for a large financial organization that has more than 12 million customers. I first met Kyle more than a decade ago to help his teams become more aligned. I was struck by how well he listened. One of the first things he said was, "I'm a banker by training. You're the expert on teamwork and leadership. I want to learn everything I can from you. What have you learned from talking with our team? What should we do?"

There's nothing passive about listening. Seeking understanding is an active, dynamic process. Although you can't technically see reality 100% the way anyone else can, your goal in listening is to get as close to that as possible.

Dynamic listening takes intense focus and purpose. Dynamic listening can be exhausting. And, yes, sometimes, it can be really boring. You'll want to jump to your ready-made conclusions.

But don't do it.

The feeling of being listened to—really listened to—is a fast track to connection. The biggest thing that gets in the way of listening with purpose is quite simple: it's offering up your complete and undivided attention. Many leaders feel they don't have time for it. If you think you don't have time for it, ask yourself: What is *not* paying attention costing you? The answer might be the wake-up call you're looking for.

Practice Being Open

Appreciating that others see and feel things differently is a prerequisite for openness. But it's just a start. Openness means being receptive to new ideas, feelings, and experiences. Such openness takes courage, and that courage looks very different for different leaders, depending on their character.

Letitia, a senior leader at a global insurance company, was adamant that her leadership team cultivate the trait of being open. As a matter of practice, whenever the team gathered for off-site meetings, she'd book a reservation at an ethnic restaurant from a part of the world that none of them had been to. It was her way to get them to expand both their palate and their thinking.

To grow your openness with others, start by being open with yourself. Do an honest reckoning: are you a leader who tends to control? Do you want to keep driving your agenda forward? Or are you a pleaser, who abdicates your own opinions around others?

Take an inventory: How open are you with your own feelings? With your own thoughts? How much do you admit to your own shortcomings? How much would you be willing to share these discoveries with others? Spending time on this kind of self-evaluation will give you valuable insights.

With practice, your capacity to be more open and present with others will increase over time. It won't feel like quite so much work. You'll also discover a whole new level of depth in your relationships, and others will enjoy a deeper connection with you.

CHIEF CURIOSITY OFFICER

In February 2014, Satya Nadella got a new job. He was promoted to be the next CEO of Microsoft. He had his work cut out for him. Founder Bill Gates had built Microsoft into a software behemoth and became the world's richest person in the process. Yet, his successor, Steve Ballmer, was unable to navigate the technology giant effectively. In his seven years as CEO, share prices of the company dropped 11.7%.[5]

By the time Nadella took over, Microsoft was well known for its culture of infighting. Intensely competitive, different product groups battled for money, talent, and visibility. As turf battles and silos grew, the company lacked a clear unifying vision.

Nadella was quite familiar the ups and downs of Microsoft. He'd been an employee since 1992, starting when he was 25 years old. He'd lived through the Gates and the Ballmer eras. When he took over as CEO, his first order of business was to change the culture. Knowing such a transformation couldn't happen overnight, he started small.

In his first meeting with the executive leadership team, he brought each person a copy of Marshall Rosenberg's landmark book *Nonviolent Communication (NVC)*. This was not what the executives expected. NVC is not your standard-issue business book. As Microsoft president Brad Smith put it, "Steve Ballmer was not somebody who brought in books. There was definitely a sense that this was something different."[6]

In fact, *Nonviolent Communication* is not just a book. It's a set of principles and practices on how to collaborate using compassion and empathy. Its ideas have been used in settings far beyond business: social change, peace talks, negotiation, education, parenting, and mediation.

Nadella realized there was no way that the Microsoft culture would change on the outside until the leadership changed on the inside. As Nadella describes, "Microsoft's culture had been rigid. Each employee had to prove to everyone that he or she was the smartest person in the room."[7] Nadella knew that in this transformation process, he wanted Microsoft "to be not a 'know-it-all' but 'learn-it-all' organization."[8]

Nadella's changes are working. He's has turned the company around, creating what's been described as the "Microsoft miracle." Microsoft is now a serious player in mobile apps, gaming, cloud services, hardware, voice recognition, and artificial intelligence. Oh, and they still do software, too. Customers and investors are liking what they see. On Nadella's first day as CEO, February 4, 2014, Microsoft's market capitalization was $301.73 billion. As of January 10, 2020, the company's value was $1.24 trillion.

Cultivate Curiosity

If you're going to be an empathic leader, you need to be curious. Curiosity, by its nature, means being engaged. You can't be curious and stay in your comfort zone at the same time.

Curiosity helps us develop empathy. When we meet new people, try new things, and go to new places, we can't help but be broadened in the process.

A key to developing curiosity is inquiry. Be like a small child, and continually ask *why?* When you get the answer, ask *why* again—keep probing to gain more insight. It will help you move beyond complacency.

If curiosity is so great, why aren't more people more curious more of the time? What's the downside?

If you're going to be curious, there are a couple of big costs to pay. The first one is time. It takes time to engage with others. If you feel as though you've already got too much on your plate, you won't have much physical or mental space to focus on taking in anything new.

The second cost is ego. If you're operating as a "know-it-all," you have an underlying belief that any new stuff really isn't of much value. Not only does it waste your valuable time, it wastes your valuable attention. In your know-it-all head, you'd rather focus on the important things that you're already familiar with. In fact, you may even see yourself as the resident expert at what you know and do. Anything new might be a threat to that expert status.

Having an uncurious attitude keeps you in the realm of the familiar. And although that might feel comfortable, it also comes with a big problem. Your habitual actions keep you stuck in a rut. Or, as Benjamin Franklin more eloquently put it, "If you do tomorrow what you did today, you will get tomorrow what you got today."

Engage with Strangers

Unless you live as a hermit, you meet new people every day. They're everywhere: in line at the coffeeshop and grocery store, waiting their turn at the dentist's office. Instead of checking your social media feed for the 20th time, why not strike up a conversation? If you ask a great open-ended question, you can get them talking. You may ask something that you notice in their appearance. Or maybe you just ask them a thought-provoking question, such as, "What do you wish you knew?" or "What's the next great adventure you're going to take?"

Then, of course, once you've asked the question you need to listen. Strive for understanding. Be open to being moved from the interaction. It may feel scary to strike up a conversation with a total stranger.

Don't think of it as a popularity contest. The point isn't to make a new best friend. Think of it as an opportunity to work on building empathy. Each time you practice, you'll hone your ability to pick up on the cues as to what people are thinking and feeling. You'll be intentional about connecting.

When I've coached leaders and assigned engaging with strangers as homework, they've reported back how enjoyable the process can be. Meng, an IT manager, noticed it helped him improve the quality of all of his conversations. He remarked, "By being so completely focused on learning about them, I got out of my own head! I used to have this running commentary wondering what people thought of me. Now, I'm so much more relaxed."

Break Your Habit Patterns

We're creatures of habit. What we did yesterday we're likely to do today. Over time, this can get us trapped in stagnation.

In the 1993 movie *Groundhog Day*, Bill Murray plays Phil Connors, a sarcastic weatherman who complains about everyone and everything around him. In a fantastical twist of fate, he's forced to relive the same day—Groundhog Day—over and over again. At first, Phil sees it as a curse. Then, Phil starts to try new things—learn to play the piano, get to really know his coworkers and the townspeople—and he slowly begins to build relationships. He even saves some lives in the process. In fact, it's only when he develops empathy for those around him that the curse is broken. Phil learns the power of connection. And because this is a movie, he lives happily ever after.

It doesn't take a paranormal experience to be able to reap the benefits of breaking your patterns. For example, have you ever noticed how much richer your day's experience is when you're on vacation? That's because you aren't coasting along, using the same neural firing patterns that you use when you eat your same breakfast off the same plate at the same seat at the same table in the same kitchen that you sit in every morning. In your routine, it's easy to slip into autopilot.

You don't need to go on vacation to break patterns. Try new things or do old things in a new way. Take a different route to get to work. Park in a different spot. Call an old friend out of the blue. Notice how you respond. When you stop going through the motions and embrace novelty, your sense of connection to people, places, things, and events will be heightened.

Spend Time in Another Person's Shoes

When Scott Moorehead graduated from college in 2001, he joined his family's business, Moorehead Communications. His parents didn't go easy on him. They had him work for a year in nearly every single position at the company. He held each of these jobs—and there were 32 of them—between a half-day to three weeks. Seven years later, Moorehead took over as CEO. His job rotation memories stuck with him. As he describes it, they "made me a very employee-centric CEO."[9]

If you want to accelerate your capacity for empathy, there's nothing like spending time in other people's shoes. You might think you know what their life is like, but when you go through the moment-to-moment experience of doing what they do, you gain a much deeper appreciation for their perspective.

When you practice this technique, you'll watch your previously held assumptions melt away. You'll no longer have to rely on second- or third-hand descriptions. You'll have your own first-person story to draw on.

One caution with this technique: although there's great value to getting to the front lines and learning from that experience, be mindful of how you spend your time there. Be a learner, not a spy. More than one manager in these circumstances has stepped into "undercover boss" mode and used it as a micromanaging opportunity.

BECOMING A CONNECTED LEADER

Empathy is a uniquely human skill. In fact, it's the most human skill. That's why it's the basis for connection and the foundation of great leadership. It will never be outsourced to a robot or an algorithm. Technologies will continue to progress, yet the demands for cognitive and affective empathy will also increase.

These six practices—listening with purpose, being open, cultivating curiosity, engaging with strangers, breaking habit patterns, and spending time in another person's shoes—are much more than just tools to strengthen your empathy. When practiced consistently, they multiply your impact. Instead of imposing your will, you'll attract others to you. With this increased influence, you'll reap the benefits of increased commitment and loyalty. You'll also get more done with less effort.

When you become a connected leader, people willingly follow. They trust you. They know that you care about them and have their best interests in mind. This bond gives them one of the greatest gifts of all: improved physical health.

The difference between a good and bad boss can literally make the difference between life and death. In a study of more than 3,100 men over a decade in typical workplaces, researchers discovered that employees who had managers who were rated as inconsiderate, unclear in giving goals and feedback, and being poor communicators were 60% more likely to suffer a heart attack or another serious heart-related ailment.[10] Disconnection promoted disease.

Although empathy is the basis for connection, it's not the complete package. People expect a lot from leaders, and if all you can offer is empathy, eventually they'll be disappointed. They need to believe in you. They want to know that you're the person who can guide them from where they are to where they want to go.

Gaining confidence from those you lead isn't something you can attain in an instant. It's a process of establishing and then building your credibility. If people are going to follow your lead, they must believe you're worth following. As such, credibility is the second major key to connection. How you gain credibility is the subject of our next chapter.

Chapter Resources

Listen with Purpose

- I remove distractions and monotask when I listen.
- I listen to the end without interrupting.
- I probe for depth when I listen.
- I ask open-ended questions.
- I don't fake listen.
- I restate thoughts and feelings.

Practice Being Open

- I maintain a list of people whose thinking is diverse from mine and I actively seek out their opinions.
- I'm willing to suspend my agenda to give others a fair hearing.
- I acknowledge others when they disagree with me.
- I'm willing to admit when I don't know.
- I tune into my own feelings.
- I tune into my own assumptions.
- I tune into the feelings of others.

Cultivate Curiosity

- I am aware of the boundaries of my comfort zone so that I can stretch beyond their borders.
- I lead with inquiry.
- I'm not afraid of looking like I don't have the answers.
- I explore unfamiliar blogs, articles, and information to get new perspectives.

Engage with Strangers

- I have some good go-to questions to start conversations.
- I use opportunities of daily interactions to meet new people.
- I ask to be introduced to others in the organization to build new connections.
- I attend networking events.

Break Your Habit Patterns

- I reach out to friends I haven't spoken to for a while.
- I find new routes to travel to everyday locations.
- I do familiar things in a new way.
- I go to a new place at least once a week.

Spend Time in Another Person's Shoes

- I ask others to show me how they work.
- I create opportunities to ride along or shadow others in their jobs.
- I volunteer to intern or learn within or at another organization.

Chapter 6

BUILDING YOUR CREDIBILITY

I met an old lady once, almost a hundred years old, and she told me, "There are only two questions that human beings have ever fought over, all through history. How much do you love me? And who's in charge?"
—Elizabeth Gilbert

In the 2002 movie *Spiderman*, there's a well-known scene that any true Spidey fan can recite from memory. If you aren't familiar with the story, here's a quick refresher: Peter Parker is a high school senior from Queens with an inferiority complex. He's an orphan, being raised by his Aunt May and Uncle Ben. While on a field trip to a genetics lab at Columbia University, he's bitten by a radioactive genetically engineered spider.

The next morning, Peter awakes to find he has new skills. Incredibly strong and quick, he can now stick to walls and ceilings and spin webs from his wrists.

Though he now has superpowers, Peter's not yet a superhero. He's still the same angst-ridden teenager who doesn't know what to do with his life. He has yet to commit to working toward a mission of justice, service, and the greater good. Amid this confusion, Peter has a conversation with his Uncle Ben. In what tragically turns out to be

91

their last conversation, Ben wisely counsels Peter, "With great power comes great responsibility."

Uncle Ben's words aren't just for his nephew. They apply to all of us who wish to wear the mantle of leadership.

This may seem like a stretch to you. What could you and Spider Man have in common? Right now, you might feel that you don't have much power at all. You might think you're "just" a supervisor. That you're "just" doing your job. That you're "stuck" as mid-level manager in a large hierarchical organization.

Many leaders take on the challenge of leadership without knowing what they're really signing up for. They think, "I just got a raise," or "I've got a new title." They don't reflect on the gravity of their role. They don't consider the power they wield and the impact that power will have on those they lead. They don't recognize their responsibility. They enter their leadership contract half-asleep.

I know this from firsthand experience. I was one of those slumbering leaders. Thankfully, I received a tremendous wake-up call from a mentor of mine right after the new millennium. It was a gift—both figuratively and literally.

THE GIFT OF LEADERSHIP

It was a blustery October day in 2002 in midtown Manhattan. The wind outside was blowing so hard that umbrellas were turning inside out. Thankfully, I was inside, in a dry, warm, bustling coffeeshop. Seated across the red-cushioned booth from me was Jeff, my leadership mentor. Every month, Jeff and I would meet here and talk shop about leadership and life.

Our waitress had just dropped the check on the sparkling Formica tabletop. "Oh, I almost forgot," said Jeff. He pulled out a small box with red and silver–striped wrapping paper around it. "Congratulations on last weekend."

The weekend before, I'd gotten certified to lead a very complex training that I'd spent years preparing for. The gift was Jeff's way of recognizing my achievement.

Jeff said, "This isn't for later. Go ahead."

Figure 6.1 The Gift: Front

I ripped open the paper and the box. There was some red crepe paper on the inside. My fingers rummaged around and hit soft cotton.

I pulled out my find. It was a t-shirt. A white, extra-large t-shirt with big block capital letters on the front (see Figure 6.1).

A wave of blood rushed to my cheeks. As I smiled, I felt that awkward mix of embarrassment and pride. In that moment, it was hard to fully take in Jeff's acknowledgment and praise. The last four years had been quite a challenging journey. Jeff knew exactly what I'd been through: he'd been certified to lead this same exact training years earlier. Since our mentor–mentee relationship had begun, we'd become very close. Jeff was like a father figure to me.

I managed to blurt out, "Thanks so much, Jeff!"

Then, with his bald head shining under the fluorescent lighting, Jeff flashed a mischievous grin and looked me dead in the eye. Coolly, he said, "Why don't you go ahead and turn the shirt around?"

I flipped the shirt over.

The first thing I saw was the large black circle. Then, the smaller rings of white, blue, and red, with the tiny yellow circle in the middle came into focus (see Figure 6.2).

It took a moment to register.

Bull's-eye.

Figure 6.2   The Gift: Back

I'll never forget what Jeff said next.

> Alain, welcome to leadership.
> As a leader, you'll always be a target.
> If you're a great leader, you'll be the target of people's hopes, dreams, even their envy.
> If you're a lousy leader, you'll be the target of people's disappointment, apathy, and blame.
> You can't *not* be a target. You'll always be a target.
> Now what type of target will you be? That's your job to figure out.

Jeff's words have stuck with me since that day. His metaphor of a leader as a target wonderfully captures the interplay between self-awareness and social awareness. You need to know how what you say and do influences the hearts and minds of those you lead. Because every business is a people business, every business is also a perceptions business. Does what you say and do connect you to others? Or does it create a rift?

Establishing credibility starts with understanding the connection between your actions and their impact on others. And here's where it gets tricky: that impact isn't the same for everyone. You need to tailor your credibility, one person at a time.

LEADERSHIP IS A ONE-ON-ONE RELATIONSHIP

Gallup is the world's oldest and most prestigious research and polling company. In 1974, Gallup decided they wanted to find out the answer to a fundamental question: "What creates the world's most successful employees?"

Gallup embarked on a gigantic research project that lasted more than 20 years. They surveyed more than one million employees around the world in over 100 countries. They questioned more than 80,000 managers, ranging from frontline supervisors to senior executives.

Gallup asked each person a series of specific questions about his or her work experience. The sum of the responses yielded a tremendous amount of data. Gallup researchers then took that data and analyzed it to see what they could find.

After their detailed analysis, Gallup discovered that there was one single factor above all others that determined what made an employee successful and effective, as defined by these characteristics:

- Customer satisfaction/loyalty
- Profitability
- Productivity
- Turnover[1]

The answer had nothing to do with employees' salary, benefits, or if they worked for one of the "Fortune Top 100 Companies to Work For."

What success ultimately boiled down to was this: the employee's relationship with his or her immediate supervisor.

Leading isn't an abstract idea that exists between you and somebody else or a group of people. It's a connection that's built through a genuine relationship. The workplace isn't an address on an office building. It's an experience that depends largely on whom one works for.

As a leader, through words and actions, you create a culture where your people succeed or flounder. You have the biggest effect. In fact, Gallup has found that 70% of the variance among lousy, good, and great cultures can be found in the knowledge, skills, and talent of the team leader. Not the players, but the team leader.[2]

Because of the disproportionate influence that immediate supervisors have, they shape the reality of the workplace. Think back on your own career. While working at one organization, have you had the experience of reporting to two (or more) different people? Depending on whom you reported to, did it feel as though you were working for two (or more) completely different companies? (Or maybe it felt like you were living on two different planets!) The power of the immediate supervisor–employee relationship is why Gallup, when publishing its findings, wrote that "it is her relationship with her immediate manager that will determine how long she stays and how productive she is while she is there."[3] People don't leave companies; they leave their direct leaders.

If you want to be a great leader and have those you lead perform at their best, the onus is on you to create an effective leader–follower relationship. You set the tone. You lay the groundwork of connection for what that relationship will become. The first step on that journey is establishing your credibility.

Credibility comes from the Latin *credibilis*, meaning, "worthy to be believed." It shares the same etymological root as the word *credit*—a loan, a thing entrusted to another. Employees don't give you their intellect, skills, and efforts; they loan them to you and your organization on a day-to-day basis.

For people to truly follow you, they must believe you're worth following. It doesn't matter how passionate, visionary, or articulate you are. The principle is so important that Jim Kouzes and Barry Posner, authors of the seminal leadership book *The Leadership Challenge*, refer to this as their first law of leadership: "If you don't believe the messenger, you won't believe the message."[4]

Belief in someone isn't an abstract idea. It's a visceral feeling. In fact, leadership is strongest when it lives close to home. It's individual and extremely personal.

When people are asked to identify their most significant leadership role models, most people choose someone from their family. The next most significant role models chosen are teachers, coaches, or work supervisors, depending on the age of the person being asked.[5] This makes sense: teachers, coaches, and bosses play such an important role because they're the people you spend the most time with on a regular basis. Their unique role comes built-in with a window of opportunity.

The people you lead would like nothing more than for you to be the leader that they've been waiting for. As they wait, they're paying attention. They want to see how you will show up. They want to see what you will do.

The fact is, no matter where you live or what your level of leadership, you're being watched. Right now. If you lead people, those you lead are studying your words and actions for signs and signals. They're seeking clues of connection. They want to know if they belong, are approved of, and if their future place in the tribe is secure.

Don't take all this scrutiny too personally. It's not just you. This happens to all leaders. It's a natural biological result of evolution. As social animals, this what all higher-order primates do. Harvard University Press editor and author Julia Kirby noted that when apes and monkeys are "threatened, subordinates glance obsessively toward the group leader, looking for indications of how to respond."[6] In fact, even when they're not in danger, baboons continue to conduct "a visual check on their alpha male two or three times per minute."[7]

However, this constant scrutiny does not work both ways. A defining feature of the alpha is how *little* attention he pays to his subordinates. Citing biologist Michael R. A. Chance's work, Kirby writes that "the whole key to a social group's hierarchy is its 'attention structure.'"[8]

Realistically, your people may not be glancing at you every twenty seconds, like baboons do. However, this doesn't negate the principle that people lower in a hierarchy watch the higher-ups far more closely and frequently than those above look down.

Come to grips with the fact that you live in a fishbowl. You're not going to change this phenomenon. You're constantly under a microscope. And although you shouldn't take the scrutiny personally, you should take the consequences of it very personally. Because people see every move you make, you'll want to make sure you're making the right moves.

Pablo, the CFO of a large financial services firm, recently brought this lesson to life. Pablo recounted to a group of newly promoted managers:

> This was during the 2008 financial crisis. I was a managing director at the time, and I was sitting at a conference table with a team of six executives in Stanley (the COO)'s office.

The team was trying to salvage a massive deal. This was our fourth day of working 16–18 hours/day. It was now 9:00 p.m. As we're working, Stanley's sitting at his desk, keeled over with his head in his hands resting on the desk. He looks like he's collapsed on the table in front of him.

Like all the rest of us on the team, Stanley is flat-out exhausted. Yet, from this prone position, he tells us all how proud he is of us and our work, and that we're making great progress on this deal. We're all excited about the work we've done.

The next morning, I'm approached by two of my team members. They've already been told the "bad news" from some other employees, and want to know:

"When are the layoffs going to start?"

I'm thinking: "What are they talking about? What layoffs?"

It took me some time and some detective work to figure out what had happened. It turns out that Stanley's office had large windows. All the meetings were completely visible from the outside.

Some other employees had seen Stanley crumpled over and with his head down on his desk the night before. They'd created a whole scenario about what was going down. Seeing his head down on the desk, they'd convinced themselves that the firm was going under. Panicked, they started spreading their own fears and "bad news" around.

Pablo finished by saying, "What I learned that day is that as a leader, your game face is always showing. So know which game face you have on. Everything you do and say sends a message."

Being perpetually alert to what you do and say is one of the most important habits for leaders to cultivate. Self-awareness takes work. Moreover, it's not enough just to be mindful of all that you do and say. It's also important to be attentive to what you don't do and don't say. After all, non-behavior also sends a message, and it also gets put under a microscope and picked apart.

For instance, a few years ago, I was in Chicago, leading a customer service conference with a group of 300 senior flight attendants from a major airline.

During a break, one of the participants pulled me aside. Her name was Francine, and, with her blue dress and red scarf, she couldn't have been any more impeccably dressed. Francine said,

> I appreciate all that you're trying to do to help us here today. But I need to tell you: it's not going to make any difference. You want to know what's wrong with this airline? They're a bunch of hypocrites!

As she was talking, Francine's face morphed from beige to pink to red. It was clear she was really upset.

Before I could even say, "Tell me more," Francine jumped in again.

> I'm based in Frankfurt, and I worked the first-class cabin on the way over here to Chicago. Those first-class passengers, they're our top-tier customers—those tickets cost a minimum of five figures, easy. And they ask us to give our all and make every customer in first class feel appreciated for [his or her] business and loyalty. I spend a lot of time upfront—prepping for the flight, reviewing the boarding list, looking at each passenger's flight history, memorizing their names, figuring out what they'll want to drink when they come on board ... all of it. It's a lot of time and a lot of effort. And I'm proud of what I do.
>
> So on this flight over here, one of our senior executives is coming over too. He's pretty high up—you'd see his picture in our in-flight magazine every once in a while. He pre-boards and sits in the first row by the window.
>
> You'd think, at the least, he'd stand up, and shake hands with the other first-class cabin passengers. He could introduce himself as a part of the airline and thank them for their business and loyalty. That's what they tell us that we need to do every day. Wouldn't a real leader do that, too?

But what does he do? He plops himself in his seat, pulls out his laptop, puts his head down, and ignores everyone around him for the next eight hours.

To make it even worse? When he gets off the plane, he doesn't even say thank you to me.

And they wonder why this industry is going down the toilet.

As I listened to Francine lambasting the airline executive, I wondered what was going through the senior executive's mind, sitting there in first class. We don't get to hear his side of the story. Maybe he was working on an important project with an urgent deadline. Maybe he was having a personal or family crisis. Maybe he was feeling ill.

We can't know for sure. But frankly, when it comes to his credibility, it doesn't matter. Francine sees what she sees, and her perception is reality. Intentions don't cut it. Ultimately, that leader sitting in first class left a strong impression with one of his employees. He may have not have known he was doing it, but he'd left one nonetheless.

From Pablo's and Francine's stories, it's obvious how crucial credibility is to leadership. But how do you build it? Where do you start? Which quality is most important for leaders to demonstrate to build credibility?

Thankfully, there's a definitive (and well-researched) answer. Jim Kouzes and Barry Posner have spent nearly 30 years studying this very question. They've surveyed more than 100,000 people around the world. They've asked these people, based on their experiences of being led by others, "What are the top qualities that you look for, admire, and would willingly follow?"

The results are surprising, not for their content, but for their stability. It turns out that the top answer has held its peak position on the list every year since 1990. The world may have changed drastically since then, but what people want most from their leaders has remained shockingly constant.

You probably already know what the answer is. You only need to ask yourself, "What's the trait that I look for and admire most in leaders I would follow?"

The quality that's most needed to build credibility is **honesty**.[9]

It makes perfect sense. Honesty gives people confidence. It enables them to believe that a connection is worth having. It's the chief ingredient of trust. Given how essential honesty is to building connection, we're going to explore what it really means and what specific actions you can take to increase it.

HONESTY

When people first think about honesty, they begin with the basic definition: telling the truth. Although this is a good start, truth-telling is Honesty 101. For leaders, this should be a given. Great leaders tell the truth, but they don't stop there. They focus on living the truth. They do this through having clear values and then acting in accordance with those values. This alignment casts a halo of integrity, which shows up in actions both big and small.

For instance, I recently hired a new electrician, Joseph, to do some work in the basement of my house. The house's previous owner had dabbled in home-rigged wiring and had left a giant wiry, tangled, and unsafe mess that needed to be cleaned up. I'd put the work off for a few years, and it was time to do something about it.

Joseph came over to meet me, check out the basement, and give me an estimate on the job. After his review, he told me that it would probably take it the better part of the day to get it done, somewhere between six and eight hours. We agreed he'd show up the following Thursday at 8:00 a.m.

Thursday morning, Joseph rang the doorbell promptly at 8:00 am. I had to work off-site all day, so I led him into the basement and told him to let himself out when he was finished.

When I returned home at 5:30, the basement looked fantastic: the giant gnarled tangle of wires had magically disappeared. In addition, Joseph had replaced the old, rusting circuit breaker panel with a shiny new distribution board and had clearly labeled every breaker switch in the house. I called Joseph to check in and let him know how pleased I was with his work. During our talk, I asked him how long the job took.

He told me, "Really, it moved along. Faster than I'd expected. I also had to stop for a bit during the day. Let's call it four hours. I'll bill you for four hours."

Four hours?

I was awestruck. I hadn't been home all day, and to me, it seemed like a lot of work. Joseph could've said, "Actually, it took nine hours," and I would have believed him. "Eight," and I would've been fine. "Six," and I would have been very happy.

Four hours?! I could barely contain my excitement. Just from my one experience with Joseph, it became clear who would be my go-to electrician from now on. And you can probably guess how many friends I've raved to about Joseph and his work. I've already referred three new customers to him.

Joseph's story shows that to begin building credibility, you don't need to perform colossal feats. You can start small. In fact, in our exchanges, Joseph demonstrated several behaviors that you can use to build connection with the people you want to lead. These include showing up on time, doing what you say you will do, and being consistent.

SHOWING UP ON TIME

If I could only choose one practice to exercise growing my credibility, I'd choose this one: showing up on time. You should treat your performance in this arena as a big deal: it is. Think about it—timeliness is the easiest and most visible thing to measure. You're either here or you're not.

Lateness is about much more than just a few wasted minutes. There's a reason one of the key metrics that kids have throughout their schooling is "days tardy." In life, being on time is the most basic social contract: that of presence. When you're late, your behavior sends the message that "I had other things going on that were a higher priority than being here with you." When you're on time, you send a message that you value the other person.

In addition, the habit of showing up on time is a keystone habit. Although all habits affect us, certain ones are particularly significant. Keystone habits have the power to spawn other habits. This in turn creates small wins, boosts motivation, and builds momentum. As Charles Duhigg, the author of *The Power of Habit*, has written,

Keystone habits influence how we work, eat, play, live, spend, and communicate. Keystone habits can start a process that, over time, transforms everything.[10]

When you practice the keystone habit of showing up on time, you can also improve the following other connection-boosting behaviors.

DOING WHAT YOU SAY YOU WILL DO

When you open your mouth to promise to do something, you immediately create expectations for those who are listening to you. For them, that promise is now a psychological loop of tension that seeks resolution. That loop will quietly keep asking them, "Will she do what she said? Or won't she?"

People crave closure. That's why kids (and adults) hate it when you tell them they must go to bed before that TV show is over. When you follow up and follow through, you bring a satisfying resolution to that tension.

Every time you show up on time, you strengthen the connection between your words ("I'll see you at 8:00 a.m.") and your deeds ("It's 8:00 a.m. I'm here.")

This is what's meant by "walking your talk." When you walk your talk, you're seen as congruent. When you don't, you're out of integrity. Something is off. This is what Ralph Waldo Emerson expressed so eloquently when he wrote, "Who you are speaks so loudly I cannot hear what you are saying."

Doing what you say you will do is the perfect definition of accountability. After all, accountability comes from the world of accounting. In finance, the two sides of the balance sheet (assets and liabilities) need to equal each other to be "in account." In leadership, the two sides of your balance sheet are "what you say you'll do" and "what you actually did." When you do what you say you will do, your two sides balance out. You're in integrity. You're accountable.

Because showing up on time is the first step of relationship building, it's a great place to practice conscious commitment making. You can start with "I'll be there at 8:00 a.m." As you master the basics, you can progress to more advanced commitments, such as, "I'll get you the report by noon Friday."

As you strengthen your accountability muscle, you can stretch into greater and greater commitments. You might also try out promises in a different context: "I'll be home for dinner by 7:00 p.m." or "I'll call you once a week, Mom."

Following through is being accountable for your actions. The key thing to remember is that your word is your promise. This means you need to stay conscious of your agreements.

> Each action you take will either strengthen or weaken your credibility and your connection.

BEING CONSISTENT

Another connection builder is consistency. This is the practice of doing what you say you will do repeated multiple times over an extended period. When you show up on time, every time, you send the message that you are someone who can be counted on.

Now, no one is going to throw you a party for showing up on time. However, it's the little things—done consistently—that make a big difference. The repetition has a multiplier effect.

Consider the example of Doug Conant. For over 40 years, starting as a marketing assistant at General Mills and rising to the ranks of CEO of Campbell Soup Company and later as chairman at Avon Products, Conant has consistently made appreciating employees a priority.

When Conant came on board as the CEO of Campbell Soup Company in 2001, the business was suffering. Conant turned the company around by making the company's employees a priority. As Conant said in an interview, "Staying close to home will take you a long way. Then you take care of your business and smartly go to where consumers of the future are or will be."[11]

For Conant, appreciation is no mere idea—it's a daily practice. Conant deeply understands the power of connection. During his tenure as CEO of Campbell Soup Company, Conant and his executive assistants spent a good 30 to 60 minutes a day scanning his mail and the internal website looking for news of people who made a difference at Campbell's.[12]

Conant then practiced a form of leadership alchemy: he transformed all that employee data into connection gold. With explicit detail, Conant hand-wrote thank-you notes to Campbell employees around the world. How consistent was his habit? In his 10-year stint as CEO, Conant wrote 30,000 thank-you notes. That works out to more than eight cards a day, seven days a week, for ten years. (By the way, the company only had 20,000 employees at the time.)

This concept of consistency is simple to understand. However, the challenge in the real world—the too-much-to-do, not-enough-time-to-do-it real world—is that consistently doing the actions that strengthen your credibility gets pushed aside by other things. What's important makes way for what is urgent.

As an example, perhaps you've worked with a leader who (somehow) managed to perpetually reschedule your regular one-on-one meetings, only to never get around to having them. Or the leader who shows up to your meetings consistently late. Part of you understands (she's busy and important, after all), but part of you trusts her a little less. And the connection weakens.

Leading today is not easy. It's easier to be distracted from your top priorities than ever because there are more distractions than ever. The sense of overwhelm can prompt you to come up with a (seemingly valid) list of reasons as to why you "can't" spend the time doing those things that are most important.

Other projects can always take top billing. But where does that leave those around you? For example, how committed are you to helping your people to grow?

I once had a leadership mentor who told me the following:

If you want to know what a person values, look at their bank statement: see what they spend their money on. If you want to know what a leader values, look at their calendar: see where they spend their time.

COMMITMENT CREATES CREDIBILITY

Susan is the CEO of a retail organization. She's been CEO for more than 20 years. Susan's company owns and manages more than 700 stores, separated into 100 regions around the United States. Each region has between five and eight stores. Each store has its own manager, and every region has a regional manager.

During her tenure, Susan has created a regional manager (RM) ritual: the regional review.

Once a year, each RM (along with the RM's boss, the regional VP) meets with Susan. To prepare for the meeting (the regional review), the RM creates a report on the state of their business: how their stores have performed against all the company metrics, what things have gone well, future market opportunities, areas for improvement, and so on.

The reports are lengthy and comprehensive: a few RMs told me they spend close to 40 hours getting their reports ready for the regional review.

The RM, her VP, and Susan all meet to discuss that RM's business. Using the report as a guide to the conversation, every review looks different. Susan can stop the process at any moment. Depending on the issue on the table, Susan will then do one or more of the following:

- Inquire or probe deeper
- Coach
- Mentor
- Congratulate
- Give feedback

According to the RMs, the district review with Susan is both the most challenging and the most rewarding part of their year. Some of the RMs told me the following:

> Nothing gets by Susan. If you don't know what's going on in your business, she'll find out you don't know.
>
> You can't fake your way through the review. If you try, you'll crash and burn.
>
> Susan's a genius. Her operational wisdom is so deep; every time I walk out of there, I know I'm a better leader.

Susan is this incredible combination of tough business savvy and warm supportive coach. She makes you feel like you're the most important person she's ever talked to. I don't know what this company would be like without her.

Each regional review with Susan lasts between two and three hours. Yes, you read that right: two and three hours per RM. Susan meets with every single one of them—*all 100*—every year. Do the math: if you average it out to 2.5 hours per RM, that's more than 250 hours in reviews. More than six weeks of Susan's year is spent on this ritual. That's quite an investment.

Susan's consistent actions create her credibility. Watching her work with her team, I saw a living, breathing model of trust in action. Susan's commitment to develop her team is reciprocated in their connection to her and their commitment to the company. More than half of the RMs have been with the company for more than 15 years, and the majority of them have been promoted from within. Susan is someone who knows her priorities.

Susan is in the leadership game for the long haul. She knows that by building capacity in her people, not only will they hit their numbers but also they'll bring the same commitment to coach and mentor the leaders they lead. She wants to do more than just run a retail business. She wants to leave a legacy that will outlast her. She understands the great responsibility that comes with her power.

One of the major faults leaders can make is to assume they get trust just because of their title. Your title might get you watched, but what will others see? The next move is yours. Your credibility exists only insofar as others believe in you: in your integrity, track record, and commitment.

Connection can't be built in an instant. It requires time, patience, and perseverance. You can't fake it: it takes sincerity and interest. It can take a long time to earn, and it can be destroyed in a moment. But thankfully, it's not some mystical innate quality. Great leaders are made, not born. They're made by practicing small habits over and over.

Be on time. Do what you say you'll do. Be consistent. These are the small things that become big things. Work at these diligently, and you may just discover your secret superpower.

Chapter Resources

Lead with Credibility

- With my leadership title comes responsibility.
- I understand how as a leader, I'm a target of others' beliefs and expectations.
- I see how leadership is a one-on-one relationship.
- It's up to me to lay the groundwork of connection.
- I know that because of my role, I'm being watched.

Show Up on Time

- I'm aware of how long it can take to get to the places I need to go.
- I include a buffer so that that I arrive promptly and calmly.
- I have a good system for tracking and updating my appointment calendar.
- I give at least 24 hours' notice when I must reschedule appointments, and I do so sparingly.
- I don't use excuses (weather, traffic, etc.) for my tardiness.
- I strive to be as on time as a Swiss watch. People should be able to set their clocks based on my behavior.
- When I am late, I own up to it and say something.

Do What You Say You Will Do

- I have a good system for tracking my commitments.
- I finish meetings by recapping next action steps and time lines.
- I offer times that I'm available to meet when I say that I'm willing and available to meet with someone.
- I use the phrase *as promised* when delivering on my commitments.
- I'm aware of (and follow through on) promises I've made even if they haven't been explicitly verbalized.

- I explicitly clarify scope of commitments upfront so all parties' promises are clear.
- If I need to renegotiate a commitment, I do so as early as possible.
- When I don't follow through on a commitment, I own up to it and say something.

Be Consistent

- I know which actions I need to demonstrate on a repeated basis.
- I check in with an accountability partner for support on developing healthy habits.
- I ask for feedback on how much I can be relied on.
- I seek coaching and support for areas where I'm inconsistent.

Part III

COMMUNICATION

L eaders spend 70% to 90% of their time in group or team interactions every day.[1] Thus, it should come as no surprise that when people are asked, "What is your biggest challenge at work?" communication is usually at the top of the list. Communication and leadership are inextricably linked.

If you see communication as just sending messages, then you're just seeing the tip of the iceberg. It's so much more. It's a skill and an art. It includes knowing how to provide appropriate context. It's reading an individual or a group. It's adapting messaging on the fly. Effective communication can inform, persuade, assure, and inspire.

In Part III, you'll learn how to grow your skill as communicator. You'll understand what it is, how it works, and the biggest obstacles to communicating well. You'll explore the multiple dimensions of communication through stories of leaders who communicated well under pressure and those who failed and why. You'll get keys that, when applied, will raise your communication skill (and your leadership ability) to a whole new level.

Communication is the next step on the leadership path after connection. Empathy and credibility create a strong bond of trust between you and those you lead. They're willing and eager to have a dialogue with you. The skills taught in Part III will help you figure out what to say, how to say it best, and how to create Shared Understanding.

Chapter 7

THE CONFUSING CONUNDRUM OF COMMUNICATION

The single biggest problem in communication is the illusion that it has taken place.

—George Bernard Shaw

On a sunny day in August 1964, the S. S. *Rotterdam* set sail from the Netherlands to New York harbor. On board was my mother, Gilberte. She was going on what she thought was a vacation. She had no idea that she would arrive in America, meet my father, begin a family, and never return to live in her home country of Belgium.

In preparation for her trip, as a native French speaker, she'd been sharpening her English-language skills. With nearly 1,500 passengers on board, she had plenty of opportunities to practice. One evening, as the sun was beginning to set across the water, she sat on the promenade deck, learning about New York City from three of her newly made American friends. With dinner being served in about an hour, Gilberte knew she still needed to shower and change into proper dining attire. As she stood up to say goodbye, she turned to her new friend, Emily, and said, "I will kiss you many times in the French way."

113

Emily stiffened and her face turned white. After a moment of shock, and some confusion on everyone's part, someone stepped in to interpret. For a French speaking–Belgian like my mother, "the French way" meant *bises*—little pecks on the cheeks, which is a customary way to say good-bye. Emily thought that "the French way" meant French kissing.

In other words, Emily thought my mom had just announced she was about to kiss her and slip her the tongue. This story, now a family classic, is exactly what's meant by "lost in translation."

If you're serious about becoming a better leader, become a better communicator. Hart Research Associates found that 93% of employers consider good communication skills more important than a college graduate's major.[1]

Communication—personal and organizational—is essential to leadership success. There are thousands of books and articles on the subject. Yet, miscommunications and missed communications abound.

In this chapter, you'll learn why being an effective communicator is so much harder than it looks and how the default settings of the human communication system have built-in flaws. You'll also learn three of the biggest obstacles to communicating well, so you can spot and avoid them in the future.

Sometimes, a little miscommunication is no big deal. The results are comical, and (like my mother's trip on the *Rotterdam*) become the stuff of family legend. Other times, however, the results can be disastrous.

CATASTROPHIC COMMUNICATION

In 2002, a General Motors (GM) engineer was tasked with designing the ignition systems for the Chevy Cobalt and Pontiac G5. The resulting ignition switch was below GM's own quality specifications. In numerous instances, when the vehicles were in motion, the substandard switch would suddenly shut off the engines in the midst of driving, as well as shut down the air bag safety system.

A safety recall was issued by GM—but not until 2014, over *11 years* later. In the interim, the faulty ignitions had caused numerous accidents and were responsible (as documented by GM itself) for 124 deaths. How could such a danger be allowed to persist for so long? Why wasn't the problem caught sooner?

GM's internal records show that the ignition issue surfaced as early as 2005. Yet, as the investigative report to GM's board of directors states, "Group after group and committee after committee within GM that reviewed the issue failed to take action or acted too slowly."[2]

The issue was killing their customers—literally. Yet the company did nothing. How could this happen? Was it a case of collective organizational insanity? Why did they fail to act?

The awful truth boils down to a choice of words: *customer convenience.*

When the ignition issues were noticed early on, the internal GM people had to classify the problem by its severity. Thinking it was only a minor flaw, they labeled it as "customer convenience": the category reserved for something believed to be merely a bother for some drivers. Because of this first misdiagnosis, later GM experts and leaders reviewing the case didn't grasp the urgency and severity of the ignition switch issue.

Had the issue been communicated as a "safety defect," GM leadership would have jumped into action. Safety defect is the industry's way to flag a significant risk, one requiring immediate response. According to the report, "cost considerations ... would have been immaterial had the problem been properly categorized in the first instance."[3]

Two words. It's horrible to think that choosing one pair of words— *customer convenience*—over another—*safety defect*—could lead to such tragic consequences. Had the second two words been chosen, 124 deaths could have been prevented. General Motors would have also avoided paying out $1.5 billion in fines and compensation.

As this story vividly shows, communication is no mere abstract concept. It is the most powerful leadership tool you have. Treat it as such. Depending on how well you use it, it will greatly expand or diminish your influence.

It doesn't take a human fatality to show the negative impact that poor communication can bring to a workplace. There's an epidemic of shoddy communication happening and its effects are far reaching. Consider these findings:

- A survey in *HR* magazine reports that of 4,000 employees, 46% said they routinely received confusing or unclear directions, and

36% of these employees reported it happening up to three times a day. Participants estimated they wasted about 40 minutes of productivity *every day* trying to interpret unclear or confusing directions.[4]

- U.S. hospitals waste more than $12 billion annually as a result of communication inefficiency among care providers.[5]
- A study by leadership consultancy Fierce, Inc. found that 86% of employees cite lack of collaboration or ineffective communications as the main source of workplace failures.[6]

Why is there such a prevalence of poor communication?

Communication is taken for granted. It's generally assumed that it's happening. After all, we have mouths that talk and ears that hear, fingers that type, and eyes that read. Assuming all these parts are in working condition, the default is to assume that we're able-bodied and able communicators. How could we be bad at something so natural? We've been doing it, in one form or another, for our whole lives.

As such, we treat communication like a basic utility. Just like the electricity in your home, it's expected that it will just be there for you when you turn it on. The process is routine. In fact, it's so routine that you only pay attention to it when it doesn't work and you're left in the dark. Not until the outage do you notice you have a real problem to fix.

Yet, although communication appears to be a utility, it's not so basic. Electricity is binary. It only offers two options: the light works when it's on and doesn't work when it's off.

Communication is a lot more complicated. Just because it's "on" doesn't guarantee that it's "working." What's heard isn't always what's said. And what's said can be different from what's meant. And sometimes, silence sends a louder message than words could ever convey.

Most leaders don't suffer from a lack of communication quantity. There's lots of communication going on. What's missing is quality. There's a shortage of effective communication.

The best leaders don't take effective communication for granted; they strive to continually improve their abilities. They know that the nature of transferring meaning from one person to another is rife with challenges. They accept obstacles as part and parcel of the process.

They just happen to know what those obstacles will be in advance, so they can proactively deal with them.

OBSTACLES TO COMMUNICATING WELL

Even with the best of intentions, communication can easily go off the rails. In part, this is by design: the human communication system comes preloaded with major bugs. The nature of the communication process contains three major obstacles: lack of alignment, lack of shared context, and overload.

Lack of Alignment

In the game of horseshoes, the goal is quite simple. It's to throw a "ringer": that is, to get your horseshoe around a metal stake. Getting one ringer takes some work. Getting three ringers in a row is a lot harder. Effective communication is the equivalent of landing three ringers in a row.

The rings represent what you, the sender of information, mean, what you say, and what the receiver hears (see Figure 7.1).

Figure 7.1   The Three Rings of Effective Communication

For the communication to be "perfect," all three rings have to land on top of each other, in complete alignment. In other words, what you mean is exactly what you say, which is exactly what I hear.

That happens about as often as a blue moon.

Why does this occur so rarely? It's because most senders make a giant mistake: they assume that what they mean is what gets heard: "Of course my meaning is blatantly clear to everyone."

Senders are confident that their intended meaning is obvious because, for them, no effort is required to make sense of the meaning. The meaning doesn't have to travel anywhere. What senders mean is crystal clear—in their own minds. They're the primary source, with zero degrees of separation. It's as if they're playing the game of telephone with themselves.

Even I—and I teach these pitfalls and know to watch out for them—am not immune. I fell into the trap of a "but it's crystal clear in my own mind!" situation recently.

My family has two longtime friends, Pam and Charlie, who came to stay with us for the weekend. They live in Washington, DC, and drove up to visit us at our home in western Massachusetts.

Our house has a driveway that allows one car to pull in from the street and then widens so that two cars can park side by side at the end. We're a two-car family, so when friends drive over, they need to park their car in the driveway behind our two cars, essentially blocking us in. It's not a big deal. We're used to it, and if we have to leave, we just do a little bit of car juggling so we can get out.

Anyway, on this particular weekend, when Pam and Charlie were visiting, I needed to leave for the airport. Because Pam's car was parked behind mine, I asked her to move her car.

She asked me, "Where do you want me to park my car?"

I replied (as I always would in this situation), "Park your car in front of the house."

Pam paused. She looked at me funny. She said, "You want me to park *where?*"

I repeated, "Park your car in front of the house."

She paused again, and gave me an even stranger look. "You're telling me you want me to park my car in front of the house."

I started to feel annoyed. I'd already repeated myself twice and it looked like I'd have to say it again. "Yes, Pam, park your car in front of the house."

Pam then publicly declared to the kitchen, as though there were not four, but 40 people assembled there, "Alright. I'm going to park my car in front of the house."

And off she went.

I went out to my car, put my suitcase in the trunk, and then got in on the driver's side. I turned the ignition and put the car in reverse.

As I slowly backed down the driveway, I cautiously looked around, careful not to bump into anything or anyone. And then something startled me, snapping my attention to the right. What was that?

Then I realized what happened. Pam had parked her car.

In front of the house.

As in, directly in front of the house.

As in, on top of the flowerbeds right in front of the house. Flowerbeds that were now crushed under Pam's wheels.

In my mind, "In front of the house" meant *on the curb of the street* in front of the house. Wasn't that obvious? What else could I have possibly meant? How could Pam have not understood what I was saying?

Psychologists refer to this phenomenon as a projection bias, when you unconsciously assume that others share your current thoughts and feelings. Because you're you, you automatically get an all-access pass into your own brain, with all the behind-the-scenes information. In your mind, what you mean is patently obvious. In fact, it's so obvious that for anyone else to doubt how obvious it is can be a source of irritation. After all, what else could you possibly mean?

However, this bias tricks you into thinking others have the same thoughts that you do. What's clear to you, however, is fuzzy for everyone else. No one else is given that same all-access view of your brain, up close and personal. They're stuck trying to make sense of what they're seeing from a seat in the rear mezzanine. Although they don't see it the way you see it, your bias convinces you that they do. Your brain's default setting mistakenly assumes that your subjective point of view is objective reality.

If you know that, as humans, we're wired for misunderstanding, you have a leg up on most other people. You don't need to look too far to watch people fall into this cognitive trap on a regular basis. People in workplaces are repeatedly astonished that what they say isn't what gets understood. You'll hear them say things such as these:

- "I sent the email. They should know what to do."
- "What's the problem? Why can't they just talk to the customer and sort things out?"
- "Senior management doesn't have a clue about what things are really like for us. Why don't they realize how stupid this new process is?"

In fact, anytime you hear someone start a sentence with "They should..." or "Don't they realize..." or "Why can't they..." the projection bias has reared its ugly head. And if it's you who does this on a regular basis, stop. It's time to give up your office romance with incredulity.

Leaders who deny that projection bias exists operate with faulty assumptions. The authors Clarke and Crossland call these "the four fatal assumptions of leaders."[7]

The Four Fatal Assumptions of Leaders

1. Constituents understand.
2. They care.
3. They agree.
4. They will take appropriate action.

I once harbored these four fatal assumptions—and paid for it, as you might recall from Chapter 1 when I lost an election to my colleague, Gary. I had assumed that the people I worked with knew what had to happen and would just get out and vote for me. I was wrong.

When communicating, you need to work with what *is*, rather than what you *think* it should be. There's no use in denying the fact that your intended meaning will change when it's received by others. It just will. To try to deny this is to deny biology.

Lack of alignment happens when what you mean is not what you say and/or what gets heard. It is the most common and most pervasive of all the obstacles to effective communication.

Lack of Shared Context

The next challenge to effective communication results from how your message is framed. Your message is precisely that: yours. You own it, and it lives in your head. In that brain of yours, you automatically construct four walls around the message. You know what it means, and even more critically, you understand why the information is important.

Communication is your attempt to transfer this information to others. In fact, this is how the dictionary defines communication: the *transfer of information*. In a static, theoretical world, this definition works just fine.

But that's not how the real world works. The minds of those you lead aren't empty vessels just hoping and waiting to be filled by your message and your wisdom.

Recently, I moderated a leadership town hall for a large pharmaceutical company. Seated on stage next to me was the CEO, Isaac. I was there to facilitate an interactive session between Isaac and his audience of 300 executives. Isaac would open by explaining the company's business strategy, and we'd end with a live question-and-answer session.

Isaac's an animated guy, and his overall knowledge of the business is brilliant. But there was a major problem: his comments were convoluted. He jumped into details without giving a rationale. There was no context to what he was saying. Random thoughts sprang out of other random thoughts. People had no sense of how anything he said mattered to them.

Looking out on the audience, I could see people nodding off and tuning out. In fact, while Isaac was rambling, I felt my own eyes drifting shut—and I was on the stage next to him! Isaac was working hard, but his information was indigestible to everyone else. It wasn't until after the town hall that I was able to offer Isaac feedback and coaching to help him clarify and structure his thinking better.

Your audience, whether it's made up of one person or 300, needs a lot more than the *what*. They also need to know the *when*, *where*, *how*, and especially the *why*. Why should they listen to you? Why does what you have to say matter? What do they need to do differently because of what you have to say?

Lack of context sets your communication adrift. It's no accident that 59% of U.S. workers say that wasteful meetings are the biggest hindrance to productivity.[8] So many of these meetings lack proper context. As a result, information flows in one ear and out the other. People feel lost, and they don't know what to do next. Confusion goes up and engagement goes down.

Overload

A few years ago, I attended a large leadership conference. With more than 2,000 people in attendance and the event spanning multiple days, there were both large plenary and small breakout sessions. After lunch on day 2, I went into a breakout workshop titled, "Leading the Next Generation of Workers." The topic intrigued me.

As I sat down, I saw that the presenter was still preparing for his session. His PowerPoint was on the screen but not yet in slideshow mode. Suddenly, Judith, the woman seated next to me, whispered in my ear.

Do you see that? I'm leaving now while I still have the chance.

I was confused. I asked her what she was talking about.

Look at his slide deck. This is scheduled to be a 60-minute session. He's got 136 slides. I don't think I can take it!

Judith got up and walked out of the room.

Judith's feeling probably feels familiar to you. People at work are suffering from information overload. Consider that every *second* there are more than

- 8,030 tweets
- 66,855 Google searches
- 73,741 YouTube videos viewed
- 2,689,607 emails sent[9]

People have plenty of other messages competing for their precious brain cells. They're not going to focus on you just because you want them to. People don't want more information—they want insight.

Too many mediocre leaders think of other people as empty vessels to be filled. As such, they ascribe to a more-is-better philosophy when it comes to sharing information. More is not better.

Herman Ebbinghaus, a 19th-century German psychologist, did pioneering research into the science of forgetting. Since his initial work, there's been controversy over the exact percentages of how much content our minds retain. However, one thing is agreed on: forgetting increases over time. Your message will dilute with each passing hour, day, and week.

The solution is not to try to cram more in. Instead, great communicators use the idea of "teach less, learn more." To get others to retain more of your message, your message needs to be simpler and clearer.

Lack of alignment, lack of context, and information overload aren't going anywhere. They will continue to trip up leaders for the rest of time. They're hard-wired into our human operating system. But, to use an IT metaphor, you don't have to live with this default configuration. There are hacks for this system. These hacks—specific practices to increase your communication quality and speed—are simple and easy to use. When you apply them, they'll take your communication—and your leadership—to a whole new level. You'll learn these practices in the next chapter.

Chapter Resources

Communicate Effectively

- I make shared context the goal of my communications.
- I include specifics into messages to avoid misunderstandings.
- I review messages before sending them to see if they could be misinterpreted.
- I remember my bias of thinking that everyone sees and thinks about things the way I do.
- When misunderstandings happen, I assume positive intent.
- I don't assume that others understand, agree, care, and take appropriate action.
- I set context for my messaging.
- I work to eliminate distractions so that people can focus on the message at hand.
- I practice the principle of "teach less, learn more."

Chapter 8

CRACKING THE COMMUNICATION CODE

Developing excellent communication skills is absolutely essential to effective leadership. The leader must be able to share knowledge and ideas to transmit a sense of urgency and enthusiasm to others. If a leader can't get a message across clearly and motivate others to act on it, then having a message doesn't even matter.

—Gilbert Amelio, president and CEO of National
Semiconductor Corp.

At its core, effective communication isn't about transferring information. It's about *transforming* information. In physics, transformation is defined as the spontaneous change of one element into another. Transformation is an incredible, active, and dynamic process. Where you end up is vastly different from where you started.

The same is true with effective communication. When you transform information, it stops being mere data, and becomes Shared Understanding. When you achieve Shared Understanding, both parties see reality in the same way. At first glance, this may not seem like a big deal, but it's the key to working well with other people.

Shared Understanding is the holy grail of communication. Leadership success depends on it. It's why you go through all the effort of communicating in the first place.

The reason Shared Understanding is so important boils down to one vital truth:

> Shared Understanding is the
> foundation for all future action.

Just as you wouldn't build a house without a proper foundation, if you make decisions without basing them on Shared Understanding, you are making decisions based on Missed Understanding.

For example, imagine I said to you, "Let's meet for lunch on Saturday at noon."

You reply, "Okay."

What's the likelihood we can pull that off?

Compare that with "Let's meet for lunch at noon on Saturday, July 2nd at Ellen's Stardust Diner on the corner of 51st Street and Broadway in New York City."

Notice the difference? In the first example, you'd need to go back and backfill a lot more information before you could take action. If you lack Shared Understanding, decision-making is compromised. As such, your results suffer.

There's a clear process between effective communication and results (see Figure 8.1).

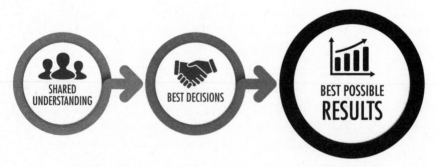

Figure 8.1 Effective Communication and Results

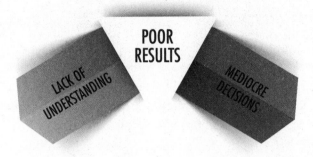

Figure 8.2 Poor Communication and Results

Good communication creates Shared Understanding, which produces better decisions, which yield better results. Better results can look like commercial success (e.g., increased profits, etc.) or cultural success (e.g., inspired employees).

On the flipside, when understanding is absent, you make poorer decisions and wind up with worse results (see Figure 8.2).

Large or small, a single communication has the potential to completely destroy the morale of your people.

COMMUNICATION GONE WRONG

I was in Atlanta to speak at an annual conference hosting the top 1,000 leaders of a global manufacturing company. The CEO was first up on day 1, kicking off the conference with a state-of-the-company address.

Now, if you were the CEO, how would you design your presentation for maximum value? Perhaps you'd prioritize these actions:

1. Making attendees feel welcomed
2. Making them feel appreciated
3. Giving them a clear roadmap of what will be covered while at the conference
4. Making them feel they're part of the larger team
5. Sharing something to inspire them and feel proud about the company

6. Providing them with the latest information about the business
7. Projecting about the future of the business
8. Providing clear calls to action to bring back to their teams after the conference ends

None of these eight items probably strike you as unusual. They're standard elements in such a conference kick-off speech. When leaders address these items, they put their audience at ease and focus them in the right direction.

For the company, this conference was a big deal. It was their one chance a year to rally their leaders, who could then in turn go back and rally their 150,000 employees around the world. The company had spent an enormous amount of money flying everyone in to be together. The CEO, in his opening address, was there to set the tone for the next few days.

Did he ever. In under 10 minutes, he turned the conference into a complete train wreck. What happened?

Imagine you're one of the 1,000 leaders at the conference. You walk into a giant hotel ballroom. It's so vast you need a map to find your banquet table, one of 100 tables in a sea of carpeting. The room quickly fills up. High-energy pop music throbs through the speakers. As you look around the room, the staging and lighting is Broadway theater–caliber quality. The music fades. The lights go black. The giant screens around the room light up.

On the monitors, an internal company video rolls. The video is an unabashed feel-good journey of your company. A feeling of pride wells up in your chest. It's extremely well produced: it looks like it was made in Hollywood. Video ends and fades to black.

A booming voice announces, "Ladies and Gentlemen, please welcome your CEO, _____!"

Huge applause. A gigantic spotlight turns on. The CEO steps behind the podium. The whole room is silent with anticipation.

The CEO begins.

No smile.

No "Hello."

No "Welcome to Atlanta."

No "Thanks for coming to spend the next four days here with us."

Instead, he blurts out, "All right, let's look at how we did last year."

With one click of a mouse, the CEO jumps into a very busy Excel slide and reviews last year's financials.

While explaining the numbers, the CEO bizarrely takes on the tone of a frustrated teacher lecturing to a group of hopelessly stupid students. He says,

> This last column here on the right of this slide, well, this represents ROIC—return on invested capital. But why am I telling you that? If you don't know what ROIC is, you shouldn't even be sitting in this room. You better know what that is.

As the CEO digs himself deeper and deeper into the hole on stage, you look around. You watch the body language of the other attendees. Even though they're seated, hands go up across chests as if to defend themselves. People exchange uncomfortable glances. Sighs become audible. You feel your own enthusiasm wane, replaced by frustration.

You think, "This can't be happening."

But, alas, it is. Another horrible business presentation was born into existence. The CEO was completely oblivious to his impact on the audience. He may have been an expert on the finances of the company, but he was a shockingly poor communicator.

This CEO is not alone. Communicating well with employees is not easy. Not only does it take skill but also will. And not everyone is up for the challenge. A recent survey conducted by Harris/Interact found that a stunning majority—69% of managers—say there is something about their role as a leader that makes them uncomfortable communicating with their employees.[1]

THE RIGHT WAY TO COMMUNICATE

This chapter will crack the communication code. It will break down the magic of communication into its component parts. You'll learn about six keys—specific behavioral practices—that you can use immediately to improve your communication skills:

1. Communicate with the end in mind
2. Have a central message

3. Create checks for understanding
4. Own and fix communication breakdowns
5. Make the implicit explicit
6. Master the medium

Key 1: Communicate with the End in Mind

The art of communication is the language of leadership.

—James Humes

Isabella was a senior VP at a large consumer goods company, facilitating a working strategy session with the senior leadership team. The
goal of the meeting was to engage, inform, and inspire the senior leaders so that they'd take full ownership of the strategy. Then, they'd be
equipped to go off and roll the strategy out to their functional teams
and execute against it for the next year.

Isabella knew the business inside and out. However, the concepts
she introduced during the session were too dense and complex. People
clearly weren't following her.

On a break, I asked Isabella how things were going. She beamed and
told me, "The meeting's going really well."

I asked her how she knew.

"We're though the first two priorities," she said proudly, "and we
only have one more to get through and there's still an hour and fifteen
minutes left."

Uh-oh. From Isabella's response, I immediately realized that her
mind-set was *content-focused*, rather than *outcome-focused*. She saw
her role as to "present" the strategy. For Isabella, this meeting was
something to get through. All she wanted was to finish up, check off
the box on her to-do list, and move on.

Isabella didn't communicate with the end in mind because she
never stopped to consider what that end should be. She didn't see the
strategy session as an opportunity to align and motivate the leaders.

She was just sharing information. In doing so, she abdicated her leadership.

Leaders work in the influence business. Every interaction is an opportunity to create value. Every act of communication should be an act toward persuading, educating, informing, inspiring, or motivating someone else to move in a desired direction.

Effective communication needs to be framed to focus on meeting the needs of those with whom you're speaking and to offer them something of value. You should never communicate for communication's sake. Rather, you should proactively develop a communication strategy. When designing your communication, ask yourself, "What could I say that would make someone choose to listen to me?"

As you prepare, step into the shoes of your audience. Ask yourself these questions:

- What's in it for them to listen to you?
- What challenges do they currently face?
- Are you credible in their eyes? If not, what do you need to do or say?
- How will you build rapport?
- What pain point or challenge will you help them overcome?
- What stories or examples can they relate to? (How will they make the biggest impact?)
- What call to action can you make that they'll respond to?

Unless you know the answers to these questions, you're likely to flop. You'll fall into the trap that many leaders do: *communicating to meet your own needs, not the needs of your audience.* This is what both Isabella and the CEO in Atlanta did. In Isabella's case, her underlying need was "I need to check my boxes." For the CEO, his need was "I need to show you how powerful I am." In both cases, it was all about them, and the audience tuned out.

You'll only be able to communicate with the end in mind if you have a genuine desire to connect. You need to talk with people, not at them. It takes a certain level of maturity to be other-focused. It means giving up insecurities that many leaders in organizations have: fear, control, and power. If you can do this, you'll bring your communication to a whole new level.

Key 2: Have a Central Message

If you have an important point to make, don't try to be subtle or clever. Use a pile driver. Hit the point once. Then come back and hit it again. Then hit it a third time—a tremendous whack.

—Winston Churchill

Anne is a client of mine, a senior executive who works in the technology industry. She shared this story with me:

Our company had the opportunity to acquire a smaller player in our market. The very next day, a bunch of us met with a bunch of them. We spent all morning going through their financials, asking them lots of questions, and seeing how this would work.

That afternoon, the group from our own company went off to meet on our own. We were pretty hyped up. We immediately started rehashing every detail of the morning meeting. Over an hour of heated discussion went by, when one member of our team suddenly stood up. He shouted, **"Hold on everybody! Can we stop for a minute? We're in the weeds. What is the purpose of this meeting?"**

It's easy to get lost in the details. So many clamor for our attention. But in the noise, the point gets lost. For example, *two-thirds* of senior managers can't name their firm's top priorities.[2]

Confusion can only be dispelled with clarity. When communicating, you need to have a clear and concise central message. It's the core theme that ties together everything you say.

There's an old three-step formula for effective communication that highlights the importance of having a clear central message:

1. Tell them what you're going to tell them.
2. Tell them.
3. Tell them what you told them.

If you're not crystal clear, how do you expect anyone else to be?

People love being given a clear central message. The clarity provides comfort. Confusion is anxiety producing: both mentally (high-alert brain waves) and physiologically (stress hormones activated). When you know what the point is, you can relax.

A clear central message also gives context. Similar to having a good map, clear context helps you to orient and navigate much more quickly. Instead of wondering where to go, you can spend your time going there.

Given the benefits of having a clear central message, it's amazing how many leaders communicate without having a clear central message. Their meetings, emails, and presentations become guessing games. They spawn meetings after the meetings, when team members try to figure out the key point.

Your central message needs to be concise. It must be about only one thing. As you prepare in advance, you need to take a machete to all of your thoughts and hack out a clear path that can be understood, remembered, and easily followed.

For example, your message can't be "discussion on quality." That's too vague. Instead it could be "product defects are killing our profits." Then, use supporting points that reinforce your central message.

There's a reason Winston Churchill encouraged repeating the message again and again. It's the same reason that advertisers say that people need to hear something seven times before they remember it. Forgetting is going to happen. You can't escape that fact. However, the more you repeat your key theme, the more likely it will stick.

When crafting your messaging, get strategic. Design your communication so that people remember the right thing. The central key message is the one thing that you need them to know and remember.

Key 3: Create Checks for Understanding

If you want understanding, try giving some.

—Malcolm Forbes

On December 11, 1998, NASA launched an unmanned spacecraft to Mars. The *Climate Orbiter* was a 745-pound robotic space probe designed to study the Martian climate and atmosphere. The cost of the *Orbiter* was $125 million.

On September 23, 1999, the mission went horribly wrong. The *Orbiter* drifted from its intended course and flew too close to Mars, where it entered the upper atmosphere and disintegrated. The mission was a total loss.

After an extensive review, NASA determined the cause of the accident. It turned out to be a communication breakdown. One of NASA's contractors, Lockheed Martin, had supplied a ground-based piece of navigation software that produced results using standard English (Imperial) measurements. The NASA navigation system used the metric system.

In other words, one group was talking pounds, and the other group was talking kilograms.[3] *Oops.*

If you find yourself frustrated and saying, "But I sent the email!" or "We had a meeting about this!" you've slid backward into the one-way communication trap. Communication isn't a static goal unto itself. Shared Understanding is.

Communication needs to be active and two-way. One of the simplest ways to ensure that your communication translates to the person you're communicating with is to use this technique: **Ask for a receipt**.

What does it mean to say you *understand*? It's word that's tossed around quite frequently, as in, "I understand you." "Got it. Understood."

Understanding depends on getting others to see reality the way you see it. You see your meaning: you want others to see the meaning in the same way. One-way communication leaves understanding to chance; others might see reality the way you see it, but they might not.

Skilled leaders know that understanding is not the default setting for communication. Rather than just hope for the best, they stack the deck in their favor. Their trick? They intentionally insert checks into their communication to guarantee that understanding takes place. They ask for a receipt.

Receipts provide proof of a complete transaction. In fact, the more important the purchase, the more likely you are to ask for a receipt. You might skip the receipt when you buy a candy bar, but you wouldn't dream of buying a house without one. It's no accident that the most important human events (birth, marriage, death, etc.) involve certified official certificates—receipts of understanding. Why should the transacting of your important business information be any different?

The best communicators know that the understanding loop isn't complete until it comes back full circle to where it started. The receipt turns one-way communication into two-way communication. The monologue becomes dialogue.

There are many ways to ask for a receipt of understanding. One of the simplest and most powerful tools is to ask for confirmation (see Figure 8.3).

Figure 8.3 Receipt for Effective Communication and Results

When the message comes back to you, you can verify: Did they get it? Is it 100% accurate? If not, you get a second (and third) chance to go back and try again.

A lesson on the power of two-way communication comes from the fast-food industry. In the 1980s, the restaurant drive-thru process was a nightmare. Tons of mistakes would be committed between the time customers would give their order and pull up to the next window. Customers would order one thing and receive something completely different.

But suddenly, everything changed. Drive-thru mistake rates plummeted. What business breakthrough led to such performance improvements? The industry discovered an innovative solution: employees started repeating the order back to the customer over the intercom. They started checking their understanding.

The next, even greater leap forward came in the 1990s, when McDonald's introduced the verification board, an electronic visual display that enabled customers to see their orders before they were put in the system.[4] Visual verification creates the ultimate in true, two-way communication. For most people, sight is their dominant sense. If you can literally see that someone understands you, then confirming that understanding becomes much easier.

Too many leaders skip this step of checking for understanding. They assume it's there, and settle for "I think they got it." Yet, the more important the information, the more important it is to verify understanding. After all, if Taco Bell will do it for a $3.19 Crunchwrap Supreme, isn't your business worth the same effort?

Key 4: Own and Fix Communication Breakdowns

> When you make a commitment to a relationship, you invest your attention and energy in it more profoundly because you now experience ownership of that relationship.
>
> —Barbara de Angelis

Not long ago, I was flying a regional jet from Cleveland to Hartford. After the plane had boarded, the flight attendant came on to the PA system and explained they were waiting for the pilot.

After 35 minutes of sitting with no updates, the side door opens and in walks someone who appears to be a pilot. He heads straight to the cockpit.

Five minutes goes by ... nothing. Ten minutes goes by ... nothing. Then, over the PA system:

> Ladies and gentlemen, this is your pilot here. Thanks for your patience. I was all the way across the airport, waiting to go on a flight to Chicago when I got the call to come over here and fly this plane. Those of you that know the Cleveland airport know how far away that is. Sorry for the delay. It's the company's fault.

I was startled by his last comment. "It's the *company's* fault?" Was the pilot saying that he wasn't to blame, but the airline was? As though, somehow, "the company" is this entity that exists separate from him?

I can imagine that the pilot was in an uncomfortable situation. Maybe his ego couldn't bear the thought that people were thinking this was his fault. Maybe this delay was all due to a company error. But, frankly, as a passenger, I really wasn't interested in assigning blame. I just wanted to get home. I'd prefer the pilot just apologize and get the plane moving.

There's an old saying that says, "Anyone can steer the ship when the seas are calm. It's when the waves are rough that leaders are tested." You can have decent communication skills and great intentions, and some-times, even then, communication will break down. These breakdowns (as painful as they seem) are opportunities. Think of them as commu-nication moments of truth. In that moment, how do you respond? Do you find the fault or the fix? It's in these moments that people see what you're really made of.

On September 29, 1982, 12-year-old Mary Kellerman of Elk Grove Village, Illinois, died after taking a capsule of Extra-Strength Tylenol. Over the next few days, seven more people died in the Chicagoland area after taking cyanide-laced capsules of Extra-Strength Tylenol, which was Johnson & Johnson's (J&J) bestselling product. The bottles had all been tampered with.

The "Tylenol murders" were a public relations disaster. Marketing experts predicted that the company would crash and burn. Yet, just one year later, J&J had regained 30% share of the $1.2 billion analgesic market. Their solution?

Courageous truth-telling, ownership of the issue, and swift action. In other words, great leadership.

It started with communication. James Burke, the CEO of J&J, appeared in numerous press conferences and gave straight talk about what had happened. He said that J&J would do the right thing. He said that customers came first. Then, he put his company's money where his mouth was.

Almost immediately after Burke made his promises, J&J halted Tylenol production and advertising. On October 5, 1982, it issued a nationwide recall of Tylenol products. Product recalls at that time were still unheard of in the United States. For perspective, there were 31 million bottles in circulation, valued at over $100 million. J&J also offered to exchange all Tylenol capsules already purchased by the public for solid tablets, free of charge.[5] James Burke owned the situation the company was in. He didn't say, "They should have told us sooner" or "It's the company's fault."

The exceptional leader puts herself on the hook: she's 100% responsible. If there's a problem, she asks, "What could I have done differently to make sure understanding happened?"

If you're genuinely committed to achieving your desired outcome, you must own the entire process of communication. It doesn't matter if you're the sender or the receiver of information. You'll do whatever it takes to make sure that information transforms into insight.

Key 5: Make the Implicit Explicit

High expectations are the key to everything.

— Sam Walton

People are good at many things. Mind reading is not one of them. If you rely on implicit hints, there's a good chance your hopes will be dashed. Create an environment in which people can say what they mean and mean what they say, and you'll go a long way to improving the quality of communication.

Lee is a sales and marketing executive. He's a master at making the implicit explicit. I've had the pleasure of working with Lee at five different points in his career, and each time he's made a move and started leading a new team. He spends the first two days with this team at an off-site retreat, establishing how they can best work together. He strives for clarity and transparency. Some items he always covers include the following:

- Personal background and preferred style of working
- Expectations he has of team members
- Expectations team members have of him
- Expectations team members have of each other

He also establishes norms of communication for the team:

- How often should the entire team meet?
- How often should subgroups meet?
- What's the best method for communication?
- What are our expectations for "timeliness" in replies?
- Are emails late nights and/or weekends off limits or within reason?

By the end of two days, everyone knows exactly where Lee stands and where he's coming from. There will be no surprises. Through his explicit candor, Lee creates a huge reservoir of trust.

Establishing explicit norms of communication increases your effectiveness. After all, don't you want people to know the rules of the road before they start driving? It takes more time up front, but it's time well spent.

Leaders who don't create clear expectations default to a "hint-and-hope" strategy. It's alive and well in Old-School command-and-control style organizations. With their rigid hierarchies, people at the top establish a norm in which they don't want to hear any bad news from below. People who have been "dinged" in the past for speaking up learn to keep their heads down. Out of fear of repercussions, they only hint at a problem issue, and then they hope that the people above them on the organization chart get the message and take the appropriate action.

Here are a few common examples of hint-and-hope in a workplace:

- Employees are afraid to speak up about customer issues they experience on the front line. Their valuable customer insights don't see the light of day. Result: any potential opportunities to improve the customer experience never occur.
- Managers who spend most of their days in meetings but only have candid conversations in those meetings after the meetings, because they won't call out the real issues in the actual meeting. Result: poor decisions get implemented.
- Executive teams who go off-site for two days of "strategy meetings" but spend the whole time discussing the crisis of the day because it's more comfortable to talk about the daily fires than tackle the big cultural and systemic issues that cause the crises in the first place. Result: the company's progress stays stuck on a treadmill.

How do you banish hint-and-hope? You start with inquiry, transparency, and honesty. You make the implicit explicit. Being genuine sets the proper tone for working together. When you keep things real, the people you work with will appreciate you treating them as adults. This will foster better teamwork and communication.

Key 6: Master the Medium

Example is not the main thing in influencing others. It is the only thing.
—Albert Schweitzer

Once you take on the role of leader, you are viewed differently. You live in the heat of a spotlight and under the focus of a microscope.

Everything you say and do (and everything you don't say and don't do) gets scrutinized. People spend their nights and weekends thinking about you, wondering what you think about them.

The irony, of course, is you're probably not thinking about them. You're thinking about all the things you need to get done.

Except for a rare few, organizations are not democracies—they're hierarchies. In a hierarchy, things aren't flat and equal. The corporate ladder, and the power that comes with each rung, are very real. If you're in a leadership role and naively act as though you're the same as those you lead, you're doing your team a disservice. You also weaken your influence.

If you're going to lead, you need to embrace the spotlight. It's an integral part of your job. Use its heat to amplify your message. Communication doesn't exist as a separate entity from you. It's an extension of you. You are the medium and the message. Your challenge is to become the best messenger you can be.

In 2006, Sir Ken Robinson gave a talk called "How Schools Kill Creativity" at the annual TED conference.[6] His 20-minute talk has been viewed online at TED.com more than 63 million times. It's the most viewed TED Talk in history.

What makes it so compelling? It engages. It delights. It teaches. It inspires. It makes you think and feel. It's not just a speech. It's an experience. Robinson doesn't just talk. He gives a bravura performance.

Robinson knows that his delivery is as important as his content. Not only is his message on creativity but also he's incredibly creative in how he shares his message. He knows that to inspire others, he must model inspiration. He knows, to paraphrase Gandhi, that he must be "the change which he seeks in the world." Robinson knows that communication is felt as much as it is heard.

There's an old proverb that states, "It's not what you say, it's how you say it." If you want to improve your delivery, you need to master the delivery medium, that is, you.

Leadership is a performing art, and you are your own instrument. To play well, you need to know how to use all the delivery tools you have at your disposal. To use music as a metaphor, your ideas and words are your "notes." Your voice and body is your "instrument" that you play those notes on.

There are many leaders who are actually quite brilliant, but they can't communicate their ideas to others without putting them to sleep. Their tragic flaw? They completely ignore their instrument, and they only focus on the notes. They wrongly assume their ideas are so interesting that they will communicate themselves. This weakens their power enormously, as do notes played through a poorly tuned instrument fall flat. To play well, you need to understand and practice using all the parts of your leadership instrument. These parts fall into two categories: your voice and your body.

The different elements of voice include the following:

- **Volume.** Are you loud enough so everyone can hear you comfortably? Do you create variety in volume so that people stay engaged?
- **Pace.** Do you speak too slowly or quickly? What impact does your speed have on your listener?
- **Intonation.** How much do you use the range (low pitch to high pitch) of your voice? Modulation in range can help to emphasize certain points.
- **Diction/pronunciation.** Do you sound easy and clear to understand? If you do, you'll come across sounding more intelligent.
- **Passion.** Are you excited by your subject? If you're not, why would anyone else be?
- **Fillers.** Do *ums*, *ahs*, and *ers* dilute your message?
- **Pausing.** Do you stop and take a breath for air? Pauses give your listener a moment to digest what you've just said. Pauses create a perception of you as confident.

Different elements of body include the following:

- **Facial expressions.** Does your face say, "I'm interested in you?" or "Speaking is more painful than root canal?" Faces are huge conveyors of emotion. Get some feedback on how yours comes across.

- **Gestures (hand, body).** Do your hand and body movements support your thoughts or get in the way of them?
- **Posture/stance.** Do you stand upright (confident) or slouch (weak)? Are you open to the people you speak to or closed off with how you stand?
- **Movement.** How do you use the space that you're in? Does movement move the message forward or hold it back?

Each element of your voice and body may seem like a small detail, but details matter. Each piece adds to or subtracts from the greater whole of your message. If you start to focus on using your instrument in an intentional way, you'll be way ahead of most leaders out there. No one's expecting you to become a Hollywood-level performer, but even a small change can make a big difference. How you come across is the foundation of your personal brand and the basis of your professional reputation.

RAISE YOUR COMMUNICATION GAME

Everyone communicates. But not everyone communicates well. By applying the following six keys, you'll be well on your way to achieving Shared Understanding:

1. Communicate with the end in mind
2. Have a central message
3. Create checks for understanding
4. Own and fix communication breakdowns
5. Make the implicit explicit
6. Master the medium

In fact, you'll be such a strong communicator that people will not only understand you but also they'll be inspired to work with you. Because of your skill at connection and communication, they'll be ready to collaborate.

Chapter Resources

Communicate with the End in Mind

- I proactively use a communication strategy.
- I frame communications around benefits received, not features given.
- When I design my communications, I make sure to find out:
  - ☐ What's in it for them to listen to me
  - ☐ Their current challenges
  - ☐ If I'm credible
  - ☐ How I can best build rapport
  - ☐ How I can help them
  - ☐ Which stories and examples will be most relatable
  - ☐ What call to action they will respond to

Have a Central Message

- I craft a clear, concise, central message in advance.
- I build my whole communication around reinforcing the central message.
- I begin with the central message.
- I repeat the central message multiple times.
- All of my stories, data, and examples are in service to the central message.
- I close my communications by reiterating the central message.

Create Checks for Understanding

- I ensure my communication is two-way.
- I ask for a receipt of understanding.
- If understanding is not 100%, I take time to reiterate and clarify it until it is.
- I focus communication on specific actions, rather than concepts, to create clarity.

Own and Fix Communication Breakdowns

- I don't blame others for missed understandings and misunderstandings.
- I'm solution oriented, rather than fault-finding, in my communication.
- I recognize that miscommunication is a default setting and it takes work to overcome the default.

Make the Implicit Explicit

- I don't expect anyone else to read my mind.
- When starting with a new team, I share my thoughts on the following:
  - ☐ Personal background and preferred style of working
  - ☐ Expectations of team members
  - ☐ Expectations team members have of me
  - ☐ Expectations team members should have of each other
- I establish team norms for communication, including these issues:
  - ☐ How often should the entire team meet?
  - ☐ How often should subgroups meet?
  - ☐ What's the best method for communication?
  - ☐ What are our expectations for "timeliness" in replies?
  - ☐ Are emails late nights and/or weekends off limits or within reason?

Master the Medium

- I recognize that everything I say and do is under a spotlight, and I use my voice and body accordingly.
- When I communicate, I use my voice to its full capacity. I make sure I do the following:
  - ☐ I'm loud enough so everyone can hear me comfortably.
  - ☐ I create variety in volume so that people stay engaged.
  - ☐ I have a good pace that's easy to follow.
  - ☐ I modulate the tone so as not to be monotone.

- ☐ I speak clearly to be understood.
- ☐ I'm passionate about my subject matter.
- ☐ I practice eliminating verbal fillers.
- ☐ I use pauses effectively.
- When I communicate, I use my body to its full capacity. I make sure to do the following:
- ☐ My face is open and inviting.
- ☐ I make eye contact.
- ☐ I use hand and body movements that support my ideas and central message.
- ☐ I stand with a tall posture.
- ☐ I have open body language.
- ☐ I use the space to help convey ideas more clearly.
- ☐ I make sure my movement increases engagement of the message.

Part IV

COLLABORATION

If there's one constant in today's workplace, it's change. VUCA (volatile, uncertain, complex, and ambiguous) has not only entered the common parlance, it's now business as usual. Technology has connected more people in more places at more times than ever before. Leaders who can't harness the power of these connections are fated to flounder. Today's leader can't stay stuck in a silo, relying on the antiquated model of top-down command and control. They need to lead collaboratively.

Effective collaboration doesn't just happen—it takes adept facilitation. Collaborative leaders need a plethora of skills. They need to know how to build a common vision and engage others to bring the vision to life. They need to inspire others to bring their whole selves to work. They need to find ways to bring a diversity of players to the table and draw out the best ideas. They need to know how and when to use which style of decision-making in which situation. If that wasn't enough, they do all these things while making it easier for their people to do their best work.

These efforts bring rich rewards. Leading effective collaboration is a win-win. Not only are employees happier, creative, and energized but also companies that promote collaboration are five times as likely to be high performing.[1]

In Part IV, you'll learn how to lead others in a collaborative environment. You'll delve into the inner workings of motivation. You'll learn what's required to meet each employee's essential needs. You'll understand the elements of the employee experience and how you can affect it. Finally, you'll gain a new set of tools to simplify your meetings and your emails, limiting the levels of needless complexity that get in your and your team's way.

Chapter 9

MOTIVATION

The Search for the Magic Pill

Motivation is the art of getting people to do what you want them to do
because they want to do it.

— Dwight Eisenhower

The famous film director Alfred Hitchcock was known for his disdain of actors. Early in his career, he became known for saying that "actors are cattle." Later in Hitchcock's life, he claimed that he had been misquoted. "I never said all actors are cattle; what I said was all actors should be treated like cattle."[1]

From Hitchcock's perspective, actors should be putty to be molded precisely as the director envisioned. Any attempts on their part to "act" just got in the way. He had a command-and-control style of leading. As Hitchcock explained,

> In my opinion, the chief requisite for an actor is the ability to do nothing well, which is by no means as easy as it sounds. He should be willing to be utilized and wholly integrated into the picture by the director and the camera. He must allow the camera to determine the proper emphasis and the most effective dramatic highlights.[2]

149

Hitchcock didn't want his actors thinking too much, and he most certainly didn't want their input. There's a story about Hitchcock working with Paul Newman in late 1965 on the movie *Torn Curtain*. At the time of filming, Newman was a bona fide Hollywood star and had already been nominated twice for a Best Actor Academy Award.

Newman came to Hitchcock and wanted to discuss the character he was playing. Hitchcock dismissed him, saying, "It's in the script." Newman persisted, asking, "But what's my motivation?" Hitchcock replied, "Your motivation, Mr. Newman, is your salary."[3]

Authoritarian leadership (the likes of which we've explored in Chapters 2 and 3) was about mandating. Collaborative leadership is about mobilizing. Eisenhower's quote that opens this chapter, "Motivation is the art of getting people to do what you want them to do because they want to do it," highlights the inherent challenge in motivation. It's that *"because they want* to do it" part that's tricky.

How do you get someone else *to want to* work toward your objectives? *Want to* isn't a request to someone's head. It's an appeal to their heart.

This chapter will explore the different dimensions of motivation. You'll see what makes motivating others so complex—and you'll learn that contrary to Hitchcock's opinion, salary and extra money isn't enough. You'll recognize some of the common traps that leaders fall into in their attempts to be inspiring. Finally, you'll learn a whole new approach to successfully motivate others.

Motivation, simply put, is the desire to do things. It's why some people will get up at the crack of dawn to run 10 miles. It's why others spend hours a day practicing a musical instrument. It's the spark that lights your engine and the gas that fuels your performance.

Effective leaders today know they can't impose their will on those they lead. For example, I remember discussing this very issue with Debra, the CEO of the U.S. division of a major international bank. I was just starting what would turn out to be a four-year engagement with the company, helping them to transform the culture of their 13,000 U.S.-based employees. The bank had been through some serious regulatory challenges, and it wanted to create a culture in which every employee took responsibility for how the bank did business with customers.

Debra joked with me about how her life would be so much easier if she could just impose her will on the organization and everyone would do her bidding. Debra knew exactly what she wanted to be different. She had a crystal-clear vision of how a transformed cultured would look, feel, and act. If it would have worked, she would happily have clicked "send" on an email that looked like this:

To: All U.S. Bank Employees
From: Debra
Subject: Culture Transformation
    Effective immediately, all employees are expected to do the following:

- Be brave and speak up
- Be motivated and inspired
- Challenge others
- Simplify the business
- Do the right thing
- Make this a great place to work

Thank you,
Debra

Of course, Debra never sent such an email. It would have accomplished nothing. Debra knew that leading people on a journey from where they are to where they need to be was a process, not an event. She also knew this undertaking would not be easy; with a 13,000-person company, it would take years to turn the organizational ship around and head in the right direction. She'd have to find a different—and better—way to motivate.

UNDERSTANDING THE DRIVERS OF MOTIVATION

Motivating ourselves is hard. Anyone who has ever set (and tried to keep) New Year's resolutions knows exactly how hard. Trying to motivate others is exponentially more complex. For starters, where do you begin? What do you say? What do you do? What works? What doesn't work? How do you discover what makes them tick? Will what works today be as effective tomorrow?

Imagine you're leading four different groups of employees who all work assembling chips in a semiconductor factory. You're trying to motivate them to produce a certain number of chips per day. Which motivator do you think would work the best?

- A $30 cash bonus
- A voucher for free pizza
- A text message from the boss reading "Well done!"
- Nothing

It turns out this isn't a hypothetical situation. This was a week-long experiment run at an Israeli semiconductor factory by the psychologist Dan Ariely. At the start of the week, employees received an email promising a cash bonus, free pizza, or a "Well done!" text message from the boss if they got all their work done that day. A quarter of the factory employees received no email and no reward, thus serving as the control group.

Ariely found that after day one, the lure of free pizza was the top motivator, increasing productivity by 6.7% (over the control group who received nothing). The email offering words of praise from the boss incited 6.6% more productivity, and the email offering the cash bonus garnered 4.9% more productivity.

As the week progressed, things got more interesting. On day two, the productivity of the cash bonus group plunged. They performed 13.2% *worse* than those in the control group. By the time the week-long experiment ended, the cash bonus group not only cost the company money but also their results were 6.5% worse than the control group.

To sum up, the cash incentive was worse than offering no incentive at all. As for the other two motivators? Over the course of the whole week, it turned out that the appreciation text message from the boss was the strongest motivator of the bunch. Pizza was a close second.[4]

Many leaders I've worked with are surprised by these results. They expected that the cash would be the best incentive. Ultimately, here's the core reason why motivation is so complicated:

The people you lead are not you.

Although that statement may seem obvious, it's worth exploring in greater detail.

If you've been raised with basic social skills, you've internalized certain norms about how to interact with other people in society. One of the biggest of these norms is what's widely known as the Golden Rule: Do unto others as you would have them do unto you. It's a guiding principle of human behavior.

Now, I have no quibble with the Golden Rule. As rules go, it's about as good as they get.

However, applying the Golden Rule in a leadership-motivational context raises a red flag. Taken literally, it translates as, "Motivate others as you would have them motivate you." And this is where things get dicey. Because, if you were to strictly apply this rule, then you're starting off with a faulty premise. You're assuming that what motivates you will motivate others. And that's not how motivation works.

Kelly, an IT manager, shared a story with me that illustrates this point. Early in his career, Kelly was the manager of 18 people for a corporate help desk. Looking for ways to motivate his team, he started a secret contest. He tracked key performance indicators (resolution rate, call-handle time, etc.) and ranked the team accordingly.

At the end of the month, Kelly called the team together to tell them about his contest and announce the first winner. After milking the suspense for as long as he could, Kelly announced the winner was Gina, a young woman who had been with the company for 10 months. In his excitement, Kelly didn't notice that Gina, still in her chair, had started to sweat, and her face had gone bright pink. Finally noticing that she hadn't come up yet, Kelly urged her, "Gina, come on up! Speech from the winner!"

Gina struggled to stand up, swaying as she did so, and then, as soon as she was stable, bolted from the room. What Kelly didn't know (and found out later) was that Gina suffered from social anxiety disorder.

Though Gina could manage her symptoms in her job, Kelly's contest pushed her over the edge.

Everyone sees "reality" through his or her own set of eyes. They've had different life experiences, which shape different values, beliefs, and behaviors. As such, they interpret and respond to events differently than you do.

To motivate others, leaders need a stronger guiding principle than the Golden Rule. Dale Carnegie, in his classic *How to Win Friends and Influence People*, shares a story that suggests a better option:

> Personally I am very fond of strawberries and cream, but I have found that for some strange reason, fish prefer worms. So when I went fishing, I didn't think about what I wanted. I thought about what they wanted. I didn't bait the hook with strawberries and cream. Rather, I dangled a worm or grasshopper in front of the fish and said: "Wouldn't you like to have that?"[5]

Carnegie's story illustrates what has come to be known as the Platinum Rule:

> Do unto others as they'd like done unto them.[6]

As good as this sounds, this isn't so easy. People are a lot less straightforward than fish. To motivate others, leaders need to unearth what others would like done unto them. This brings up more questions than answers. For starters:

- Who is the "they" you're hoping to motivate?
- Is it an individual or a group?
- If it's a group, what do you do if different people like different things?
- What if some of these things stand in direct opposition to other things?
- Is it possible to pick one thing that everyone would like?
- If not, whom do you start with?
- What do you do first?

In order to lead collaboration, you need to take a page from Sherlock Holmes's playbook and become a motivation detective.

THE SECRET ABOUT MOTIVATION

The world is full of obvious things which nobody by any chance ever observes.

—Sherlock Holmes

Here's the dirty little secret about motivation you need to know: you can't really motivate anyone else. Think about it: if you want to "make" someone be motivated, you've regressed back to Old-School leadership, trying to use force to impose your will.

There's only one person you can truly motivate: yourself. In the same way, there's only one person who can motivate any other person: that person alone. Your job isn't to motivate that person.

Now, just because that's not your job doesn't mean you get a total pass. You don't get to bail on all things motivational, using the excuse, "Well, I can't really motivate anyone else anyway." If you're going to be effective as a leader, you need a motivated workforce. People do better work when they're inspired to do so. High performance springs from motivated performance.

So, on the one hand, you can't motivate people. On the other hand, you need them to be motivated to do great work. How are you supposed to solve this puzzle?

Thankfully, there is a solution. As Sherlock Holmes says, it's obvious, but not easily observed. That's because the answer is a paradox.

Although you can't motivate anyone else, there is something you can do. You can create the conditions in which motivation is most likely to happen. This means creating an environment loaded with specific cues that will nudge people toward being motivated.

If "loaded with cues that nudge people," sounds confusing, you're in good company. "Environment creation" is not a skill listed on a new leader's job description. Very few new leaders have any practice in doing this. You'll learn how to do this important work in the next chapter.

Chapter Resources

Motivate Effectively

- I recognize that real motivation comes from commitment, not compliance.
- I practice inviting and including rather than mandating.
- I employ the Platinum Rule rather than the Golden Rule.
- I work to create an environment that will be motivating.

Chapter 10

LEADING BY DESIGN

The Primary Needs

A choice architect has the responsibility for organizing the context in which people make decisions.

— Richard Thaler

For all the free will we humans think we have, we're surprisingly susceptible to influence. Do you want to get people to eat smaller amounts of food? Serve it on smaller plates. Do you want people to sign up to be organ donors? Make the default option a yes rather than a no.

These two illustrations come out of the field of behavioral economics, examples of what's known as choice architecture. In both cases, someone thought about a situation and designed a specific environment to unconsciously influence (or, to use Nobel Prize–winning economist Richard Thaler's word, *nudge*) others toward a specific result).

If you want to create a highly motivated team, you can't leave it to chance. You have to operate as a motivational choice architect. This takes tact, finesse, and an understanding of the subtleties and nuances of human behavior.

In this (and the following) chapter, you'll gain tools and specifics into the process of intentional motivational design. You'll learn about fundamental human needs, as well as how they set the tone for high performance and effective collaboration. You'll also explore potential tools to help you meet those needs. Armed with these tools and some deliberate practice, you'll be ready to create a culture in which those you lead will make the switch from doing something because they have to do it to doing something because they want to do it.

MOTIVATIONAL DESIGN

Traditional architects design structures. In their work, they use the elements of point, line, shape, form, space, color, and texture. Motivational architects work in an entirely different medium. Their goal is not the design of physical structures; they design environments for the people that they lead to work in.

If the environment is designed well, people can thrive and perform at their best. If the design is poor, people wither and results suffer. Instead of using lines, colors, and textures, leadership architects work with the foundation of behavior: human needs.

HUMAN NEEDS

Needs are fundamental to human existence. The first understood needs were biological: food, water, clothing, shelter. The reason for this is obvious: they are all visible, external, and tangible. If you don't meet these needs, you'll die.

However, there are other needs—social and psychological—that are required to function and develop as a member of society. Take the need for attachment, for example. An infant needs to develop a relationship with at least one primary caregiver for the child's successful social and emotional development. Children who don't get their need for attachment met are more likely to develop an attachment disorder, leaving them feeling isolated and unsafe. Later in life, they're generally less trusting of others, possess lower self-esteem, and have difficulty forging close relationships.

Our human needs are so important, they must be continually met on an ongoing basis. In addition, although each need is essential to our being, none happen in abstract isolation from the others. They coexist in a dynamic, interconnected system.

In the past century, many models and theories on human needs have been created. Some of the best known are Maslow's hierarchy of needs, Erickson's eight stages of development, and Piaget's theory of cognitive development. However, no matter the framework, all agree on one thing: all humans have universal needs. You'll find needs wherever you find people.

Human needs are so fundamental that they've remained unchanged for all of human history. For example, people have always had a need for subsistence. However, *how* we've gone about meeting that need has changed. Hunter-gatherers on the savannah didn't meet their subsistence needs at the McDonald's drive-thru. In fact, it's the expression of how these needs are satisfied that differentiates one culture from the next.

As a leadership architect, your goal is to design a high-performance culture. You'll use a structured yet flexible process so you can respond to the varying needs of different people. This need-satisfying process is simple and cyclical: once you finish the last step, you arrive back at the start and begin again. The process is as follows (see Figure 10.1):

1. Prioritize which human need to address.
2. Choose which satisfier can best meet that need.
3. Decide how that satisfier will be expressed.
4. Observe the impact of that satisfier on the people and the environment.
5. Adjust and reprioritize (repeat step 1).

Before you get started, you'll want a detailed understanding of the materials you'll be designing with. There are four human needs that are central to effective collaboration:

- Safety
- Energy
- Purpose
- Ownership

Figure 10.1 The Need-Satisfying
Process

The first two, safety and energy, are primary employee needs and the subject of this chapter. Similar to air and water, you won't last long if these needs remain unmet. If you're going to motivate people, you need to start here.

Once the primary needs are met, you can turn your attention to the performance needs—purpose and ownership. Built on a foundation of the primary needs, these higher-level needs are what ultimately improve performance. They will be the subject of Chapter 11.

Primary Need 1: Safety

At our core, everyone needs safety. If we're unsafe, we feel at risk, living in a danger zone. Trying to work (let alone achieve high performance) without feeling safe is nearly impossible.

Safety is a multilevel concept. The most basic level is that of **physical safety**. People don't want to come to work and get hurt or sick. Potential physical safety satisfiers include answering yes to the following questions:

- Is the work environment well-lit and well-ventilated?
- Are there no obstructions that could cause an injury?

- Is the workplace located in a geographically safe location?
- Is the physical building secure?
- Is the furniture ergonomic?

Ensuring these needs are met is the reason that OSHA (the Occupational Safety and Health Administration) was founded.

After physical safety comes **fiscal safety**. People need a return for their labor. Satisfiers here include the following:

- Is there fair compensation?
- What kinds of benefits are offered?
- What kind of job security comes with the position?

In today's world, meeting baseline physical and fiscal safety needs is expected. And although these needs are necessary and important, they're not sufficient by themselves. As Alfred Hitchcock heard from Paul Newman (see Chapter 9), salary alone was not an adequate motivator.

The next level area of safety is much more complex, much less understood, and most important. It's also the area where you as a leader have the most direct influence. This is **psychological safety**.

Psychological safety can be defined as "being able to show and employ one self without fear of negative consequences of self-image, status or career."[1] It's the ability, as one CEO I worked with put it, "to bring your whole self to work." You don't have to check a part of yourself at the door when you enter the building in the morning.

Psychological safety is a visceral experience people have (or don't have) working in teams. When people feel psychologically safe, they believe that they can take risks and try new ideas. They feel supported and respected by the team. They feel their team has their back.

When team members feel psychologically safe, they are more likely to do the following:

- Admit, look at, and learn from mistakes.
- Offer feedback, both positive and negative.
- Generate new ideas that can be of value.

- Share best practices.
- Be more supportive and encouraging of others.

When psychological safety is not present, the following reactions can happen:

- Team members are excluded from information sharing and/or decision-making.
- Ideas that are offered up are "assassinated."
- People don't share their ideas and/or perspective for fear of criticism.
- People who disagree withdraw from discussion and opt to gossip and avoid directness.

Google is not known as a company that relies on intuition, emotion, or psychology. On the contrary, Google is world-famous for harnessing the power of data to drive decision-making. This ability is reflected in their mission: to organize the world's information and make it universally accessible and useful.

In 2011, Google decided to invest their data-hunting power to answer this important question: "How can you build the best team?"

The findings of their research (named Project Aristotle) were recently shared by author Charles Duhigg. Project Aristotle's researchers started by looking at 50 years of academic studies on teamwork. What was the hidden factor that made the best teams the best?

As they pored over the studies, they kept looking for patterns. They created numerous hypotheses. Was the greatness due to similar interests? How much they socialized outside of the office? Similar educational backgrounds? Personality types? The gender balance of the team? As they analyzed and reanalyzed the data, they were flummoxed: they couldn't find any patterns.

Finally, they focused their attention on group norms: the unwritten rules of how people behave. As they dove deeper into the group norms of teams, they discovered two specific norms that stood out among great teams:

1. Team members had approximately the same amount of air time, that is, they spoke in roughly the same proportion.

2. Team members were skilled at picking up on how others felt based on tone of voice, body language, and other nonverbal cues. They were sensitive to each other's moods.

These two norms are key tenets of psychological safety. The best teams create a culture in which people feel comfortable speaking up and taking risks.

So how can a leader create a culture that promotes these norms? You can satisfy the need for psychological safety through the behaviors you model. One Google leader, Matt Sakaguchi, attended a presentation on the findings of Project Aristotle. The project's findings intrigued him. He had just taken over leading a new team of engineers, and a survey had shown that many of his team members were feeling unfulfilled in their jobs. Specifically, they didn't have a clear vision of how their work contributed to the larger whole.

Sakaguchi gathered his team at an off-site location and started by asking everyone to share something personal about themselves. He decided to go first:

> I think one of the things most people don't know about me is that I have Stage 4 cancer.[2]

Not an easy thing to share. Sakaguchi's honesty and vulnerability broke the ice for the team. Things got very real, very quickly. As their conversation unfolded, they shifted to talk about the things at work that bothered them. Suddenly, their workplace annoyances and conflicts seemed smaller and more manageable in the grand scheme of things.

One Google engineer, Sean Laurent, shared his insight into this need to feel safe:

> The thing is, my work is my life. I spend the majority of my time working. Most of my friends I know through work. If I can't be open and honest at work, then I'm not really living, am I?[3]

Modeling openness—especially when tensions are high—is the most important thing you can do to promote psychological safety on your team. As a leader, when you're vulnerable, you give others permission to be vulnerable too. The resulting culture of candor eliminates the need to keep up the appearance of the corporate façade of everything and everyone being okay. Instead, you can cut to the chase and deal with what's really going on.

It seems particularly relevant to also include that psychological safety means that people are free from bullying and sexual harassment. These behaviors are criminal. People who are bullied and harassed do not feel safe. As a leader, if you see or hear instances of this happening, you need to respond, investigate, call it out, and address it appropriately.

Primary Need 2: Energy

Energy is the fuel of high performance. For people to achieve great results over a sustained period, they need to be enthusiastic about the effort they put into their work. Although this may seem intuitively obvious, it's not the norm. Consider this all-too-common story of Sage, a manager at a manufacturing company that I worked with.

I'm convinced that my company tried to turn me into a zombie. When I started, I was excited, curious, creative. I was ready to help the company change and grow. That's what I talked about in my job interview. That's why I thought I was hired. So when I started, I spoke up in meetings, shared my ideas, looked to connect with people outside my function, and make things happen.

At my first performance review, my boss told me, "You need to dial it back a little." If I read between the lines, what he was really saying was that he was upset that I was outshining him.

That review was a wake-up call. I started looking around at how everybody else worked. I started noticing who gets ahead here. What's rewarded is effort, not results. It's the people who get in early and stay late and sit quietly in their cubicle all day long. It's the people who respond to their boss's emails within five minutes on the weekends or late at night. The ones who spit back exactly what their boss tells them.

After that review, I was completely demoralized. I figured if that's the way the game is played, then I can play it that way too.

I've tried it for a few weeks now. I hate it. I feel so fake ... and so drained. This isn't what I signed up for. I don't know what I'm going to do.

The cultural and behavioral norms Sage describes sound like they were taken straight from the pages of the *Dilbert* cartoon series. There's a reason *Dilbert* is wildly popular: it hits a little too close to home. Most people have firsthand experience with the zombie workplace—it's the standard at most companies.

There's a worldwide employee energy crisis. The zombies have become the silent majority. Global studies have found that the percentage of employees who are "involved in, enthusiastic about and committed to their work and workplace" is only 15%.[4]

The energy crisis doesn't just impact morale. It affects every aspect of your organization. Low energy and commitment influence turnover, productivity, revenue, quality, safety, absenteeism, shrinkage, team performance, and customer satisfaction. This crisis costs the overall U.S. economy as much as $350 billion every year. That boils down to at least $2,246 per zombie employee.[5] As a leadership architect, you're going to need a range of tools to combat this energy drain. The following sections explore nine techniques to help you build an energized culture.

Lead by Example

If you want the people around you to be energized, you need to be energized. People pick up on the energetic cues of those around them, and they pay special attention to the energy of their leaders. If you're positive, people pick up positivity. If you're stressed out, you'll infect your team with anxiety.

As someone who leads groups of 10 to 2,000 people multiple times a week, I can testify to the importance of self-care. I've made showing up energized, focused, and positive a habit. My rituals around this include planning my travel schedule to get at least 8 hours of sleep a night; eating lean, healthy whole foods; and exercising daily.

When you show up to work, what behaviors do you model? How much gas do you have in your tank? What things do you do on a regular basis to renew and recharge? Do you get enough sleep? How's your nutrition? How often do you engage in physical activity? How often do you do things that you're passionate about? Find and cultivate the habits that will fuel you.

Use the 90-minute Rule

Have you ever noticed you hit an energy breaking point during long meetings and/or conference calls? Symptoms of this include your body getting fidgety, loss of focus, and becoming cranky. This breaking point usually happens at about 90 minutes. Proceed past this mark at your own peril. On the far side of this threshold, information processing and decision-making quickly degrades in quality.

These signposts are your body's way of telling you that your physical systems need to renew and recharge. If you want to avoid this energy collapse, stop and take a break at least every 90 minutes. "Pushing on through" does more harm than good. Although it might seem counter-intuitive, you (and your team) will end up getting better work done in less time if you include breaks.

Stop Unnecessary Interruptions

When you ask someone, "Hey, do you have just a second?," that "one second" comes with a tremendous cost. First off, there's the time of the interruption itself—which is never just a second. Then, there's the time it takes to get back to the point they were before the interruption. Research has shown that the average time it takes to refocus is 23 minutes and 15 seconds.[6] Basex, an economy research firm, reports that interruptions at work consume an average of 2.1 hours per day per employee.[7] Based on that lost time, the subsequent lost productivity costs the U.S. economy $588 billion dollars per year.[8]

If you work in an interrupting culture, you're not alone. A recent study shares a startling finding: 71% of people report frequent inter-ruptions when they're working.[9] Beyond the time loss, there's the burnout factor. Workers who are frequently interrupted reported 9% higher exhaustion rates.[10]

When someone's in your face asking if you have a second, it's hard to say no. It's especially hard to say no when that person is your boss. If you want to remedy the ills of interruptions, stop being part of the problem.

Next, help the rest of your team minimize interruptions. Encourage people to turn off auto-notifications. Set norms around what "prompt" response times are. Agree to call someone's mobile only in cases of true urgency.

You can also create stretches of dedicated time so people can get to the important work that demands deeper thinking. Set up office hours for questions. Create no-email Friday afternoons, or no-meeting Tuesday mornings. Put up yellow "POLICE LINE DO NOT CROSS" tape around your space so people know to leave you alone. Your ability to help people protect their time and focus is as boundless as your imagination.

Direct Less and Facilitate More

As a rule, adults don't like to be told how they should do something. They prefer being self-directed. Collaborative leaders find ways to get people involved.

As you plan your meetings, town halls, one-on-ones, ask yourself, "How can I structure these so my team members are more involved and engaged?" Look for opportunities that offer minimum instruction and maximum autonomy. Draw on the expertise of those you lead. They have years of experience and a rich bank of knowledge. You just need to ask them to share it.

There's no need to shout out that you're the team leader—everyone knows that already. Being overly directive when you don't need to be doesn't enhance your leadership aura—it ticks people off. If you want to get more done with less effort, start thinking and acting like a facilitator.

Create Variety

Do you have a regularly scheduled meeting that should win the award for "most dull meeting ever"? Anything, no matter what it is, if unchanged, gets stale over time. Remember this simple rule: Boring = Bad. Energized = Good.

One of the key drivers of energy is fascination. Novelty, by its nature, takes people by surprise. Find ways to spice up your experience with seeking and applying the new. This takes some planning and creativity.

For example, what if you were to start each meeting by asking each team member a thought-provoking question? Or watching a relevant TED Talk and discussing it? Mix it up. Once you get into the flow of variety, there's no limit to your creativity.

Include Humor

When it comes to increasing energy, laughter may indeed be the best medicine. Studies have shown that employee humor is associated with enhanced work performance, satisfaction, work group cohesion, health, and coping effectiveness, as well as decreased burnout, stress, and work withdrawal.[11]

Humor is a double-edged sword. Although the benefits are clear, if used incorrectly, it creates hurt feelings, animosity, and divisiveness. As a leader, your best rule of thumb regarding humor is to be self-deprecating. You'll never run the risk of hurting someone else's feelings if you make fun of yourself. You'll also never run short on content for your material.

Tell Stories

When the first groups of people gathered together in caves and around fires, they told stories. This was no accident: stories are one of the most powerful forms of human communication. Good stories draw you in. They have interesting characters. They take you on a journey, involve a challenge or conflict, and bring illumination in their resolution. Skilled storytellers know how to craft their stories to leave their listeners with a powerful message.

Not only do great stories make you think but also, more importantly, they make you feel. When you hear a good story, you don't just listen. You see the images. Mirror neurons in your brain are activated, and you identify with the characters in the story. You experience the action as though it's happening to you. This multisensory combination makes stories vivid in a way that a series of data points and graphs just can't do.

The visceral effect that stories have brings added benefits. Not only are you held rapt as it's being told, you'll remember the story long afterward. In a world of information overload, messages can drown easily in a sea of data. Stories are your best hope to get your point of view across. They help others hear your signal amid the noise.

Get People Moving

In physics, energy is defined as the capacity to do work. Similarly, if the people you lead are more energized, they can perform better. Unfortunately, in this age of doing more with less, fatigue has become the norm rather than the exception.

A study published in the *Journal of Occupational and Environmental Medicine* found that 38% of American workers surveyed experienced "low levels of energy, poor sleep or a feeling of fatigue" during their past two weeks at work.

Not only do they feel worse, they perform worse. The study found that total lost productive time averaged 5.6 hours per week for workers with fatigue, compared to 3.3 hours for their counterparts without fatigue. In addition, tired employees are less able to concentrate, have more frequent health problems, and are more likely to have a job-related safety incident.[12]

Although it may seem counterintuitive, one of the best ways to increase energy is by using energy, specifically through low to moderate physical activity. Researchers at the University of Georgia found that when a group of sedentary people were exposed to low-intensity aerobic exercise for 20 minutes three times a week for six weeks, their fatigue levels dropped by 65% and their energy levels rose by 20%.[13]

To optimize collaboration, design an environment that involves movement. There are lots of ways to do this:

- Have a Stand-Up Meeting: you'll be amazed how focused and succinct people will become.
- Start a meeting with a few minutes of gentle stretching.
- If you're meeting with just one or two other people, consider turning the conversation into a walking meeting (grab a notepad to record ideas).
- Walk to colleagues' offices rather than using a phone or email.

- Encourage a culture of standing up periodically.
- Use the stairs instead of the elevator.

Remember, adults aren't just thinking machines. They have bodies attached to their cerebellums. They can only absorb so much while sitting still. Find ways to keep your team moving to keep a high level of focus.

Appreciate

If you think appreciation is crucial in the workplace, you're right: 66% of employees say they would "likely leave their job if they didn't feel appreciated." This is up significantly from 51% of employees who felt this way in 2012.[14] The research firm OC Tanner has found that lack of appreciation is the number-one reason people leave jobs (78%).[15]

Appreciation is key to boosting engaged collaboration. However, too many leaders don't take the time or make the effort to acknowledge good work that gets done on a regular basis. As soon as one goal is achieved, they focus on the next goal. This drains the team of morale and energy, leaving them feeling taken for granted.

You don't have to be the highest-ranking executive in charge to foster a culture of appreciation. All you need to do is take action. Consider the case of Laila, who managed a major engagement with one of her firm's largest clients. The size and scope were massive—30 live events run in 10 cities for 2,000 people, delivered in just over a month. Each event had custom components that had to be tailor-managed. The client continued to make revisions right through the first week of deployment, and in order to keep the planes flying smoothly, Laila put in 70-hour workweeks.

The project ran without a single major problem. The client and their 2,000 people were thrilled. When the project ended, Laila hoped that the partners in her firm would stop and celebrate the work done by the 30-person team who pulled it off. Although Laila had influence with the team, she had zero authority. None of these 30 people reported to her. Which senior person would stop and recognize their accomplishment?

Laila quickly realized (based on past experience) that no one was going to fill the vacuum. So she sent out an email to the entire team:

Dear Team,
    Today marks the end of our project!
    Kudos to everyone involved in the experience.
    Thank you to each of you for being so strong in your role. As we all know, there were lots of updates and things to learn on this project. Together, each working expertly within our roles, we accomplished the goal and made a huge difference to our client. I'm so relieved everyone on our team made their assigned sessions and that each event and delivery has received rave reviews.
    Here's to working as a team. It's an honor to work with each of you,

Laila

Laila's email started a "reply-all love-fest" that everyone got involved in. The positive energy was infectious. One member of the team was so inspired by Laila that he wrote an email to the entire firm, providing context and details so the larger company could also join in the celebration. In that email, he singled out Laila for her superb leadership and going above and beyond the call of duty.

Afterward, Laila told me:

> I could get upset about the fact that our team wasn't being recognized the way I wanted it to—or I could do something about it. This experience taught me that I have a lot more power than I realize.

MEETING THE PRIMARY NEEDS

Feeling safe to bring your whole self to work. Having energy to have that whole self be your best self. These primary needs seem so obvious.

Yet, in many organizations, these needs are forgotten, neglected, or taken for granted. As a leader, you have the power to change the game. You now have plenty of design tools. You can reshape your environment and make sure these needs get met. Then, you can move on and find ways to address your employees' next set of needs: the performance needs.

Chapter Resources

Apply the Human Need-Satisfying Process

1. Prioritize which human need to address.
2. Choose which satisfier can best meet that need.
3. Decide how that satisfier will be expressed.
4. Observe the impact of that satisfier on the people and the environment.
5. Adjust and reprioritize (repeat step 1).

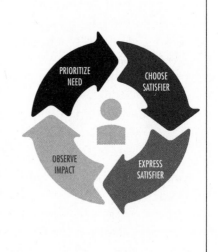

Satisfy Primary Need 1: Safety

- **Physical Safety**
  - ☐ The work environment is well-lit and well-ventilated.
  - ☐ There are no obstructions that could cause an injury.
  - ☐ The workplace is in a geographically safe location.
  - ☐ The physical building is secure.
  - ☐ The furniture is ergonomic.

□ No one is asked to perform duties that put his or her safety at risk.

□ All safety protocols are clearly communicated and followed.

- **Fiscal Safety**
  □ Compensation is fair.
  □ Benefits are appropriate for my team.
  □ Employment contracts are clearly stated and agreed on.
- **Psychological Safety**
  □ I model openness and vulnerability for my team.
  □ If speaking up on an issue requires courage, I speak up first.
  □ I work to make sure there's equal air time for all team members.
  □ I listen to tone of voice and watch body language to pick up on the moods of others.
  □ I'm vigilant about noticing any bullying or harassment.

Fulfill Primary Need 2: Energy

- I show up with energy and lead by example.
- I'm aware of what boosts and drains my energy, and I work to create a surplus reserve of energy.
- I keep my meetings and conference calls to less than 90 minutes.
- If meetings go longer than 90 minutes, I plan to include breaks.
- I minimize unnecessary interruptions for myself and my team.
- I encourage my team to turn off auto-notifications.
- I set dedicated office hours and boundaries for work times, meeting times, and email times.
- I save emergency responses for actual emergencies.
- I look to structure my collaboration to get others as involved and self-directed as possible.

- I remember that those I lead have lots of experience and wisdom, and I tap into it regularly.
- I find ways to break up monotony and create variety for my team.
- I inject humor into my leadership.
- I look to use stories to convey messages.
- I hold walking meetings occasionally.
- I hold stand-up meetings occasionally.
- I set time for stretching and walking throughout the day.
- I appreciate each team member at least once a week.

Chapter 11

LEADING BY DESIGN

The Performance Needs

The highest levels of performance come to people who are centered, intuitive, creative, and reflective—people who know to see a problem as an opportunity.

—Deepak Chopra

One of the most viewed TED Talks of all time is Simon Sinek's "How Great Leaders Inspire Action." In his talk, Sinek explains that although all organizations know what they do, and most of them know how they do it, only a very few organizations know *why* they do what they do. Sinek suggests that what separates great leaders from the rest is that great leaders start with *why*.

Having and communicating a clear *why*—a clear purpose—is a requisite for high performance. When people know why they do what they do, and believe in it, they operate at a whole new level of engagement. They know what they're doing matters and makes a difference.

When people act on purpose, they commit to what they're doing. This commitment helps them meet their next performance need: ownership. When what you do means something to you, it's yours. You do whatever it takes to get to your result.

175

People don't just come to work for a buck. They want these higher-level needs of purpose and ownership met. Knowing how to help your people meet these needs will influence their behavior and affect their performance.

PERFORMANCE NEED 1: PURPOSE

Purpose is the reason for which something is done or created or for which something exists. Some years ago, I got the chance to work with a company that produces medical devices and surgical supplies. I would be leading a series of communication workshops for groups of their mid-level managers at locations all around the United States. My client contact in Minnesota asked if I wanted to take a tour of the factory. I jumped at the chance.

The factory makes medical devices for cancer patients. On the tour, I saw a fascinating mix of cutting-edge technology and old-fashioned assembly. The level of precision required to ensure product quality was amazing.

At one point, the tour stopped to watch April, an assembler on the line. The guide explained that April is a hand-piece operator. She welds covers around a motor and then carefully aligns two cannulas. A cannula is a thin tube that will be inserted into a vein or body cavity to administer medicine, drain off fluid, or insert a surgical instrument. Next, April glues the cannulas in place on the device.

The work required a tremendous amount of concentration. Watching April was like watching an artist. I wanted to learn more about her demanding assembly work. I approached her and introduced myself, explaining that I was on a tour. "What exactly do you do here?" I asked.

I was expecting April to detail the assembly line process. I thought she might explain the difference between the inner and outer cannula. Maybe she'd tell me about how the cover had to be aligned just so. I thought she'd give me a technical explanation. I never expected to hear what April said next.

She said, "My name's April. I help save people's lives. What do you do?"

* * *

People benefit from having a clear purpose. Employees who derive meaning and significance from their work are more than three times as likely to stay with their organizations as those who don't. These employees also report 1.7 times higher job satisfaction.[1] Compared to non-purpose-oriented employees, purpose-oriented employees have 64% higher levels of fulfillment, are 50% more likely to be in leadership positions, and are 47% more likely to be promoters of their employers.[2]

Most leaders recognize the power of purpose. But when it comes to making purpose a reality, there's a big gap between what they know and what they do. A global survey of 474 executives found that although 89% agree that an organization with shared purpose will have employee satisfaction, only 46% of those same leaders said it informs their company's strategic and operational decision-making.[3]

Creating a purpose-filled workplace doesn't happen by chance. April wasn't a random fluke employee; the leadership of her company is very conscious about creating a purpose-filled culture. Once a quarter, leadership holds a company-wide town hall. At this meeting, they bring in customers who use the company's products. They stand up and tell their stories about how their lives had been helped or even saved because of the medical products they used.

Good intentions won't create an environment of purpose: strong actions do. The following sections examine four things you can do to help satisfy the need for purpose.

Tell the Origin Story of Your Company—and Your Leadership

Your company wasn't hatched in one day. There's a compelling, passionate story behind the organization. Who are you? Where did you come from? What's your reason for being?

Origin stories become mythic folklore. Bill Hewlett and Dave Packard in a garage in Palo Alto. Michael Dell in his college dorm room. Fred Smith getting a C on a paper at Yale that would be the seed of the idea for FedEx.

Every company has a compelling origin story—even yours. If you don't know what it is, go out and find it. Then, craft it so it's tuned to resonate strongly with your listeners.

Once you've crafted a good company origin story, start working on your own leadership story. Who are you? Where did you come from? What's your reason for leading? Great purpose stories help the listener viscerally connect with their own sense of purpose. Your story reminds people why they choose to work here versus somewhere else.

Have Your Customers Share Stories Firsthand

It's easy for employees to feel disconnected from the impact their company's product or service has on customers. This is especially true for non-customer-facing employees. One of the best ways to remind employees of your purpose is to hear it straight from the customer's mouth.

Consider an example from Lyft, the San Francisco–based ride-sharing company with a mission "to reconnect people through transportation and bring communities together."[4] In a *Harvard Business Review* article, Erica Keswin describes how Lyft uses the power of customer stories to strengthen the company's purpose:

> During an all-hands meeting of 500 Lyft employees, a woman stood on a stage and told the story of the Lyft driver who not only drove her daughter to safety from a violent roommate situation but actually helped her pack and unpack her belongings into a hotel room.[5]

A firsthand customer story is a powerful way to kindle purpose. Storytelling is a living, breathing, emotional way to demonstrate your organization's values in real-time action. You don't have to be the organizer of an all-company meeting to reach out to customers. Who can you find to share how what your team does has made a difference in their lives?

Co-create a Purpose Statement with Your Team

You're probably familiar with organizational mission statements. Most established companies have one. They're created to focus the company's direction, shape the strategy, and provide a guide for decision-making. Although the structure of mission statements can vary, most have two parts: a vision of what the organization wants to become and the actions it takes to get there.

For example, one steel company's mission is to be the preferred supplier in the steel industry by being the benchmark for safety, quality, service, and on-time delivery.

This mission (like many others) is internal and company facing. For the employees of the company, it tells them who they are, what they want to become, and how they'll do it. Although that's not bad, it misses a huge motivational opportunity. What difference do employees make in the lives of the people who use their products and/or services? Why does what they do matter?

In contrast to a mission statement, a purpose statement is outward facing. It's an expression of the effect that we have on those whom we serve. It looks at the organization from the perspective of the customer.

As an example, consider IKEA. They could have created a statement that reads, "To be the number-1 furniture retailer in the world through quality, design, and low cost." This would tell people what they do, and how they do it.

Instead, their statement reads, "To create a better everyday life for the many people."[6] Their purpose statement starts with why. It's designed to appeal to the heart, not the head. IKEA's purpose shares a vision: to help people live better lives. This vision taps into the belief of anyone and everyone who yearns for something better. When people feel connected to making a vision like this a reality, they've tapped into something much bigger than themselves. They're meeting their need for purpose.

Unless you're the CEO in your company, there's good chance that you don't have a lot of say in changing your organization's mission statement to craft it into a purpose statement. But that shouldn't stop you from taking these ideas and using them with the people you lead.

As a team, you can cocreate a purpose statement. Use your company's mission statement as a starting point. From there, step into the shoes of your customer and get a good sense of how their lives are influenced by the work that you do.

Acknowledge Progress

In 2011, researchers from Harvard University published the findings of an extensive study on motivation at work. Over a four-month span, they worked with 238 knowledge workers from seven companies.

Figure 11.1   The
Effort-Progress-Reward
Cycle

The subjects went about their day-to-day jobs as usual. However, at the end of each workday, they were asked to fill out an email diary/questionnaire with these questions:

- What events stood out that day?
- What was your mood?
- What were your perceptions?
- What was your motivation?

The research netted out close to 12,000 individual diary entries. After analyzing all the data, the researchers found that the strongest motivator of human behavior was making progress in meaningful work.[7] They called this the progress principle.

Intuitively, this principle makes sense. Progress in meaningful work creates a virtuous cycle: seeing your effort produce small wins inspires you to keep working to achieve bigger and bigger wins (see Figure 11.1). This effort-progress-reward cycle is a natural momentum builder.

If you can understand and use the progress principle, you may have discovered your secret motivational weapon. Work to create an environment where people can make (and feel) meaningful progress.

Mark, a senior leader at a New York–based financial services company, described his progress-facilitating role this way:

> My job is to be a bulldozer. I push all the crap out of the way so my people have a smooth road to travel on to get where they need to go.

PERFORMANCE NEED 2: OWNERSHIP

How do you treat a rental car?

I've asked that questions to thousands of people. It almost always gets a big cackle of nervous laughter. Those giggles indicate a truth response—we've touched a nerve. It seems I'm not the only one who treats his rental car differently from his regular car.

Full disclosure: here are some examples of things I've done with rental cars:

- I've tossed trash on the floor or the backseat, as though it was a garbage can.
- I've accelerated much faster than I usually would, pushing the RPMs on the tachometer into the red zone.
- I've been less careful about bumping the tires against the curb when parallel parking.
- I've gone over the speed bumps at the airport at speeds much higher than prescribed by the road signs.

I would never do these things in my car, but I've done them with rental cars. Why? It's quite simple: it's a rental.

Once I drop that car off, I'm done. I won't think about it ever again. If something goes wrong with that car later, it won't be my problem. In those moments, I'm operating with *psychological rentership*. When I have this mind-set, my internal dialogue says, "I don't care. This doesn't belong to me. Someone else can take care of this."

You can spot psychological renters at work. When asked, "How are you?" they respond with "Two days until Friday." They refer to Wednesday as *hump day*. They never speak up in meetings unless called on.

Psychological rentership is a state of indifference, a feeling of apathy, a lack of purpose or meaning. Physical signs include low-energy, lack of initiative, and poor focus. Cynics use psychological rentership as a coping mechanism, a hard shell to protect themselves from further frustration, disappointment, and stress.

However, leaders who encourage an ownership mind-set not only wind up with better employees but also they deliver better results. Research has shown positive links between psychological ownership for the organization and employee attitudes (organizational commitment, job satisfaction, organization-based self-esteem) and work behavior (performance and organizational citizenship).[8] Given these benefits, there are five things you can do to satisfy the need for ownership, and the following sections explore each of them.

Expect the Best

In 1964, psychologist Robert Rosenthal received permission to administer a new form of IQ test at an elementary school in California. Based on the results, Rosenthal told the school's principal, Beverly Cantello, that he'd identified small groups of tested children who were about to flourish academically. Their teachers were informed about their budding high potential.

Did they flourish? Did they ever. Over the next year, the first-graders in this select group increased their IQ scores by 27 points on average.

But, it turns out the whole thing had been a giant experiment. Cantello and her staff learned that Rosenthal had lied. That "new" IQ test? Just an ordinary IQ test. The high-potential students? Chosen at random. The reason that the students improved so much was because the teachers had believed in their budding abilities and had nurtured them as such.[9]

Beliefs and expectations create operating norms. If you believe that your employees are capable of handling big ambitious projects, the likelihood of them succeeding is so much higher than if you believe they are incapable of doing so. Obviously, you don't want to set them up to fail. Train them on the needed skills, then show your belief in them and let them go. They just may surprise you and ask for more.

Ask

Diego had always been a "middle of the bell curve" employee. An engineer for a technology company, Diego had been a solid performer for 32 years. Solid, but never outstanding. Given his performance, Diego had been passed over for promotions and formal leadership development training for decades.

Then, the company was hit with a gigantic product recall. Billions of dollars and the company's reputation were at stake. This was a crisis the likes of which they'd never dealt with. Diego's manager, Flora, was stretched thin. She asked Diego to step up and help.

Flora asked Diego to be responsible for setting up four new product recall service centers and lead a team of 40 people. Diego took on the new role and exceeded everyone's wildest expectations. After the recall crisis ended, Flora pulled Diego into her office to discuss his terrific work. She asked him, "How come you never stepped up to this level earlier?"

Diego replied, "I was never asked."

You can't expect behavior you haven't asked for. Not everyone steps up and shows initiative naturally. If you want people to be proactive, you need to state that upfront.

Focus on the Ends, Not the Means

No two people are going to do a task the exact same way. Clarify the destination, but allow people to pick their own route to get there.

Take Roberta, for example. The chief marketing officer for a large pharmaceutical company, Roberta would find her stomach churning when her direct reports would present ideas in meetings that weren't presented the way she would do it. The physical pain got so bad she sought out help.

In my coaching work with Roberta, I helped her to realize she was attached to her identity as a perfectionist. Having been seen and rewarded as a high-achiever early on in her career (and, frankly, all throughout her childhood) Roberta had mistakenly internalized the belief that there was only one right way to do things: her way.

When it comes to achievement the goal is excellence, not perfection. I asked Roberta to try on a new label: recovering perfectionist.

(That got a smile and sigh of relief.) Through our work together, Roberta learned to stop micromanaging. She discovered that when she let people choose their own path, their level of ownership and commitment skyrocketed.

Have a Clear Decision-making Process

Business results are achieved based on the decisions we make. If your employees depend on you to make all (or most) of the decisions, then you don't have a true culture of ownership.

A tool that can help improve decision-making is called the decision tree model. The model clarifies and communicates where people are free to make decisions on their own, with input, or not at all. It also provides direction to help them grow and increase their ownership. It also helps them increase their sense of personal accountability.

The decision tree model uses a simple visual analogy of a tree: leaf, branch, trunk, and root (see Figure 11.2). The parts indicate

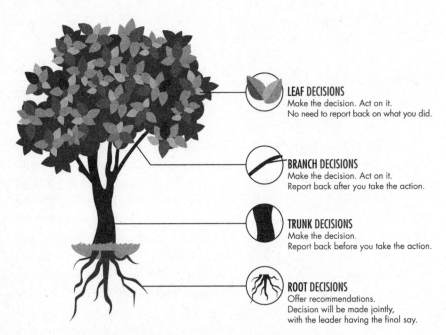

LEAF DECISIONS
Make the decision. Act on it.
No need to report back on what you did.

BRANCH DECISIONS
Make the decision. Act on it.
Report back after you take the action.

TRUNK DECISIONS
Make the decision.
Report back before you take the action.

ROOT DECISIONS
Offer recommendations.
Decision will be made jointly,
with the leader having the final say.

Figure 11.2 The Decision Tree Model

the potential impact the decision could have on the health of the overall organization. A tree can withstand a leaf being pulled off it, but damage to the trunk or roots can be life-threatening.

Not only does using the decision tree clarify decision-making authority but also employees take more ownership and the load of leaders becomes lighter and lighter as work is delegated out.

Ask for Feedback

Jenny is the operations director of a conference center in St. Louis where I've worked numerous times. (I should mention that I've worked at similar centers hundreds of times in my career.)

As far as I'm concerned, when it comes to venue organizers, Jenny's the gold standard. She goes completely above and beyond anyone else. The key to her performance? Feedback.

Jenny always wants to make things better. As each day begins, she asks, "Any special requests for today?" Every single day, when we finish, she asks, "What changes or tweaks for tomorrow?" "What else do you need?" "What else can I or my staff do that can help you?"

Not only does she ask, she then listens to the responses. She writes them down. She acts on them. And she commits preferences to memory, so when I come back to town two months later, everything is updated.

Think back on all the leaders you've ever worked with over the years. How many of those leaders have, unsolicited, asked you for feedback on how they could do a better job of supporting you? If you're like most people I've asked, you can count the number of those leaders on one hand.

Feedback offers a fast track to improved performance. When you seek input from your team on what's working well and what can be improved, you send a very clear message: it's not about me. It's about us. When employees see that the team takes priority over the leader, and they have a say in the team's direction, their sense of ownership increases.

There's a peculiar phenomenon that happens to people when they own things. Social psychologists call it the "mere ownership effect." It's a cognitive bias in which we assign more value to things just because we own them. If you can help those you lead satisfy their need for ownership, they'll find more value in their work.

SATISFYING PERFORMANCE NEEDS SATISFIES PERFORMANCE

People may labor because they have to, but they perform because they want to. When you recognize that people have hidden performance needs that yearn to be satisfied, you'll see employees in a whole new light. You'll work as a performance architect, designing an environment to meet their needs for purpose and ownership. By taking on this design thinking mind-set, you can transform your leadership and those you lead. Your ability to foster and facilitate collaboration will multiply exponentially.

Meeting the needs of the people you lead is not a static endpoint. There are ways to engage and inspire people even more. In today's world, employees crave much more than just having their needs met. They want employment to be a dynamic and rewarding experience. Exceptional leaders understand what makes great experiences and how to go about building them. You'll learn how to do this in the next chapter.

Chapter Resources

Satisfy Performance Need 1: Purpose

- I know and tell the origin story of my company.
- I know and tell the origin story of my leadership.
- I get customers to share their experiences with us firsthand.
- I cocreate a purpose statement with my team. I revisit this regularly.
- I acknowledge progress on a regular basis.

Fulfill Performance Need 2: Ownership

- I believe in and expect the best from people.
- I ask people to take on greater responsibilities.
- I focus on the ends, not the means.
- I use a clearly defined and communicated decision-making process.
- I ask for candid feedback.

Chapter 12

CREATING GREAT EMPLOYEE EXPERIENCES

The purpose of life is to live it, to taste experience to the utmost, to reach out eagerly and without fear for newer and richer experience.

—Eleanor Roosevelt

I was hired by the communications department of a large pharmaceutical company. On my first day, I arrived in the lobby just before 8:30 a.m., excited to begin my new job. I told the security guard my name and told him I was to meet Melissa, my new boss.

The guard found Melissa's name in the directory and called her desk. No answer. He told me to have a seat and wait. Twenty minutes passed. I started to feel frustrated. I'd been told to be there at 8:30 a.m., and had gotten up extra early to make sure no hiccups could happen during the commute.

At 9:05, a woman entered the waiting area and asked, "Are you Tim?" When I jumped up and said "yes," she brusquely told me to follow her. I had no idea who this was. She took me to what turned out to be the security office so I could get my ID badge. This took about an hour to finish up. Then, she took me

187

up to the fifth floor and ushered me into an empty cube. No phone, no computer, just a chair and a desk. She handed me a stack of forms to fill out and an employee handbook. "Someone will be by in a bit to get these from you."

At this point, I felt as though I was in a doctor's office. I hate doctor's offices.

An hour later, a guy named Stuart showed up. Stuart told me he works in communications. He told me that Melissa was out of the office this week on a business trip, and she's called and asked Stuart to show me around.

Stuart took me on a walk up and down the rows of cubes. In the next ten minutes, I met at least 20 people. It was like a blur of faces and names going past. I didn't remember anyone's name, and I had no idea what any of them did.

Stuart walked me back to the cube and told me to wait, since IT would be by soon to set me up. I waited until about 12:30. At that point, I'm starving, so I hurried down to the cafeteria to grab something to bring back up so I wouldn't miss IT. Turned out I didn't need to rush. IT didn't show up until after 2 p.m.

Ben, the guy from IT, came by with a used laptop. He was the first person to stop and take a moment to really talk with me. Ben was really nice, but he wasn't the sharpest of IT professionals. He didn't know how to get me logged on to the system.

During Ben's third phone call to the help desk, Stuart stopped by and told me that Melissa would be back on Wednesday. I didn't make it that long. I quit the next day.

Tim's a client of mine. The story of his terrible, horrible, no-good, very bad day is all true. In the span of less than eight hours, his tank of enthusiasm went from overflowing to completely empty. His new position at a stable company with a good salary and benefits didn't matter when stacked against the interactions he had on his first day on the job.

Although Tim's day may be an extreme example, just a couple of these offenses would demoralize most people. Tim saw the writing on the wall and left. What about those people who had a similar onboarding and chose to stay? How does it affect them? And how does it affect how engaged they're willing to be at work?

Tim's day was not a product of bad luck. It was a product of bad leadership. Melissa completely dropped the ball in ensuring Tim had a great experience. As a result, Tim and the company both lost out.

In this chapter, you're going to learn the ins and outs of experience and why it's important to create great experiences for those you lead. Most important, you'll gain a new set of tools to create great employee experiences in the future.

WHAT IS AN EXPERIENCE?

Reality, at a human level, is quite subjective. What we perceive as "reality" is the sum of the inputs to our five senses, our reflections on those inputs, and the feelings and thoughts we ascribe to those inputs. When you add all of that up, you're left with your experience of something or someone.

Experiences are the foundation of every type of human relationship. What we think and how we feel about someone (family members, colleagues, neighbors, etc.) or something (airlines, sports teams, types of soap, etc.) is entirely shaped by the exchange we have with or about that person or thing. Each contact leaves an impression: positive, negative, or neutral. Jan Carlzon, the former CEO of SAS (Scandinavian Airline Systems), called these contacts *moments of truth*. To give you a sense of the cumulative power of these moments of truth, consider Carlzon's perspective:

> Last year each of our ten million customers came in contact with approximately five SAS employees, and this contact lasted an average of 15 seconds each time ... These 50 million "moments of truth" are the moments that ultimately determine whether SAS will succeed or fail as a company. They are the moments when we must prove to our customers that SAS is their best alternative.[1]

In the customer journey, their overall experience is created by every touchpoint where your company interacts with them. This isn't limited to their exchange with a customer service representative. It's much broader, including aspects such as your online presence, how easy your website is to navigate, how quickly you respond, the quality of your product or service, and your relationship post-sale.

WHAT DOES CUSTOMER EXPERIENCE HAVE TO DO WITH LEADERSHIP?

Understanding the customer experience is critical for leaders. Moments of truth aren't just for customers. They happen for employees as well. Think of poor Tim, who opened this chapter.

If the customer experience is the basis for how customers think and feel about a brand, the employee experience is the basis for how your employees think and feel about you.

Today's employees have incredible choices. If an employee can jump ship and head down the street to work for another company for 15% higher base pay and similar benefits, the employee experience becomes a tremendous differentiator of value. The more positive the employee experience, the more likely your employee is going to be dedicated to your organization. Employees who are engaged put in 57% more effort on the job and are 87% less likely to resign than employees who are disengaged.[2]

The key to creating a great employee experience is to leverage the power of peak moments. Peak moments are touchpoints where employee expectations are particularly high. If you get these right, you'll build loyalty and commitment. Get them wrong and engagement wanes. Let's begin by looking at what makes for a peak moment and where they exist for the people you lead.

THE POWER OF PEAK MOMENTS

Think back to the last vacation that you took. If a friend asked you about your trip after you came home, what would you tell them? You wouldn't walk them through everything you did. Instead, you would go through your memory, pick specific moments to share, and edit out the rest. A lot of the boring everyday bits would be left on the cutting room floor.

What you'd wind up sharing are peak moments. Peak moments are those vivid instants that get seared into our brains. They're heightened reality, life with the dull parts taken out. Memories of peak moments are rich in emotion, sensory detail, and/or surprise.

In life, there are some communal peak moments that everyone experiences. Counting down the last ten seconds until the new year. Waking up to find the money left by the tooth fairy. Heading off to the first day of school. Graduation. As a society, we've created rituals to celebrate peak moments and guide us through times of transition.

Compared to personal lives, most professionals' lives are shockingly devoid of peak moments. No wonder so much of work seems so ... plain. Not investing in these peak moments is a missed leadership opportunity. The employment life cycle is full of natural points at which such moments would be of great benefit:

- Sourcing and recruiting candidates
- The interview(s)
- The employment offer
- Preboarding
- First day on the job
- First team meeting
- Compensation and benefits
- Initial training
- Performance coaching and feedback
- Project kickoffs
- Continued professional training
- Mentoring
- Organizational communication
- Appreciation, recognition, bonuses
- Promotion
- Resignation
- Termination
- Retirement

Each of these junctures represents a window of opportunity to deepen and enrich the employee experience.

Take, for example, Tim's peak moment—the first day on the job. When it comes to a new hire, this is your one chance to make a first impression. Proportionally, it counts for a lot more than just one day.

How that new employee feels about you and the company is formed and solidified in the first full-day encounter. Employees don't walk in the door fully committed. They have their radar up, watching and waiting to see how you show up for them.

Unfortunately, Tim's bad experience is far too common. A bad first day sets the tone for what the days to come would be like. According to a February 2014 survey by Bamboo HR, one-third of approximately 1,000 respondents said they had quit a job within six months of starting it. Of those that quit, more than 16% left within the first week.[3]

On the flipside, there are lots of companies that realize creating an incredible first experience can set their new employees on the path to success. One of my clients, a global consulting firm, brings hundreds of new hires from around the United States together for their first week on the job. They stay in a large hotel and spend the next eight days immersed in an intensive simulation to learn basic consulting skills.

But skill building isn't really why the firm puts this event on. Martin, the North American head of learning, described it to me this way:

> By the end of these eight days, we want them to have the most positive experience possible of our firm. We want them to feel that their decision to join up was the best choice they've made in their entire lives. It should feel that good.

Although a week-long offsite orientation immersion might be nice, it's not required. Google's analytics team pays special attention to which leadership actions have the biggest impact on a new hire. In *Work Rules*, Laszlo Bock, head of Google's people function, shares a simple email reminder alert that is sent out to managers on the Sunday night before they have a new employee starting the next day. The email tells them to do the following:

- Have a role-and-responsibilities discussion.
- Match your new hire with a peer buddy.
- Help your new hire build a social network.
- Set up onboarding check-ins once a month for your new hire's first six months.
- Encourage open dialogue.

What Block and his team have found is that sending this reminder alert can reduce the new hire's time to full productivity by a month. This is 25% faster than it would be otherwise.[4]

The first day on the job, although important, is but one of many professional milestones. Each one of these markers represents a moment of truth. These are the moments when you must prove to your employees that your company is their best option.

LEAVE THEM WITH A *WOW* EXPERIENCE

The online shoe retailer Zappos knows a thing or two about creating great experiences. Since their founding in 1999, Zappos has grown enormously. From the start, they knew they weren't in the shoe industry. They were in the happy customer industry. Their business was shaped by their core values, the first of which is Deliver WOW Through Service.[5]

Some of examples of Zappos' WOW in action with their customers:

- Zappos sent flowers to a woman who had ordered six different pairs of shoes, who was recovering from foot pain due to harsh medical treatments.[6]
- When Zappos ran out of stock, a customer service rep left the call center and traveled to a rival shoe store to get a specific pair of shoes for a customer staying at the Mandalay Bay hotel in Las Vegas.[7]
- It overnighted a free pair of shoes to a best man who had arrived at a wedding without shoes.[8]

Zappos' WOW is not limited to their customers. They also believe employees need a WOW experience—otherwise they can't deliver WOW to customers. As an example, to help ensure there's a good cultural fit, new employees are offered $4,000 to leave the company during their new hire orientation to make sure they really want to be part of the Zappos team. When Amazon acquired Zappos in 2009, they also adopted the Zappos' "Pay to Quit" offer.[9]

How do you create an enjoyable experience? In instance after instance, two core themes consistently show up: generating positive emotions and creating delight. The remainder of this chapter will share multiple tips, tools, and techniques in each of these areas. With these skills and deliberate practice, you can make creating great experiences part of your leadership job description.

MASTERING GREAT EXPERIENCES: GENERATE POSITIVE EMOTION

Conventional wisdom tells us that business and emotions do not mix. Many organizations operate with an unwritten "check your feelings at the door" policy. The fact is, no one ever checks his or her feelings at the door. What employees do is *suppress* their feelings at the door. This leaves them feeling like a work-bot, not a human.

Emotions have a huge impact on how we perform. In his book *The Happiness Advantage*, Shawn Achor cites research showing that happiness improves nearly every business outcome: raising sales by 37%, productivity by 31%, and accuracy on tasks by 19%.[10] In addition, positive emotions help us to be more innovative. In a positive state of mind, you're more able to generate new ideas and be open to the ideas of others. Some keys to generating positive emotion include modeling positivity, flipping the negative script, and acknowledging and celebrating small wins.

Model Positivity

There's an exercise that I've done many times that's a variation of one that we reviewed in Chapter 1. You can try it now. Think about a leader in your life whom you've known and worked with personally and whom you especially admire. This could be a teacher, coach, mentor, or manager. What words would you use to describe that leader?

In all the times I've done this activity, the answers I get back generally include words such as these:

- Dynamic
- Engaging
- Enthusiastic

- Kind
- Thoughtful
- Considerate
- Confident
- Inspiring
- Caring

What do all these words have in common? They're all positive traits.

No one has ever told me, "I had this amazing leader, and you know what I loved about him? He used to get so anxious every time a deadline would approach. I really miss that."

If you want to create positivity, be positive. Now, I recognize this sounds like a worn-out cliché. Being positive is easy to do, *once*. The challenge comes in consistency: How do you show up day after day with a reliably positive attitude?

To learn how, consider the experience of a professional stage actor. Actors serve as a valuable teaching model because their industry—live theater—specializes in the business of creating compelling experiences. If the experience is dull, the show closes. Professional actors on Broadway perform in their shows eight times a week. Do you think they "feel" like giving a full-out performance night after night, week after week, month after month? Not necessarily.

But what the pros do is find ways to make each performance—whether it's the first or the 301st—fresh. They know that it's their job to be completely present and focused. If you go through the motions without caring, everyone will know.

You may not feel like it, but conveying emotions is part of your job. Take a moment to think about which feelings you're sending out to others. The business world has far too many leaders who can't be bothered. Ultimately, being positive means choosing positivity. The choice is yours to make.

Flip the Negative Script

Julian leads the safety team for a statewide transportation system. In preparation for his annual all-team off-site meeting, I asked him what were the biggest challenges that got in the way of his team working better together. He said:

> We have an epidemic of negativity here. I've got some really smart people on my team, but all they look for is what's wrong. If there are 10 things going on and 9 are working just fine, they'll rip into that one thing that's not working well. You'd think that everything around here is horrible. If that wasn't enough, after meetings, they get into their little cliques and complain about other people and what a problem they are. It brings morale and effectiveness way down.

Julian's team is not unusual. Focusing on what's not working is the brain's default setting. Human brains are wired with a negativity bias. This bias means you have a stronger response to negative information and emotions than positive ones.

From an evolutionary perspective, this negativity bias makes sense. Our wiring gave us a heightened sensitivity to potential threats, allowing us to respond quickly to flee from danger. It literally kept us alive.

Negativity bias is part nature, but also part nurture. Negativity is multiplied by how we're trained to think. For instance, to succeed in your professional life, you've been taught to become a good problem-solver. That means you've honed your skills at identifying what the problem is, analyzing the causes, analyzing potential solutions, and testing out hypotheses to find a worthwhile solution.

These analytical skills are great for solving problems but lousy for creating a positive culture. Analysis is an abstract separation of a whole into its constituent parts to study those parts and how they relate. Positivity springs from synthesis—building bridges and making connections. It's the very opposite of analysis.

Psychologist Barbara Frederickson has done some pioneering research into the science of positive emotions. Her studies have found that positivity "broaden(s) people's attention and thinking, enabling them to draw on higher-level connections and a wider-than-usual range of percepts or ideas."[11] In other words, being positive enables people to see more options and possibilities. When you have more options, you can make better choices.

To create a great experience, you're going to have to flip the script. Instead of always fixing what's wrong, seek out what's right. Next time you have a team meeting (or a one-on-one) try questions like these:

- What energizes our organization and helps it function at its best?
- What are the things that make future progress possible?
- What are the most momentous stories in your life?
- What things are going well in your life?
- Where am I making a difference?

By framing questions through the lens of appreciative inquiry, you'll tip the scales toward the positive.

Acknowledge and Celebrate Small Wins

If organizations are suffering through a negativity epidemic, they're also in the middle of a celebration drought. Karen, a senior manager at a technology company, shared a common refrain:

> Everyone here is working hard and constantly on the go. We've got a ton of projects going on, and as soon as we finish one thing, it's on to the next one. Stop and celebrate? There's barely enough time to catch my breath. It'd be great to celebrate more. It's just not something we do.

Why don't companies like Karen's celebrate more? I've asked this same question to hundreds of leaders. The typical first response is, "We don't have time." Consider the belief behind that statement. It harkens back to that industrial age mind-set view of employees. "We don't have time" really is code for "We don't understand small wins are the ideal opportunity to create future motivation and achievement."

Celebration doesn't have to involve a big awards banquet, a major outlay of cash, or a full day out of the office. Sometimes the simplest handshake or word of praise will do the trick. Think back to the Israeli semiconductor factory in Chapter 9. Among pizza, cash, or a text message from the boss that read "GOOD JOB!," the text message was the strongest motivator. Whether you want to celebrate on an individual or group level, acknowledgment is 90% of the effort required. The rest is just the frosting on the cake.

Without acknowledgment, people's mental energy is stuck in an open loop that yearns to be closed. Not being recognized for one's achievement is demoralizing. After all, if a win happens but no one ever notices it, is it really a win?

The lack of recognition and celebration of wins is a bigger problem than you might think. Most leaders think they're actually pretty good at this skill. But the research finds otherwise. Studies have found that more than 80% of supervisors claim they frequently express appreciation to their subordinates, whereas less than 20% of the employees report that their supervisors express appreciation more than occasionally.[12]

Support for making progress toward meaningful work is the most effective employee motivator. Acknowledging and celebrating wins is a powerful way to offer that support. If you think back on the peak experiences in your life, there's a very good chance that celebrating was part of them. It's key to generating positive emotion.

MASTERING GREAT EXPERIENCES: CREATING DELIGHT

The ability to generate positive emotion is an essential leadership skill. Positivity should be the default for every high-performing work environment. Yet, if you want to make the employee experience even more outstanding, you need to master the ability to delight.

Delight is not an abstract concept. It's a feeling—highly subjective and deeply personal. It's the unabashed pleasure that comes when preconceived expectations are exceeded in wonderful ways. It's, to borrow from Zappos, a WOW!

Some ways you can create delight:

- Start with sizzle
- Use surprise
- Create rituals
- End with a bang

Start with Sizzle

When an experience starts, you have a tiny window of opportunity to grab people's attention. If you don't hook them quickly, you'll lose them. In most business settings, boring is business as usual. The standard for engagement in business settings is quite low. If you try something—anything—you'll stand out from most of your peers.

I was at a conference where Ralph, the CEO of a health-care company, got up to speak. His topic: the need for the company to adopt new technology. Ralph's subject matter—dealing with change—was not a revolutionary topic. I've seen many other leaders present on the same issue. Most of them start off with something like, "The world is changing, and so is our industry. These are the things you need to know. Next slide." These presentations are doomed from the start.

Ralph was different. Next to him on stage was a small table with numerous objects:

- A rotary dial phone.
- An eight-track player.
- A Commodore 64 computer.

Ralph used his antique props for comic effect. He got the whole crowd laughing about what life would be like if we were still using these tools at work. Ralphed hooked his audience, and they were open to him from there on.

Tools to help you start with sizzle are detailed in the following sections.

Use a Relevant Icebreaker Activity

When done well, icebreakers get people moving, interacting, and building relationships. They can relax a potentially formal or tense atmosphere.

However, when executed poorly, icebreakers are cheesy wastes of time. Does anyone really want to listen to a room full of their colleagues go around one at a time and share the name of their first pet? There's nothing like a bad icebreaker to transform a group of willing participants into prisoners.

The first key to leading an effective icebreaker is clarity. The rules need to be easy to understand and follow. People need to be able to fully engage without confusion. Your directions need to be so precise that there's no possibility for misunderstanding. The best way to get to this standard of precision is to practice. Find a few friends or family and try it out on them first. Don't let showtime be your first dry run.

The second key for an effective icebreaker is relevance. Don't just do an icebreaker for the sake of breaking the ice. Choose an activity with useful subject matter that connects to who you are, why you're there, and what you hope to accomplish. For example, when facilitating workshops on leading change, I often start the workshop by saying, "Follow the instructions on the next slide." The slide is shown in Figure 12.1.

After they move, we debrief their experience: what happened and what their internal reaction was. Through dialogue, we discover how the activity was an analogy for how people feel and respond to being told to change when that change is sprung on them suddenly. The activity hooks people in a way that just discussing the concepts never could.

Poll the Group Using ART

When it comes to sizzle, use technology to your advantage. Audience response technology (ART) is an interactive means for you to create engaging, real-time interaction with your audience. There are hardware, software, and cloud-based systems to choose from.

There are plenty of benefits to using ART. First, ART works at the speed of our instant-gratification culture. In seconds, you can collect and analyze participant feedback to any question that you pose. Because people don't see the results of others until you reveal them, the individual polling process prevents groupthink.

MOVE TO A DIFFERENT TABLE
AND SEAT IN THE ROOM.
NOW.

Figure 12.1   Example Icebreaker

Second, the technology enables you to turn traditional one-way communication into two-way communication. This interactive dialogue builds credibility and trust, because you're showing people that you're interested in what they think. Given the anonymity, people feel safe to answer honestly, and both introverts and extroverts have a chance to be heard.

The key to a successful ART session is to have genuine thought-provoking questions. For example, if you ask, "What's the biggest issue our customers would say we have?" you'll prompt a rich discussion. If you use softball questions such as, "Who's happy to be here? Press 1 for yes, Press 2 for no," it'll be a failure. Be creative. You can certainly create a mix of lighter fun questions, as well as challenging questions that cut to the heart of your subject.

Ask Them a Question about Themselves, Get Them Talking, Then Listen

Research tells us that people do have a favorite subject to talk about: themselves. Based on your understanding of the audience, craft a compelling question for them to discuss.

Here are some quality generic questions:

- What's the biggest challenge you face in your role?
- If you were CEO, what would you change first?
- Who has been your strongest leadership mentor and why?

You can have people pair up and spend a few minutes interacting, then ask for a few replies, which you will (through clever preparation) use to transition into your next point. Redirecting the communication flow so you do more listening than talking will build rapport. In addition, the interactivity will increase engagement.

Play a Video

Everyone in your audience has grown up watching movies. They are fluent in the language of cinema. Perhaps more than any other medium, movies have the power to make us feel. Moviemakers are experts in their ability to take us on an emotional journey. As a leader, why not leverage what already exists to your advantage?

Choose a video that's relevant to your message. With the internet, you have boundless options. For example, if you are about to hold a meeting to establish team communication norms, maybe you'd want to show "A Conference Call in Real-Life."[13] Here's a tip: let your participants know how long the video will last. Saying "we're going to watch a short video" is vague. Short to you might be 20 minutes. To me it's three. Instead, say, "We're going to watch a video that runs about four and a half minutes." Then people can settle in for the ride.

Use Surprise

There's something wonderful about the experience of being surprised. Sneaky by nature, surprise is an encounter with the unexpected. Not only do surprises grab our attention but also we remember them far longer than everyday events. The novelty of the moment interrupts typical neural firing patterns. The surprise tells our brains: WATCH HERE!!! PAY ATTENTION!!! It epitomizes the *peak* of a peak experience. Tania Luna and LeeAnn Renninger, authors of the book *Surprise*, write, "We feel most comfortable when things are certain, but most alive when they're not."[14]

In addition, surprise can change our moods. The momentary shock of a happy surprise can move someone from a current state to a more positive state. This can make that person more open, curious, and receptive to new ideas.

To create surprises, you don't need to be an artistic genius or wait for a flash of inspiration. Because surprises are built on interrupting predictable patterns, all you need to do is to find alternatives to the usual assumptions people would have about a situation. Ask yourself, "What's ordinarily true about this situation?" Then, brainstorm alternatives to how things are usually done.

For example, at large conferences, it's not terribly unusual to kick off the conference with a local marching band. I've seen it done dozens of times. It's fun and high energy, but somewhat predictable.

One client took this marching band idea and turned it into something truly original. I was working as the master of ceremonies for a conference of 350 flight attendants. In the middle of my opening remarks, I was "interrupted" by 10 members of a local percussion ensemble.

However, instead of coming out and playing percussion instruments (predictable), they came out with airline beverage carts and banged on the carts using various tools and implements you'd find on an airplane. The flight attendants loved it.

Another way to surprise people is through humor. Whether it's a great visual, video, or anecdote, humor is built on a setting up a premise (predictable situation) and then taking it to an unexpected conclusion. Advanced tip: rehearse your surprise in advance. In the moment, you want it to go smoothly.

Create Rituals

Labor Day weekend is a big deal in my house. Not because it's Labor Day, per se. It's because it's the weekend of the three-county fair in my town. The oldest continuous running fair of its kind in the United States, it's got agricultural exhibitions, displays, competitions, and demonstrations. It's got food booths, amusement park rides, and midway games. My kids (who are currently 14 and 11) have been going since they were born. They love it. Every year there are must-dos at the fair. We always go and see Granny's Racing Pigs. Alex, my son, always gets a moo-nut: a donut filled with soft-serve ice cream. Miranda, my daughter, always wants us to watch the talent show. We end the day with the whole family going up on the Ferris wheel. Whenever I've broached the subject of going away for the whole Labor Day holiday, they've begged and pleaded to stay. For them, the fair is a powerful ritual.

A ritual is a ceremonial act or action set in a precise manner. Performing a ritual is a transformation of sorts. It moves those involved in the ritual out of the mundane, everyday into a heightened version of reality. It creates a peak moment.

For example, consider the ritual of a birthday cake. If you observe the goings-on for most of the party—food, beverages, conversation, and so on—it's a pretty typical social gathering. Now, notice how things change when the cake comes out with the candles lit. There's a quiet focus. Someone begins to sing. Everyone joins in. The song ends. Then there's that lovely pause while the birthday boy or girl makes a wish. The candles get blown out. There's applause. And we return back to our ordinary experience.

A mentor of mine once said, "A ritual is anything that worked that got repeated." There are all sorts of different types of rituals, and there's nothing stopping you from creating your own rituals with your teams at work. All it takes is your intention.

For example, one small company I worked with had a ritual that, at their monthly all-staff meeting, they'd invite anyone who had joined the company since the last meeting to stand in the middle of the circle of the team. Then, they had to sing a song—any song, of their choosing. After they were done, they'd get a huge round of applause, a certificate with the company's values on it, and a company t-shirt. It was a rite of passage.

If you think about the biggest rituals in life: birthdays, graduations, weddings, baby showers, funerals—they nearly all revolve around transitional moments. Rituals demarcate boundaries. They also support us as we cross thresholds and move from one phase of life to the next. They're a way to honor achievement, change, and growth.

Don't all of those professional transitional moments in the career life cycle deserve to be honored as well? In most organizations, these moments are forgotten. Remembering and ritualizing these moments is a way to re-humanize work. The key to using rituals is to be less concerned with getting them right than doing something at all. Get started. Like family holiday celebrations, rituals will grow and evolve over time.

End with a Bang

There's a reason that Shakespeare wrote a play titled *All's Well That Ends Well*: it's true. When you design your experiences, make sure you leave people on a high note. What do you want impress on them? Some things you can do include sharing a story, showing a video, doing some ritual of appreciation or celebration, or showing appropriate humor. Whatever mode you choose, the mood should be positive. You want to be remembered—for the right reasons.

For example, have you seen leaders give presentations that end in a mumbled puddle of apologies? Or refer to handouts that they forgot to bring? Or, maybe instead of an uplifting message, they leave you with a mess of logistics to sort out? In all these cases, the ending sabotages everything that was done before.

Although it's true that you only get one chance to make a first impression, you also only get one chance to make a *last* impression. And that ending carries extra weight. Psychologists refer to this bias as the *peak-end rule*, which means you evaluate an overall experience based on how you felt at its peak and at its end. Those moments matter most.

Spend some time really thinking about "What's the final message I want to leave people with?" Then, craft and plan your ending accordingly. For example, when I lead two-day facilitator boot camps, I end with a very specific checkout. I ask everyone to briefly share what they're most proud of having accomplished in the last two days. It's a quick and easy way for the group to connect one last time, generate positivity, and leave on a high note.

TAILORING A PERSONALIZED EXPERIENCE

As an experience creator, you can make work a dynamic place, filled with purpose and meaning. As Pine and Gilmore, authors of *The Experience Economy*, put it,

> experiences are inherently personal, existing only in the mind of an individual who has been engaged on an emotional, physical, intellectual, or even spiritual level. Thus, no two people can have the same experience.[15]

The relationship experience between you and those you lead is deeply personal. When it all goes well, it should be tailored specifically for them. Yet, you don't need to create each new experience from the bottom up. You can mix and match these tools and techniques in new combinations to engage and collaborate at an entirely new level. You're only limited by your imagination.

When I've shared these tools with leaders in workshops, a common response has been, "This experience creation stuff is all fine and well and good, but I'm already super-busy. I can barely keep up with what I'm doing now. How can I be expected to use these new techniques when my plate is already overflowing?"

Understood. You can't take on more when you're already full. Being too busy is one of the biggest hindrances to collaboration. To lead smarter, sometimes the best thing you can do is to *not* do something—to streamline, minimize, or eliminate. We'll explore how. you go about doing this in the next chapter.

Chapter Resources

Capitalize on Peak Moments

- Sourcing and recruiting candidates
- The interview(s)
- The employment offer
- Preboarding
- First day on the job
- First team meeting
- Compensation and benefits
- Initial training
- Performance coaching and feedback
- Project kickoffs
- Continued professional training
- Mentoring
- Organizational communication
- Appreciation, recognition, bonuses
- Promotion
- Resignation
- Termination
- Retirement

Generate Positive Emotion

- I consistently model positivity.
- I use inquiry to reframe negative scripts to find solutions.
- I acknowledge and celebrate small wins.

Create Delight

- I start with sizzle by doing the following:
  - ☐ I use a relevant icebreaker activity.
  - ☐ I survey groups using ART or other means.
  - ☐ I ask great starter questions to get groups talking.
  - ☐ I show videos as a way to engage and inspire.
- I include the element of surprise to engage.
- I create rituals that my team adopts and celebrates.
- I end events with a memorable bang.

Chapter 13

MAKING THINGS SIMPLE

Simplicity is the ultimate sophistication.

—Leonardo da Vinci

While on the phone with Rachelle, a senior learning and development executive for a global manufacturer, our conversation turned to her company's workplace competencies. Workplace competencies refer to behaviors or skills that are used to define and measure an employee's effectiveness.

Rachelle casually mentioned that her company uses 600 different formal competencies.

Yes, you read that right: 600.

How can anyone possibly remember 600 of anything?

Rachelle and the 600 competencies are but a symptom of a larger disease. Accelerating growth and technologies have created a new organizational malady: complexity. Leaders and employees alike are feeling overloaded and overwhelmed.

For the past few years, I've been helping people escape the complexity trap. I've had the good fortune to work with Lisa Bodell, CEO of Futurethink and author of the bestselling book *Why Simple Wins*. Lisa spent five years researching her book on overcoming complexity. We then teamed up to bring the content in workshop form to numerous organizations. My thinking owes a debt to Lisa and all the leaders who've participated in the Killing Complexity workshops.

THE SIMPLE ADVANTAGE

It's ironic, but with all the new technology, software, and applications people have access to, what do people crave most? Ease of use. Consider your own experience. For example, if you visit a website that's confusing to navigate, what do you do? First, you get frustrated. Second, you leave. And you don't come back.

The rise of digital technology introduced a new acronym: UX, or user experience. UX designers work to plan all aspects of an end user's interaction. Design goals include making the user experience consistent, satisfying, and enjoyable. However, the most important goal is to make the experience simple.

There's a reason why Apple is one of the most valued companies on the planet. Apple customers are loyal to Apple in part because its products are intuitively easy to use. This is no accident. As Apple founder Steve Jobs said, "It takes a lot of hard work to make something simple, to truly understand the underlying challenges and come up with elegant solutions."[1]

UX is a good metaphor for your leadership. You're looking to collaborate well with the people you lead. If things are unnecessarily complex, people get frustrated.

If you can make simplicity part of your leadership operating system, you've got a competitive advantage. A survey of more than 14,000 people in nine countries found that only one out of five employees finds his or her workplace truly simple. Of those, 30% describe their workplace as complex and difficult to navigate.

The survey found that in a "simple organization," 95% of employees are more likely to trust their company's leadership, 54% find it easier to innovate, 65% are more likely to refer someone to work at their company, and 84% of employees plan to stay longer in their job.[2]

Not only does complexity drain morale but also it drains performance. A typical frontline supervisor or mid-level manager works 47 hours per week. A 2016 survey found that of this time, he or she devotes 21 hours to meetings involving more than four people. Another 11 hours is spent processing e-communications. If you subtract time periods of less than 20 minutes between meetings or processing emails as "unproductive time," it leaves them with less than 6½ hours per week of uninterrupted time to get work done.[3]

Many things can create unnecessary complexity, but there are two titans that play an outsized role in complicating the workplace: **meetings** and **emails**. They suck time and energy more than just about anything else.

The good news is it doesn't have to be that way. This chapter is full of ideas that are easy to implement. Once you apply these tools, you'll never want to go back to the way things were before. Let's get cracking.

MEETINGS

If it seems like being booked into back-to-back meetings is becoming more of the rule than the exception, you're right. Technology has made creating and sending out meeting invites as easy as the touch of a button. But meeting quantity should never be confused with meeting quality. More is not better.

To create a better meeting experience, you're going to have to be intentional about creating meeting norms. Better meetings won't happen by themselves. Create your norms with your users in mind. The following sections provide some suggested norms you can use.

Require Meeting Agendas in Advance

One of the keys to simplicity is clarity. Meetings with no agendas are mediocre at best. "Because it's 10:30 a.m. on a Tuesday" is not a valid reason to meet. The agenda should clearly state the purpose of the meeting. It's not enough just to list a subject, such as "this year's budget." Attendees need to know what they're there to do: get updates? Share information? Give input? Make decisions? The agenda should be specific.

Be bold. Set the ground rule that if there's no agenda set out in advance, the meeting does not happen.

Make It OK to Say No

Jill, a quality manager at a large pharmaceutical company, said, "Everyone's really nice here. No one ever turns down a meeting invite, even if they've got other things going on. Everyone does it, so no one feels comfortable to say no."

It's easy to get lulled into conformity. But not every meeting needs everybody there. Buck the trend. Once you've established clarity in agendas (see previous section), give permission for your people (and yourself) to decline meeting invites. Your life will thank you for giving it some time back.

Have a Strong Facilitator

Leading a meeting well is harder than it looks. Effective meeting facilitators are skilled at managing the content (what is being discussed) and the process (how it's being discussed).

Just because you're the leader doesn't mean you are always the right person to lead the meeting. You may be better served to have someone else facilitate. This can free you up to fully immerse as a participant.

Avoid Multitasking

If everyone pulls his or her phone or laptop out during a meeting, how much genuine listening is going on? How much useful dialogue is likely to occur? What's happening is not a meeting; it's a pseudo-meeting, where people are just biding their time until it's their turn to report out. They're going through the motions of meeting.

There's one big reason people multitask in meetings. The meetings are of such poor quality already that they don't feel as if they're missing anything. If you design meetings so they're truly valuable, people will appreciate the new norm of powering off devices before you start. Be explicit about your new policy. Some of my clients have even placed baskets by the door for people to leave their devices.

Multitasking becomes especially challenging for people working in a remote setting. If you are going to engage your virtual attendees, you have to find more ways to make the meeting interactive. You may want to consider using video so people can't disappear.

Start Promptly

Your CFO would not stand for you taking 16% of your budget and flushing it down the toilet. Yet, when you start an hour-long meeting ten minutes late, that's exactly what you're doing: 16% of your time is gone.

As a leader, you set the tone. If you tolerate lateness, that's what you'll get. You'll also get resentment from the people who consistently show up on time and feel their time is being wasted.

Have Stand-Up Meetings

There's nothing like challenging gravity to get people to focus. When people stand up, they don't get to relax the way they do in a chair. Not surprisingly, they cut to the chase much more quickly. A study published in the *Journal of Applied Psychology* found that sit-down meetings were 34% longer than Stand-Up Meetings—with no difference in the quality of decisions made.[4]

Appoint Timekeepers and Scribes

Being the leader doesn't mean doing everything yourself. When you delegate out roles at meetings, not only do you share the load but also you empower people to take responsibility for the quality of the meeting outcome.

It's amazing how many meetings take place where nothing gets written down. A scribe who can capture the essence of what happened is worth his or her weight in gold. Great timekeepers do more than look at their watch. They challenge the group to increase its sense of urgency and to hold fast to boundaries.

Many leaders who've deputized others into these roles have found it to be a huge support. In addition, they're often surprised to find that the people who take on these roles do a better job than they did themselves.

Change the Default Times

There's nothing magical about 30- and 60-minute increments. They are, however, the default settings in iCal and Outlook for meetings.

One of the biggest complaints people make about their meeting culture is the stress that comes from back-to-back scheduling. In the course of one second, one meeting ends and the next one starts. Although this works fine on paper, it doesn't work in real life. People may have to travel from one room to the next, dial in to a new conference line or weblink, or use the facilities. They may also need time for a mental break to refocus on to the next subject.

Cyril Parkinson once wrote, "Work expands so as to fill the time available for its completion."[5] Parkinson's law, as it's come to be known, means that if you have an hour scheduled for a meeting, that's how long it will take. Amazingly, if you schedule a 45-minute meeting, that's what people will get used to. Giving people a humane amount of transition time before their next meeting may make you the most popular leader in your organization.

Distribute Materials in Advance

Depending what you're meeting about, you may have reports or other items that people need to review in advance. ("Advance" means at least a day or two—not five minutes before you start.) Make it clear that attendees are expected to spend time going over materials before you meet, rather than use valuable time during the meeting.

In addition, look for ways to cap the volume of preread materials. People are busy. People need enough data to be informed, not overwhelmed. When it comes to prework, less is more. Not only is a three-page synopsis easier to read than a 30-page report, the likelihood of the prework getting done increases exponentially.

Use the Parking Lot

One of the things people hate most about bad meetings is the way they go off on tangents. You thought you were meeting to discuss A, B, and C, but the discussion has veered off into X, Y, and Z. X, Y, and Z may be meaningful topics, but because they were never part of the agenda, what are you supposed to do?

Due to the nature of discussions, tangents happen. But that doesn't mean you should be ruled by them. If you find yourself heading toward X, use a parking lot. Have a flipchart or whiteboard that's titled "Parking Lot" and write X on it. Say, "I hear you talking about X. Let's park X for now, and let's find another time and place where we can really focus on dealing with X."

People respect leaders who set healthy boundaries. A parking lot is a clever tool to help you acknowledge new ideas without letting the outliers derail your focus.

End the Meeting if It's Going Nowhere

It's hard to admit, but some meetings are just plain useless. Try as you might, you can keep talking around and around a subject, but it's clear that you're not getting any closer to new insights or solutions. Rather than persisting at hitting your head against the wall, just stop.

End early. Pick it up again at a different time and place. In the interim, maybe there's someone or something else that has information that could be relevant. For now, there's no need to stick with it just because you said so.

Follow Up

People don't meet just for meeting's sake, even though it may feel like it at times. Ideally, meetings are catalysts to future action. Because of this meeting, who is going to do what? By when? If it's not measured, it won't be managed.

If you've discussed ideas, but don't make time and place for action steps and follow-up, you've wasted most of your time. Budget 10% to 15% of your time toward the end of a meeting to document next steps. Then, find ways after the meeting to keep these commitments out in the open.

Create One Meeting-Free Day a Week

It turns out the best way to run some meetings is to not meet at all. It's obvious that one of the biggest costs of constantly moving from meeting to meeting is time. However, another huge drawback of being in perpetual meeting mode is that you're robbed of your ability to stay focused on one thing.

A meeting demands more of your cognitive capacity than just the time spent in the meeting. The meeting cycle also includes the preparation time before meeting and the synthesis time afterward. When you're in multiple meetings a day, it's hard to break this cycle of thinking and dedicate mental energy to more complex, long-term project work. A meeting-free day gives you (and your team) the space and time to get to those things that are important, but not urgent.

Many clients I've worked with have used this technique with great success. Manny, an operations manager at a manufacturing organization, said, "Meeting-free Thursdays has given me my life back." It's especially useful for people who are strong self-starters and like to stay focused on one thing. A word of warning: not everyone functions well with a full day of unstructured time. For people in this camp, it may be more helpful to go with a meeting-free half-day. Try it out, see how it works, and adjust as needed.

EMAIL

In the era known as BE (Before Email), also known as the 1970s, the average executive dealt with about 1,000 external communications a year. Assuming a 50-week work year, that works out to about 20 communications a week. Four a day. Given the type of technology available at the time, most of these communications were phone calls, with some telexes.

Fast forward to the 2010s. Now, the average executive deals with 30,000 external communications a year.[6] That's 120 a day, scattered across a variety of platforms: voice mail, email, Instant Messaging, videoconferencing, and so on.

Think back to when you received your first emails. Ding... you've got mail! How novel and charming it all seemed. Instant magic! Then, that slow drip of email turned into a stream that turned into a river that turned into a tidal wave.

If it feels as though you're drowning in email and communication complexity, you're not alone. Technology is a great servant but a lousy master. Here are some ways to harness the beast of email. You can use these tools with your team to make their experience of work simpler and less stressful.

> Technology is a great servant but a lousy master.

Turn Auto-Notifications Off

Your computer has default settings when it arrives. These settings aren't the ones that serve you best. One of those default settings is the one in which your mail program alerts you with a sound and/or a screen that tells you something new has just arrived. Change it—get rid of that alert. Every ping and ding sabotages your concentration and derails your momentum. And while you're changing the defaults on your computer, pull out your smartphone and change those settings as well.

Create Email-Free Time Zones

Irma, an auditor for a financial services firm, agreed to a one-week experiment. For five days, she decided to set up email-free time zones. She changed her way of working so she would process emails only three times a day: two hours after she started working in the morning, once after lunch, and once at the end of the day. "That first morning," Irma reported, "it was really hard not to open my inbox. I'm so used to doing that first thing when I come in. I felt like a drug addict in withdrawal."

Irma's description of an addict is not far off. Many people feel compelled to constantly check their devices. Three-quarters of workers report replying to email within an hour or less of receiving it.[7] That means they're constantly checking their inbox.

Why so often? There's actually a moment of checking the inbox that brings with it intense pleasure. It's a similar moment that someone playing a slot machine experiences just after they pull the arm and before the wheels stop spinning. It's the thrill of anticipation, which releases the chemical dopamine. Dopamine—the hormone of craving—is one of the most addictive chemicals on the planet. It's hard to quit cold turkey.

However, perpetual email checking has its downsides. As was the case with chronic meetings, chronic email checking destroys your focus. In addition, inbox hypervigilance creates stress. Most of the emails in your inbox want something from you—your time, attention, or both. Jumping to view these requests without a thought-through plan of action triggers your fight-or-flight response. Before you know it, you're operating from a false sense of urgency. This urgency not only hurts your performance but also stresses everyone around you who has to work with you.

Just because emails can be sent back and forth in an instant doesn't mean they should. If you reply to others' emails instantly, you set up an expectation that immediate response is the norm. Although this may satisfy the part of your ego that wants to be seen as dutiful and hard-working, it sabotages the part of you that has other things to do. By setting email-free time zones, you can begin to tame the email dragon. Dedicating times of day means you take back control. The dragon only comes out when you say so, and on your own terms. It no longer gets to run the show and wreak havoc on your workday.

Create Norms for Response Times

Another cause of false urgency is the lack of norms for response times. Now, certain jobs and roles need an immediate response. For example, an emergency room doctor works in an environment where the quick decisions she makes can mean life or death.

This is not the case for every role. Think about your own work. Although an immediate reply might be a nice to have, is it a *need to have*? Create some team norms and rules for response times. What makes sense in your culture? Is it to respond to all emails within 24 hours? Four hours? One hour? When you create and clarify boundaries for people, you free them up to focus on what matters, rather than worry about second-guessing their decisions.

Save as Draft, Delay Delivery, and Send Later

Not only can email be sent and received at lightning speed, it can do so at any time of day, on any day of the week. This is both a blessing and a curse. It creates a tremendous amount of flexibility for where and when you work. At the same time, it can make any distinctions between work and life disappear.

By all means, use the flexibility that email provides to its utmost advantage. For example, if you have small children and want to get home and put them to bed, and then get back to work between 9:00 p.m. and 11:00 p.m., go for it.

However, just because those are your optimal working times doesn't mean you should make anyone else work those same hours. As a leader, if you don't set clear expectations, the people who report to you will feel compelled to get back to you. (After all, you're the boss.)

Jill, an executive for a regional airline, thought she had a handle on this practice. She said to me, "I've told my people, I work best at night. I don't expect you to respond to me until the next business day."

Although Jill's intentions are admirable, she's missing an important piece of the equation. As a leader, your actions carry more weight. Even if you've told people that they don't need to reply right away, just receiving an email from the boss places psychological baggage on your team members. Now, they're thinking about the issue you've written about in your email. Their downtime is not as down as it was before your email arrived.

Instead of sending emails at all hours of the day, you can compose them, and save them as drafts, and send the next day. Or you can opt to delay delivery, so they're not received until a specified time. Either way, it helps put the boundary back between work and life.

Limit CC Recipients and Do Not Reply All

The more people you send emails to, the more emails you're going to get back. Hence, if you want to get fewer emails, send fewer of them. One of the keys to reducing email quantity is limiting CC recipients and not replying to all.

Rick, a salesperson for an auto parts distributor, told me, "Around here, we have serious CC disease. Everyone does it for everything. They're afraid of not having a paper trail. I think we should change the name of the email function from CC to CYA (cover your ass), because that's what it really is."

Some clients I work with have a rule they can CC no more than three people on an email. They've also become vigilant at asking, "Who really needs to see this?" It isn't that they're withholding valuable information; they're just not overwhelming people with irrelevant information.

They know that fewer emails means getting time back elsewhere. In a study published in the *Harvard Business Review*, it was concluded that when a team lowered email output by 54%, 10,400 annual worker hours were gained.[8]

Write a Clear Subject Line

The advent of email has brought with it a new sport: subject fishing. It's that game you play when what's currently in the subject box makes no sense, and you have to dive deep and scroll through all of the FW:FW: FW: FYI SEE BELOW to figure out what this content is really supposed to be about. People hate playing this game. It's a giant frustrating waste of time.

However, when I ask groups of leaders to honestly admit if they ever perpetuate the game by forwarding the confusion on to the next innocent bystander, most of the hands in the room go up. They do it because it's easier and quicker for them to do in the moment.

Instead of subject fishing, choose to write (or rewrite) a clear subject line. If your subject line is good, you may not need a whole lot more in the body of your email. Futurethink, Lisa Bodell's innovation consultancy, practices what they preach here and are masters of the great subject line. Many of the emails I receive from them are standalone subject lines.

For example, if Futurethink wants to inquire if I'm available to deliver a session for a client, the subject line reads: Date check: Friday, November 17 full day NYC? That's the entire email. The subject line tells me exactly what I need and how to respond.

Utilize One-Screen Emails

There's a reason Twitter is such a popular social media platform. Its limited character length forces you to get to the point. To make your emails simpler, consider the Twitter model—keeping your emails to one or two sentences. As a rule of thumb, limit your email text so it can all be read on one screen (as read on a standard laptop). Scrolling should not be needed.

The more concise your messaging is, the more likely it will be easily understood. Everyone's attention is scattered today—don't make things harder than they already are. If you have additional information that takes up more than one screen, attach it as a separate document. Then, in your email, briefly explain the purpose of the document.

SUMMING UP SIMPLE

Making things simple shouldn't be confused with making them easy. Too many leaders multiply organizational complexity for the sake of personal ease. It's easier to invite everyone to attend the meeting than to really consider who needs to show up. It's easier to institute a one-size-fits-all policy than it is to have a difficult conversation with the person who doesn't exercise personal judgment. It's easier to hit *fw: FYI see below* than it is to take a minute to extract and summarize the essence of a message.

Technology and its countless tools have made all this easier than ever before. But, just because you can doesn't mean you should. Although new tools might make certain tasks quicker in the short term, quicker is not necessarily better. If tools aren't deployed thoughtfully, they actually make things harder for everyone else in the long run.

Be willing to challenge the process. Question the status quo. Make "because we've always done it that way" a wake-up call and a rallying cry for change.

The rewards of making things simple are well worth the effort. Making things simple shows off your thoughtfulness and intentionality. You'll be someone people want to work with.

Collaboration can include many things: motivation, meeting needs, and creating experiences. Making things simple can be a guiding principle through each of them. When you reduce unnecessary complexity, you're leading by example. You're modeling how to create effective groups and work well together. You'll facilitate better communication, teamwork, and innovation. People will be more engaged, deliver better results, and have a whole lot more fun in the process. Given that you spend more time with your work colleagues than your own family, doesn't that seem like a worthwhile goal?

Chapter Resources

Establish Better Meeting Norms

- I require meeting agendas in advance.
- I make it OK to decline meeting invites.
- I make sure meetings have a strong facilitator.
- I set up guidelines so people don't multitask during meetings.
- I start meetings promptly.
- I hold Stand-Up Meetings.
- I appoint timekeepers and scribes for meetings.
- My meetings last for 25 or 50 minutes.
- I send out meeting materials in advance.
- I create a parking lot and use it.
- I end stalled meetings.
- I follow up after meetings.
- I create one meeting-free day a week.

Simplify Email

- I turn auto-notifications off.
- I create email-free time zones.
- I institute a 24-hour rule (or other clear time frame) to reply.
- I don't send emails at off-work hours. I save the emails as drafts, delay delivery, and send later.
- I limit CC recipients and use of Reply All.
- I make sure each email has a clear subject line.
- My emails can be read on one screen.

EPILOGUE

Time to Leap

It's through a leader's actions—what he or she does and says on a daily basis—that the essence of great leadership becomes apparent.

—Travis Bradberry

When you embrace leadership as a journey of constant and never-ending improvement, sometimes the lessons come in the unlikeliest of places. Such as the dentist's chair.

First, a disclosure: the reason I keep going to the same dentist has nothing to do with my dentist. It's because Jackie, the hygienist, is amazing. Equal parts entertaining and educational, Jackie sees each tooth as a canvas and she's a da Vinci. Calling her skilled is an understatement. If you want to know anything about dental care, Jackie is your go-to.

One day, as I sat in the chair, I asked her, "With all of this new dental technology, with the sonic-powered and battery-powered and free-floating bristle head toothbrushes, what do you recommend? What's the best toothbrush out there?"

Jackie paused as she lifted her protective goggles to look me eye to eye. "The best toothbrush?" she grinned. "Oh, that's easy. It's the one that you'll use twice a day."

Jackie's wisdom has application far beyond the bathroom sink. Any tool is only as good as its user's commitment to using it. And not just once—but consistently, over time.

THE MYTH OF LEADERSHIP DEVELOPMENT

It's easy to look at leaders you admire, those you deem "successful," and put them up on a pedestal. As you bask in their radiant glow, you might imagine that their journey to greatness was a straight shot, with each victory building on the one before it. Every opportunity, every step, every advancement perfectly aligned with the one before. In comparison, how could imperfect you measure up?

The idea that effective leaders can plot their progression on a straight line is a myth. Progress is messy. Sometimes it's frustrating. Sometimes it's painful. Sometimes it feels like failure. You need to learn to accept the messiness and all the feelings associated with it. It's a surefire sign that you're growing.

Let go of the fallacy that everything will go according to plan. Nothing could be further from the truth. The road of progress only looks like a straight line when you look at it in reverse. It takes time, perspective, and synthesis to connect the dots in a linear fashion (see Figure E.1).

Each one of these squiggles represents the falls, faults, and failures along the way. That's what progress looks like when it's not airbrushed and Photoshopped. Exceptional leaders are exceptional learners—imperfect people who take each mistake along the way and figure out what they need to learn from it. Then, they do something to get back on course and keep moving.

For example, George Washington, the first president of the United States, will undeniably stay on the short list of fantastic leaders for centuries to come. Yet, he was anything but brilliant as a leader when he began. Early in his career, he failed miserably during the French-Indian War.

Leading a British troop, Washington ordered his company to erect a fort for defense: Fort Necessity. It was built in a most indefensible spot: a muddy creek bottom with higher ground around them on three sides. It was a terrible plan. On July 3, 1754, the 22-year-old Washington lost the battle for Fort Necessity. Disgraced, he resigned his post. In letters home, he shared the fear that his military career was over.

Figure E.1 The Road to Success Fallacy

Yet, as history has shown, Washington had a lot of improvement left in him. Not only did he grow into an exceptional leader but also he had the competence and foresight to lay the groundwork for what the presidency should look like for centuries to come. One of his defining traits as a general and later as president was his humility—a trait learned in part through his humbling experience in that muddy creek.

It's been said that "experience is the best teacher." That's partially true. Experience is the best teacher if it's reflected on and learned from. That's why some people have 20 years of experience, and other people have one year of experience 20 times. If you can extract the lesson that each experience offers, you'll correct your course more quickly on the road to progress.

THE POWER OF SMALL CHANGES

If you want to be something different, you have to do something different. Try something. Notice what happens. If it works, then keep doing it. If it doesn't, notice it, and change your approach. For example:

- Try giving people your complete time and attention, like Matt the DM you met in the introduction.
- Try going on an extended listening tour, like Angela Ahrendts did when she became VP of retail stores at Apple (Chapter 4).
- Try asking for an understanding receipt rather than assuming everyone knows what you mean, as you saw in Chapter 8.
- Try making your implicit expectations explicit, like Lee, the sales executive you met in Chapter 8.
- Try using the "Platinum Rule," like Kelly (the IT manager in Chapter 9) learned to do after his epic failure motivating his staff.
- Try starting a culture of appreciation by publicly celebrating a win with the team (like Laila, the project manager, did in Chapter 10).
- Try changing the default times for meetings to 25 or 50 minutes (a technique from Chapter 13).

The key is to try something. Anything. The magic comes from your effort.

Peter Sims, author of *Little Bets: How Breakthrough Ideas Emerge from Small Discoveries*, writes, "Most successful entrepreneurs . . . operate in this experimental way when trying new ideas. They think of learning the way most people think of failure."[1]

Sims gives the example of Howard Schultz, the long-time CEO of Starbucks. When Schultz opened his first stores, he modeled them after the coffeehouses of Milan, Italy. Not everything went according to plan. Some of Schultz's missteps along the way included these:

- The original name of Schultz's cafes: *Il Giornale*. Difficult to pronounce.
- Baristas wearing bowties. Baristas were uncomfortable.
- Stores piping in opera music. Customers complained.
- No chairs. More customer complaints.

Schultz admits he made lots of mistakes, but he learned from them. This is precisely what John F. Kennedy meant when he said, "Leadership and learning are indispensable to each other."[2]

YOU'RE AS READY AS YOU NEED TO BE

On your journey through these pages, you've gained numerous insights into leadership. You can now put leadership in its proper historical context. You've been witness to numerous examples of challenges and failures that have revealed a common theme:

> To succeed as a leader, focus on others, not on yourself.

You know that leadership is a relationship. People need to feel connected to you. If they're going to fully engage, they need to believe in your influence, not your authority. You can increase your influence through cultivating your empathy and your credibility.

You've discovered how much more there is to communication than just talking. You can now identify the biggest barriers to communicating well. You have tools to help you ratchet up your communication skill and raise your game.

You know that to thrive, you're going to need to lead collaboratively. You recognize that although you can't motivate anyone else, you can design the conditions in which they motivate themselves. You can use your understanding of human needs and the employee experience to lead a team of joyful, engaged, and high-performing people.

You have an abundance of tools to apply these principles. You've learned numerous pitfalls that will try and trip you up, despite your best efforts. You hold the keys to lead in your hand.

Don't just hold the keys: use them. Start unlocking doors. Use these skills. See what happens. Some of the doors you try will open easily. Others will remain shut. If they stay closed, find a different approach and try again.

You can choose any number of places to start. But before you do, here's a little secret that leaders know: you'll never be 100% ready.

When it comes to preparation, there's always something else you can do. When it comes to gathering information, there's always more you can get. When it comes to getting input from others, there's always someone else to talk to.

Believe in yourself. Walking the path of leadership takes courage. Stepping out without being ready is scary, yet necessary.

Years ago, I participated in a daylong outdoor adventure high-ropes course. The course included several elements that involved using mountain climbing harnesses and ropes. These components served as physical metaphors for the obstacles of leadership.

When I arrived at the final element, I could see they had saved the best for last. This element was called "The Leap of Faith." This element involved a wooden pole (picture a telephone pole), about 50 feet high, with metal rungs like a ladder on the side. On the top of the pole was a small platform, which was the size of a pizza box. The climber (wearing a full body harness) climbs to the top, stands on the platform, and then leaps out to grab a trapeze bar that is only reachable if you fully extend. It's a literal "leap of faith."

I was with a group of five other climbers. I chose to go last, and as each person went in front of me, I could feel my pulse quicken. Finally, it was my turn.

The metal rungs felt cold in my hands. As I heaved myself up, the breeze wafted across my face and as I climbed higher and higher I was able to see over the tops of the trees and see the hills in the distance. My heart rate climbed along with my elevation. By the time I got near the top, it felt as though my heart would explode out of my chest. My adrenaline was surging.

I stepped onto the platform, trying to gain my balance as the wind swirled around me. My heart was pounding, my legs shook, and my vision blurred. The trapeze bar was out in front of me.

I just stood there. Waiting. When was the right time to go? A full minute seemed to pass as I waited for a sign to make my move. Would the clouds part and a beam of sunlight pour down? Or would I hear Alec Guinness's voice in my head saying, "Use the force. Trust your feelings"?

I kept waiting. But no sign ever came.

Then, a chill ran down my spine and the hairs on the back of my neck stood on end in a flash of insight. Suddenly, I got the lesson.

In that moment, I realized that there would be no "right time." No perfect convergence. No preordained moment. This moment is as good as any. As a leader, sometimes you just go. You choose: now is the time. You don't need permission.

So I leapt. My fingertips brushed off the trapeze bar as I missed it and fell. My team kept me safe in my climbing harness.

When I got down to the bottom, I asked if I could go again. Having done it once, I knew what adjustments I needed to make to succeed this next time. The second time out, I was ready. I leapt and caught hold of the bar.

Decide. Leap. Go. Watch. Reflect. Learn. Apply. Go again.

After all, if not now, then when?

If not you, then who?

We need a new type of leader, one who can excel at navigating this exciting new world.

Go be one of them.

NOTES

INTRODUCTION

1. USPS, *Strategic Information Plan 2006–2010* (September 2005), 60, http://about.usps.com/strategic-planning/stp2007revisedfinal 12_31_07.pdf.

2. USPS, *Strategic Information Plan*, 60.

3. USPS, "About the United States Postal Service," accessed June 6, 2018, http://about.usps.com/who-we-are/leadership/about-usps .htm.

4. Kara O'Connor, "Out of Time Residents Not Happy about Post," *The Hour* (September 15, 2010), http://www.thehour.com/wilton/ article/out-of-time-residents-not-happy-about-post-8295123.php.

5. Ketchum, *Leadership Communication Monitor 2016* (2016), http://www.ketchum.com/pt-br/special-report/leadership-com munication-monitor-2016.

6. "Edelman Trust Index," Edelman, accessed February 9, 2017, http://www.edelman.com/executive-summary.

7. "The Engaged Workspace," Gallop, accessed June 6, 2018, http:// www.gallup.com/services/190118/engaged-workplace.aspx.

8. Christine Porath, "Half of Employees Don't Feel Respected by Their Bosses," *Harvard Business Review* (November 19, 2014), https://hbr.org/2014/11/half-of-employees-dont-feel-respected- by-their-bosses.

9. Karyn Twaronite, "Global Generations: A Global Study on Work-Life Challenges across Generations," *EY* (2015), http:// www.ey.com/Publication/vwLUAssets/EY-global-generations-a- global-study-on-work-life-challenges-across-generations/$FILE/ EY-global-generations-a-global-study-on-work-life-challenges- across-generations.pdf.

10. Laci Loew, "State of Leadership Development 2015: Time to Act Is Now," Brandon Hall Group (August 2015), http://www .ddiworld.com/DDI/media/trend-research/state-of-leadership-development_tr_brandon-hall.pdf?ext=.pdf%2520.

11. Annamarie Lang and Bradford Thomas, "Where Are Your "Ready-Now" Leaders?" *Development Dimensions International* (February 20, 2013), http://www.ddiworld.com/ddi/media/white-papers/whereareyourreadynowleaders_wp_ddi.pdf.

12. Laci Loew, "Study Shows Leadership Development Rated below Average or Poor in More than One-Third of Organizations," *Training* (May 28, 2015), https://trainingmag.com/study-shows-leadership-development-rated-below-average-or-poor-more-one-third-organizations.

13. Lou Solomon, "Two Thirds of Managers Are Uncomfortable Communicating with Employees," *Harvard Business Review* (March 9, 2016), https://hbr.org/2016/03/two-thirds-of-managers-are-uncomfortable-communicating-with-employees.

CHAPTER 1

1. Daniel Goleman, "What Makes a Leader," *Harvard Business Review* (January 2004).

2. J. Bathurst and D. Walton, "An Exploration of the Perceptions of the Average Driver's Speed Compared to Perceived Driver Safety and Driving Skill: Accident Analysis and Prevention," *PubMed* 30 (November 1998): 821–830.

3. John Wooden, "First, How to Put on Your Socks," interview by Devin Gordon, *Newsweek* (October 24, 1999), http://www .newsweek.com/john-wooden-first-how-put-your-socks-167942.

4. Wooden, "First, How to Put on Your Socks."

5. John Yaeger, "John Wooden" (October 1, 2009), http://donyaeger .com/john-wooden.

6. W. Edwards Deming, Four-day seminar, Phoenix, Arizona (February 1993) (via the notes of Mike Stoecklein), http://quotes.deming .org/authors/W._Edwards_Deming/quote/10091.

CHAPTER 2

1. Michael Mankins, Chris Brahm, and Greg Caimi, "Your Scarcest Resource," *Harvard Business Review* (May 2014), https://hbr.org/2014/05/your-scarcest-resource.

2. Niall McCarthy, "A 40 Hour Work Week in the United States Actually Lasts 47 Hours," *Forbes* (September 1, 2014), https://www.forbes.com/sites/niallmccarthy/2014/09/01/a-40-hour-work-week-in-the-united-states-actually-lasts-47-hours/#4022e569f5e4.

3. Mary Madden and Sydney Jones, "Most Workers Use the Internet or Email at Their Jobs, but They Say These Technologies Are a Mixed Blessing for Them," Pew Internet and American Life Project (September 24, 2008), http://www.pewinternet.org/files/old-media//Files/Reports/2008/PIP_Networked_Workers_FINAL.pdf.pdf.

4. Frederick Winslow Taylor, *The Principles of Scientific Management* (New York: Harper & Brothers, 1911).

5. Ibid.

6. Ibid.

7. "The United States in 1900," Digital History, accessed June 7, 2018, http://www.digitalhistory.uh.edu/disp_textbook.cfm?smtID=2&psid=3175.

8. Michael Perelman, "Henry Ford Double's His Worker's Wages," Delancey Place (January 29, 2016), https://delanceyplace.com/view-archives.php?p=2991.

9. Sarah Cwiek, "The Middle Class Took Off 100 Years Ago ... Thanks to Henry Ford?" *Economy* (January 27, 2014), https://www.npr.org/2014/01/27/267145552/the-middle-class-took-off-100-years-ago-thanks-to-henry-ford.

CHAPTER 3

1. Susan Fowler, "Susan Fowler's Plans after Uber? Tear down the System That Protects Harassers," Interview by Sam Levin, accessed June 8, 2018, https://www.theguardian.com/technology/2018/apr/11/susan-fowler-uber-interview-forced-arbitration-law.

2. Susan Fowler, "Reflecting on One Very, Very Strange Year at Uber" (February 19, 2017), https://www.susanjfowler.com/blog/2017/2/19/reflecting-on-one-very-strange-year-at-uber.

3. Jessica Guynn, "Some Uber Riders React to Sexism Claims with Their Wallets," USA Today (March 8, 2017), https://www.usatoday.com/story/tech/news/2017/03/08/more-uber-riders-ditch-ride-hailing-app-over-susan-fowler-harassment-discrimination-charges/98862784/.

4. Oxford Economics, "Global Talent 2021: How the New Geography of Talent Will Transform Human Resource Strategies," Oxford Economics (2012): 6.

5. IBM, "Leading through Connections: Insights from the Global Chief Executive Officer Study," IBM (2012), 21.

6. Daniel H. Pink, "Revenge of the Right Brain," WIRED (January 1, 2005), https://www.wired.com/2005/02/brain/.

7. The New Palgrave Dictionary of Economics, ed. Steven Durlaf and Lawrence Blume (London: Macmillan, 2008), 841.

8. "GDP per Capita," World Bank, accessed June 6, 2018, https://data.worldbank.org/indicator/ny.gdp.pcap.kd.

9. "Life Expectancy at Birth," World Bank, accessed June 6, 2018, https://data.worldbank.org/indicator/SP.DYN.LE00.IN?end=2015&start=1960.

10. Richard A. Easterlin, "The Worldwide Standard of Living since 1800," Journal of Economic Perspectives 14, no. 1: 7.

11. "More than Half the Homes in U.S. Have Three or More TV's," Nielson (July 20, 2009), http://www.nielsen.com/us/en/insights/news/2009/more-than-half-the-homes-in-us-have-three-or-more-tvs.html.

12. Adam Minter, "Somebody's Making Money off of All Our Junk," Bloomberg (August 28 2017), https://www.bloomberg.com/view/articles/2017-08-28/the-self-storage-business-is-booming-here-s-why.

13. Bruce N. Pfau, "What Do Millennials Really Want from Work? The Same Things the Rest of Us Do," *Harvard Business Review* (April 7, 2016), https://hbr.org/2016/04/what-do-millennials-really-want-at-work.

14. Geoff Colvin, "Humans Are Underrated," *Fortune* (July 23, 2015), http://fortune.com/2015/07/23/humans-are-underrated/.

15. James Manyika, Susan Lund, Byron Auguste, and Sreenivas Ramaswamy, "Help Wanted: The Future of Work in Advanced Economics," McKinsey Global Institute (March 2012), 12, https://www.mckinsey.com/~/media/McKinsey/Featured%20Insights/Employment%20and%20Growth/Future%20of%20work%20in%20advanced%20economies/Help_wanted_future_of_work_full_report.ashx.

16. Daniel H. Pink, *To Sell Is Human: The Surprising Truth about Moving Others* (New York: Riverhead Books, 2012), 83–89.

17. Grace Nasri, "Solving Information Asymmetry: How Today's Companies Are Empowering Consumers and Creating More Efficient Markets," *Huffpost* (November 9 2013), https://www.huffingtonpost.com/grace-nasri/solving-information-asymm_b_3870302.html?guccounter=1.

18. Lucinda Shen, "United Airlines Stock Drops $1.4 Billion after Passenger-Removal Controversy," *Fortune* (April 11 2017), http://fortune.com/2017/04/11/united-airlines-stock-drop/.

19. Amy Martinez, "Tale of Lost Diamond Adds Glitter to Nordstrom's Customer Service," *The Seattle Times* (May 11, 2011), http://old.seattletimes.com/html/businesstechnology/2015028167_nordstrom12.html.

20. Ashley Lutz, "Nordstrom's Employee Handbook Has Only One Rule," *Business Insider* (October 13, 2014), http://www.businessinsider.com/nordstroms-employee-handbook-2014–10?IR=T.

PART II

1. Jim Kouzes and Barry Posner, *The Leadership Challenge* (Hoboken, NJ: John Wiley & Sons, 2012), 30.

CHAPTER 4

1. Evan Sinar, Richard S. Wellins, and Matthew J. Paese, "What's the Number 1 Leadership Skill for Overall Success?" *DDI* (February 23 2016), https://www.ddiworld.com/global-offices/united-states/press-room/what-is-the-1-leadership-skill-for-overall-success.

2. Ashley Lutz, "How Trader Joe's Sells Twice as Much as Whole Foods," *Business Insider* (October 7, 2014), http://www.businessinsider.com/trader-joes-sales-strategy-2014–10?IR=T.

3. Fariss Samarrai, "Human Brains Are Hardwired for Empathy, Friendship, Study Shows," *UVA Today* (August 21 2013), https://news.virginia.edu/content/human-brains-are-hardwired-empathy-friendship-study-shows.

4. "The Business Case for Trust," Franklin Covey, accessed June 8, 2018, http://www.speedoftrust.com/how-the-speed-of-trust-works/business_case.

5. Jennifer Reingold, "What the Heck Is Angela Ahrendts Doing at Apple?" *Fortune* (September 10, 2015), http://fortune.com/2015/09/10/angela-ahrendts-apple/.

6. Sabrina Son, "Effective Employee Retention Strategies for the Retail Industry," TINYcon (August 11, 2016), https://www.tinypulse.com/blog/effective-employee-retention-strategies-for-the-retail-industry.

7. John Naisbitt, *Megatrends* (New York: Warner Trends, 1984), 25.

8. Reingold, "What the Heck."

CHAPTER 5

1. Tony Schwartz and Christine Porath, "Why You Hate Work," *New York Times* (May 30, 2014), https://www.nytimes.com/2014/06/01/opinion/sunday/why-you-hate-work.html.

2. Jerry Useem, "Power Causes Brain Damage: How Leaders Lose Mental Capacities—Most Notably for Reading Other People—That Were Essential to Their Rise," *The Atlantic* (July 2017), https://www.theatlantic.com/magazine/archive/2017/07/power-causes-brain-damage/528711/?utm_source=nhfb.

3. Michael Inzlicht and Sukhvinder Obhi, "Powerful and Cold-hearted," *New York Times* (July 25, 2014), https://www.nytimes.com/2014/07/27/opinion/sunday/powerful-and-coldhearted.html?ref=opinion&_r=1.

4. Stephanie Vozza, "10 Unique Ways Leaders Bond with Their Employees," *Fast Company* (September 18, 2015), https://www.fastcompany.com/3050651/10-unique-ways-leaders-bond-with-employees.

5. Jacob Davidson, "How Microsoft Became a Market Darling, in Two Charts," *Money* (May 5, 2015).

6. AP, "Satya Nadella Aims to Make Microsoft Mighty—and Mind-ful," *USA Today* (September 25, 2015).

7. Satya Nadella, "Satya Nadella: The C in CEO Stands for Cul-ture," *Fast Company* (September 21, 2017).

8. Satya Nadella, "We Sat Down with Microsoft's CEO to Discuss the Past, Present and Future of the Company," interview by Krzysztof Majdan and Michał Wasowski, *Business Insider* (April 20, 2017), http://uk.businessinsider.com/satya-nadella-microsoft-ceo-qa-2017-4?r=US&IR=T.

9. Joann S. Lubin, "How to Be a Better Boss? Spend Time on the Front Lines," *The Wall Street Journal* (February 9, 2012), https://www.wsj.com/articles/SB10001424052970203824904577212951446826014.

10. A. Nyberg, L. Alfredsson, T. Theorell, H. Westerlund, J. Vahtera, and M. Kivimäki, "Managerial Leadership and Ischaemic Heart Disease among Employees: The Swedish WOLF Study," *Occupational and Environmental Medicine* 66, no. 1 (January 2009): 51–55.

CHAPTER 6

1. Marcus Buckingham and Curt Coffman, *First Break All the Rules: What the World's Greatest Managers Do Differently* (London: Simon & Schuster UK, 2005), 257.

2. Jim Clifton, "Are You Sure You Have a Great Workplace Culture?" (April 27, 2017), http://news.gallup.com/opinion/chairman/2090 33/sure-great-workplace-culture.aspx?g_source=EMPLOYEE _ENGAGEMENT&g_medium=topic&g_campaign=tiles.

3. Buckingham and Coffman, *First Break All the Rules*, 36.

4. James M. Kouzes and Barry Z. Posner, *The Truth about Leadership: The No-Fads, Heart-of-the-Matter Facts You Need to Know* (Hoboken, NJ: John Wiley & Sons: 2010), 24.

5. Ibid., 9.

6. Julia Kirby, "Beware the Baboon Boss," *Harvard Business Review* (May 22, 2009), https://hbr.org/2009/05/baboons.

7. Ibid.

8. Ibid.

9. Jim Kouzes and Barry Posner, *The Leadership Challenge* (Hoboken, NJ: John Wiley & Sons, 2012), 25.

10. Charles Duhigg, *The Power of Habit: Why We Do What We Do and How to Change* (New York: Random House, 2013), 100.

11. Deborah Sweeney, "3 Ways Handwritten Notes Impact the Workplace," *Forbes* (April 24, 2012), https://www.forbes.com/ sites/deborahsweeney/2012/04/24/3-ways-handwritten-notes-impact-the-workplace/#30fcbf22b4fd.

12. Douglas R. Conant, "Secrets of Positive Feedback," *Harvard Business Review* (February 16, 2011), https://hbr.org/2011/02/secrets-of-positive-feedback.

PART III

1. R. G. Eccles and N. Nohria, *Beyond the Hype: Rediscovering the Essence of Management* (Boston: Harvard Business School Press, 1991).

CHAPTER 7

1. Hart Research Associates, "It Takes More Than a Major: Employer Priorities for College Learning and Student Success," Association

of American Colleges and Universities, accessed June 8, 2018, https://www.aacu.org/publications-research/periodicals/it-takes-more-major-employer-priorities-college-learning-and.

2. Anton Valukas, "Report to Board of Directors of General Motors Company Regarding Ignition Switch Recalls," Jenner and Block (May 29, 2014), http://s3.documentcloud.org/documents/1183508/g-m-internal-investigation-report.pdf, 2.

3. Ibid., p. 2.

4. David Woods, "Poor Communication between Managers and Employees Wastes Time and Impacts Productivity," *HR* (January 15, 2010), http://www.hrmagazine.co.uk/article-details/poor-communication-between-managers-and-employees-wastes-time-and-impacts-productivity.

5. Ritu Agwar, Daniel Z. Sands, and Jorge Díaz Schneider, "Quantifying the Economic Impact of Communication Inefficiencies in U.S. Hospitals," *Journal of Healthcare Management* 55, no. 4 (July–August 2010): 267.

6. "For Workplace Failures," Press Room, Fierce (May 4, 2011), https://fierceinc.com/employees-cite-lack-of-collaboration-for-workplace-failures.

7. Boyd Clarke and Ron Crossland, *The Leaders Voice: How Your Communication Can Inspire and Get Results!* (New York: Select Books, 2004), 6.

8. "The State of Enterprise Work," Harris Poll, Workfront, accessed June 8, 2018, https://www.workfront.com/resources/the-state-of-enterprise-work.

9. "Internet Live Stats," accessed June 6, 2018, http://www.internetlivestats.com/one-second/.

CHAPTER 8

1. Lou Solomon, "Many Leaders Shrink from Straight Talk with Employees," Interact (February 2015), http://interactauthentically.com/new-interact-report-many-leaders-shrink-from-straight-talk-with-employees/.

2. "Two Thirds of Senior Managers Can't Name Their Firms' Top Priorities," London Business School (December 7, 2015), https://www.london.edu/news-and-events/news/two-thirds-of-senior-managers-cant-name-their-firms-top-priorities#.VwVwgfmLTb0.

3. Linda Grossman, "Metric Math Mistake Muffed Mars Meteorology Mission," *Wired* (November 10, 1999), https://www.wired.com/2010/11/1110mars-climate-observer-report/.

4. Karl Taro Greenfeld, "Taco Bell and the Golden Age of Drive-Thru," *Bloomberg Businessweek* (May 5, 2011), https://www.bloomberg.com/news/articles/2011–05–05/taco-bell-and-the-golden-age-of-drive-thru.

5. Judith Rehak and *International Herald Tribune*, "Tylenol Made a Hero of Johnson & Johnson: The Recall That Started Them All," *The New York Times* (March 23, 2002), https://www.nytimes.com/2002/03/23/your-money/tylenol-made-a-hero-of-johnson-johnson-the-recall-that-started.html.

6. Ken Robinson, "Do Schools Kill Creativity?" TED (February 2006), https://www.ted.com/talks/ken_robinson_says_schools_kill_creativity.

PART IV

1. Adi Gaskell, "New Study Shows That Collaboration Drives Workplace Performance," *Forbes* (June 22, 2017), https://www.forbes.com/sites/adigaskell/2017/06/22/new-study-finds-that-collaboration-drives-workplace-performance/#26e9ce303d02.

CHAPTER 9

1. "All Actors Are Cattle," Quote investigator, accessed June 7, 2018.

2. Francois Truffaut, *Hitchcock: A Definitive Study of Alfred Hitchcock* (New York: Simon & Schuster, 2008), 111.

3. Richard Brody, "Tippi Hedren and Alfred Hitchcock," *The New Yorker*, accessed June 7, 2018, https://www.newyorker.com/culture/richard-brody/tippi-hedren-and-alfred-hitchcock.

4. Dan Ariely, *Payoff: The Hidden Logic That Shapes Our Motivation* (Simon & Schuster, 2016).

5. Dale Carnegie, *How to Win Friends and Influence People* (New York: Simon & Schuster, 1981), 41.

6. Tony Allesandra and Michael J. O'Connor, *The Platinum Rule: Discover the Four Basic Business Personalities and How They Can Lead You to Success* (New York: Grand Central Publishing, 1998), 3.

CHAPTER 10

1. William A. Kahn, "Psychological Conditions of Personal Engagement and Disengagement at Work," *Academy of Management Journal* 33, no. 4 (January 1, 1990): 708.

2. Charles, Duhigg, "What Google Learned from Its Quest to Build the Perfect Team," *New York Times* (February 25, 2016), https://www.nytimes.com/2016/02/28/magazine/what-google-learned-from-its-quest-to-build-the-perfect-team.html?_r=1.

3. Ibid.

4. Gallup, "U.S. Employee Engagement" (July 30, 2017), http://news.gallup.com/poll/214961/gallup-employee-engagement.aspx%20accessed%20October%2020,%202017.

5. Susan Sorenson and Keri Garman, "How to Tackle U.S. Employees' Stagnant Engagement," Gallup (June 11, 2013), http://news.gallup.com/businessjournal/162953/tackle-employees-stagnating-engagement.aspx.

6. Gloria Mark and Donald Bren, "Too Many Interruptions at Work?" Gallup (June 8, 2006), http://news.gallup.com/businessjournal/23146/too-many-interruptions-work.aspx.

7. Jonathan B. Spira and Joshua B. Feintuch, "The Cost of Not Paying Attention: How Interruptions Impact Knowledge Worker Productivity," BaseEx (2005), http://iorgforum.org/wp-content/uploads/2011/06/CostOfNotPayingAttention.BasexReport.pdf.

8. Bing C. Lin, Jason M. Kain, and Charlotte Fritz, 78.

9. Mark Murphy, "Interruptions at Work Are Killing Your Productivity," *Forbes* (October 30, 2016), https://www.forbes.com/sites/markmurphy/2016/10/30/interruptions-at-work-are-killing-your-productivity/#6708a8981689.

10. Bing C. Lin et al., "Don't Interrupt Me!," 77.

11. Jessica Mesmer-Magnus, David J. Glew, and Chockalingam Viswesvaran, "A Meta-analysis of Positive Humor in the Workplace," *Journal of Managerial Psychology* 27, no. 2 (2012), 155–190, https://doi.org/10.1108/02683941211199554.

12. Judith A. Ricci, E. Chee, A. L. Lorandeau, and J. Berger, "Fatigue in the U.S. Workforce: Prevalence and Implications for Lost Productive Work Time," *Journal of Occupational and Environmental Medicine* 49, no. 1 (2007): 1–10.

13. CBC News, "Low-Intensity Exercise Can Boost Energy, Curb Fatigue: Study" (February 29, 2008), http://www.cbc.ca/news/technology/low-intensity-exercise-can-boost-energy-curb-fatigue-study-1.714677.

14. "THANKS, BUT NO THANKS: Survey Reveals Strangest Forms of Workplace Recognition; Research Also Finds Two in Three Employees Would Leave Their Job If They Didn't Feel Appreciated," Robert Half, accessed June 7, 2018, http://rh-us.mediaroom.com/2017–04–12-THANKS-BUT-NO-THANKS-Survey-Reveals-Strangest-Forms-of-Workplace-Recognition-Research-Also-Finds-Two-in-Three-Employees-Would-Leave-Their-Job-If-They-Didnt-Feel-Appreciated.

15. David Sturt and Todd Nordstrom, "Yes, You Should Celebrate Employee Appreciation Day," accessed June 7, 2018, https://blog.octanner.com/appreciation-2/yes-you-should-celebrate-employee-appreciation-day.

CHAPTER 11

1. Tony Schwartz and Christine Porath, "Why You Hate Work," *New York Times* (May 30, 2014), https://www.nytimes.com/2014/06/01/opinion/sunday/why-you-hate-work.html.

2. LinkedIn, "2016 Global Report: Purpose at Work," LinkedIn (2016), https://business.linkedin.com/content/dam/me/business/en-us/talent-solutions/resources/pdfs/Global-Report-on-Purpose-at-Work.pdf.

3. EY, "The Business Case for Purpose," *Harvard Business Review* (2015), http://www.ey.com/Publication/vwLUAssets/ey-the-business-case-for-purpose/$FILE/ey-the-business-case-for-purpose.pdf.

4. Lyft (@lyft), "Our Mission Is to Reconnect People through Transportation and Bring Communities Together" (March 16, 2015), https://twitter.com/lyft/status/577558134698348544?lang=en.

5. Erica Keswin, "Use Stories from Customers to Highlight Your Company's Purpose," *Harvard Business Review*, June 22, 2017, https://hbr.org/2017/06/use-stories-from-customers-to-highlight-your-companys-purpose.

6. IKEA, "Welcome Inside Our Company," accessed June 7, 2018, https://www.ikea.com/ms/en_US/this-is-ikea/company-information/index.html.

7. Teresa Amabile and Steven J. Kramer, "The Power of Small Wins," *Harvard Business Review* (May 2011), https://hbr.org/2011/05/the-power-of-small-wins.

8. Linn Van Dyne and Jon L. Pierce, "Psychological Ownership and Feelings of Possession: Three Field Studies Predicting Employee Attitudes and Organisational Citizenship Behavior," *Journal of Organizational Behavior* 25 (2004): 439–459.

9. Katherine Ellison, "Being Honest about the Pygmalion Effect," *Discover* (December 2015), http://discovermagazine.com/2015/dec/14-great-expectations.

CHAPTER 12

1. Jan Carlzon, *Moments of Truth* (New York: Harper Perennial, 1987).

2. The Staff of the Corporate Executive Board, "The Role of Employee Engagement in the Return of Growth," *Bloomberg*

(August 13, 2010), https://www.bloomberg.com/news/articles/2010–08–13/the-role-of-employee-engagement-in-the-return-to-growth.

3. Jeana Quigley, "Do You Care about Onboarding? You Should," Bamboo HR (April 23, 2014), https://www.bamboohr.com/blog/onboarding-infographic/.

4. Laszlo Bock, *Work Rules! Insight from Inside Google That Will Transform How You Live and Lead* (London: John Murray, 2015), 295.

5. Zappos, "About Zappos Culture," accessed June 7, 2018, https://www.zappos.com/core-values.

6. Mary Beth Quirk, "Zappos CSR's Kindness Warms Our Heart," *Consumerist* (January 17, 2011), https://consumerist.com/2011/01/17/zappos-customer-service-reps-kindness-warms-our-cold-hearts/.

7. Armando Roggio, "The Zappos Effect: 5 Great Customer Service Ideas for Small Businesses," Practical Ecommerce (March 11, 2011), https://www.practicalecommerce.com/The-Zappos-Effect-5-Great-Customer-Service-Ideas-for-Smaller-Businesses.

8. Ben Popken, "Zappos Saves Best Man from Going Barefoot at Wedding," *Consumerist* (May 19, 2011), https://consumerist.com/2011/05/19/zappos-saves-best-man-from-going-barefoot-at-wedding/.

9. David Burkus, "Why Amazon Bought into Zappos's 'Pay to Quit' Policy," *Inc.* (June 15, 2016), https://www.inc.com/david-burkus/why-amazon-bought-into-zappos-pay-to-quit-policy.html.

10. Shaun Achor, "The Happiness Dividend," *Harvard Business Review* (June 23, 2011), https://hbr.org/2011/06/the-happiness-dividend.

11. Barbara J. Fredrickson, Michael A. Cohn, Kimberly A. Coffey, Jolynn Pek, and Sandra M. Finkel, "Open Hearts Build Lives: Positive Emotions, Induced through Loving-Kindness Meditation, Build Consequential Personal Resources," *Journal of Personality*

and Social Psychology 95, no. 5 (November 2008): 1045–1062, https://www.ncbi.nlm.nih.gov/pmc/articles/PMC3156028/.

12. Carolyn Wiley, "What Motivates Employees According to Over 40 Years of Motivation Surveys," *International Journal of Manpower* 18, no. 3 (1997): 263–280.

13. Tripp & Tyler, "A Conference Call in Real Life," *YouTube* (September 21, 2017), https://www.youtube.com/watch?v=kNz82r5nyUw.

14. Tania Luna and Leeann Perringer, *Surprise: Embrace the Unpredictable and Engineer the Unexpected* (New York: Tarcherperigee, 2015), 198.

15. B. Joseph Pine II and James H Gilmore, "Welcome to the Experience Economy," *Harvard Business Review* (July–August 1998), https://hbr.org/1998/07/welcome-to-the-experience-economy.

CHAPTER 13

1. Walter Isaacson, "How Steve Jobs' Love of Simplicity Fueled a Design Revolution," *Smithsonian Magazine* (September 2012), https://www.smithsonianmag.com/arts-culture/how-steve-jobs-love-of-simplicity-fueled-a-design-revolution-23868877/.

2. Siegel & Gale, "Simplicity at Work: Demonstrating the Positive Impact of Simplicity on the Workforce" (2017), https://simple.siegelgale.com/acton/attachment/9371/f-03e7/1/-/-/-/-/Simplicity%20At%20Work.pdf.

3. Michael Mankins, "Is Technology Really Helping Us Get More Done?" *Harvard Business Review* (February 25, 2016), https://hbr.org/2016/02/is-technology-really-helping-us-get-more-done.

4. Alan. C. Bluedorn, Daniel B. Turban, and Mary Sue Love, "The Effects of Stand-Up and Sit-Down Meeting Formats on Meeting Outcomes," *Journal of Applied Psychology* 84, no. 2 (1999): 277–285.

5. "Parkinson's law," *The Economist* (November 19, 1955), https://www.economist.com/news/1955/11/19/parkinsons-law.

6. Mankins et al., "Your Scarcest Resource."

7. McCarthy, "A 40 Hour Work Week in the United States Actually Lasts 47 Hours."

8. Brown, Chris, Killick, Andrew, and Renaud, Karen, "To Reduce E-mail, Start at the Top," *Harvard Business Review* (September 2013), https://hbr.org/2013/09/to-reduce-e-mail-start-at-the-top.

EPILOGUE

1. Peter Sims, *Little Bets: How Breakthrough Ideas Emerge from Small Discoveries* (New York: Random House, 2012), 9.

2. John. F. Kennedy, "Untitled Speech" [Undelivered], Trade Mart, Dallas TX (November 22, 1963), https://www.jfklibrary.org/Research/Research-Aids/JFK-Speeches/Dallas-TX-Trade-Mart-Undelivered_19631122.aspx.

BIBLIOGRAPHY

Achor, Shaun, "The Happiness Dividend," *Harvard Business Review* (June 23, 2011), https://hbr.org/2011/06/the-happiness-dividend.

Agarwal, Ritu, Sands, Daniel Z., and Schneider, Jorge Díaz, "Quantifying the Economic Impact of Communication Inefficiencies in U.S. Hospitals," *Journal of Healthcare Management* 55, no. 4 (July–August 2010): 267.

"All Actors Are Cattle," Quote investigator, accessed June 7, 2018.

Allesandra, Tony, and O'Connor, Michael J., *The Platinum Rule: Discover the Four Basic Business Personalities and How They Can Lead You to Success* (New York: Grand Central Publishing, 1998).

Amabile, Teresa, and Kramer, Steven J., "The Power of Small Wins," *Harvard Business Review* (May 2011), https://hbr.org/2011/05/the-power-of-small-wins.

AP, "Satya Nadella Aims to Make Microsoft Mighty—and Mindful," *USA Today* (September 25, 2015).

Ariely, Dan, *Payoff: The Hidden Logic That Shapes Our Motivation* (Simon & Schuster, 2016).

Bathurst, J., and Walton, D. "An Exploration of the Perceptions of the Average Driver's Speed Compared to Perceived Driver Safety and Driving Skill: Accident Analysis and Prevention," *PubMed* 30 (November 1998): 821–830.

Bluedorn, Alan. C, Turban, Daniel. B, and Love, Mary Sue, "The Effects of Stand-Up and Sit-Down Meeting Formats on Meeting Outcomes," *Journal of Applied Psychology* 84, no. 2 (1999): 277–285.

Bock, Lazslo, *Work Rules! Insight from Inside Google That Will Transform How You Live and Lead* (London: John Murray, 2015).

Brody, Richard, "Tippi Hedren and Alfred Hitchcock," *The New Yorker*, accessed June 7, 2018, https://www.newyorker.com/culture/richard-brody/tippi-hedren-and-alfred-hitchcock.

Brown, Chris, Killick, Andrew, and Renaud, Karen, "To Reduce E-mail, Start at the Top," *Harvard Business Review* (September 2013), https://hbr.org/2013/09/to-reduce-e-mail-start-at-the-top.

Buckingham, Marcus, and Coffman, Curt, *First Break All the Rules: What the World's Greatest Managers Do Differently* (London: Simon & Schuster UK, 2005), 257.

Burkus, David, "Why Amazon Bought into Zappos's 'Pay to Quit' Policy," *Inc.* (June 15, 2016), https://www.inc.com/david-burkus/why-amazon-bought-into-zappos-pay-to-quit-policy.html.

"The Business Case for Trust," Franklin Covey, accessed June 8, 2018, http://www.speedoftrust.com/how-the-speed-of-trust-works/business_case.

Carlzon, Jan, *Moments of Truth* (New York: Harper Perennial, 1987).

Carnegie, Dale, *How to Win Friends and Influence People* (New York: Simon & Schuster, 1981).

CBC News, "Low-Intensity Exercise Can Boost Energy, Curb Fatigue: Study" (February 29, 2008), http://www.cbc.ca/news/technology/low-intensity-exercise-can-boost-energy-curb-fatigue-study-1.714677.

Clarke, Boyd, and Crossland, Ron, *The Leaders Voice: How Your Communication Can Inspire and Get Results!* (New York: Select Books, 2004).

Clifton, Jim, "Are You Sure You Have a Great Workplace Culture?" (April 27, 2017), http://news.gallup.com/opinion/chairman/209033/sure-great-workplace-culture.aspx?g_source=EMPLOYEE_ENGAGEMENT&g_medium=topic&g_campaign=tiles.

Colvin, Geoff, "Humans Are Underrated," *Fortune* (July 23, 2015), http://fortune.com/2015/07/23/humans-are-underrated/.

Conant, Douglas R., "Secrets of Positive Feedback," *Harvard Business Review* (February 16, 2011), https://hbr.org/2011/02/secrets-of-positive-feedback.

Cwiek, Sarah, "The Middle Class Took Off 100 Years Ago . . . Thanks to Henry Ford?" *Economy* (January 27, 2014), https://www.npr.org/2014/01/27/267145552/the-middle-class-took-off-100-years-ago-thanks-to-henry-ford.

Davidson, Jacob, "How Microsoft Became a Market Darling, in Two Charts," *Money* (May 5, 2015).

Deming, W. Edwards, Four-day seminar, Phoenix, Arizona (February 1993) (via the notes of Mike Stoecklein), http://quotes.deming.org/authors/W._Edwards_Deming/quote/10091.

Duhigg, Charles, *The Power of Habit: Why We Do What We Do and How to Change* (New York: Random House, 2013).

Duhigg, Charles, "What Google Learned from Its Quest to Build the Perfect Team," *New York Times* (February 25, 2016), https://www.nytimes.com/2016/02/28/magazine/what-google-learned-from-its-quest-to-build-the-perfect-team.html?_r=1.

Easterlin, Richard, A., "The Worldwide Standard of Living since 1800," *Journal of Economic Perspectives 14*, no. 1: 7–27.

Eccles, R. G., and Nohria, N., *Beyond the Hype: Rediscovering the Essence of Management* (Boston: Harvard Business School Press, 1991).

"Edelman Trust Index," Edelman, accessed February 9, 2017, http://www.edelman.com/executive-summary.

Ellison, Katherina, "Being Honest about the Pygmalion Effect," *Discover* (December 2015), http://discovermagazine.com/2015/dec/14-great-expectations.

"The Engaged Workspace," Gallop, accessed June 6, 2018, http://www.gallup.com/services/190118/engaged-workplace.aspx.

EY, "The Business Case for Purpose," *Harvard Business Review* (2015), http://www.ey.com/Publication/vwLUAssets/ey-the-business-case-for-purpose/$FILE/ey-the-business-case-for-purpose.pdf.

"For Workplace Failures," Press Room, Fierce (May 4, 2011), https://fierceinc.com/employees-cite-lack-of-collaboration-for-workplace-failures.

Fowler, Susan, "Reflecting on One Very, Very Strange Year at Uber" (February 19, 2017), https://www.susanjfowler.com/blog/2017/2/19/reflecting-on-one-very-strange-year-at-uber.

Fowler, Susan, "Susan Fowler's Plans after Uber? Tear down the System That Protects Harassers," Interview by Sam Levin, accessed June 8, 2018, https://www.theguardian.com/technology/2018/apr/11/susan-fowler-uber-interview-forced-arbitration-law.

Fredrickson, Barbara L., Cohn, Michael A., Coffey, Kimberley A., Pek Jolynn, and Finkel, Sandra M., "Open Hearts Build Lives: Positive Emotions, Induced through Loving-Kindness Meditation, Build Consequential Personal Resources," *Journal of Personality and Social Psychology* 95, no. 5 (November 2008): 1045–1062, https://www.ncbi.nlm.nih.gov/pmc/articles/PMC3156028/.

Gallup, "U.S. Employee Engagement" (July 30, 2017), http://news.gallup.com/poll/214961/gallup-employee-engagement.aspx%20accessed%20October%2020,%202017.

Gaskell, Adi, "New Study Shows That Collaboration Drives Workplace Performance," *Forbes* (June 22, 2017), https://www.forbes.com/sites/adigaskell/2017/06/22/new-study-finds-that-collaboration-drives-workplace-performance/#26e9ce303d02.

"GDP per Capita," World Bank, accessed June 6, 2018, https://data.worldbank.org/indicator/ny.gdp.pcap.kd.

Goleman, Daniel, "What Makes a Leader," *Harvard Business Review* (January 2004).

Greenfeld, Karl Taro, "Taco Bell and the Golden Age of Drive-Thru," *Bloomberg Businessweek* (May 5, 2011), https://www.bloomberg.com/news/articles/2011-05-05/taco-bell-and-the-golden-age-of-drive-thru

Grossman, Linda, "Metric Math Mistake Muffed Mars Meteorology Mission," *Wired* (November 10, 1999), https://www.wired.com/2010/11/1110mars-climate-observer-report/.

Guynn, Jessica, "Some Uber Riders React to Sexism Claims with Their Wallets," *USA Today* (March 8, 2017), https://www.usatoday.com/story/tech/news/2017/03/08/more-uber-riders-ditch-ride-hailing-app-over-susan-fowler-harassment-discrimination-charges/98862784/.

Hart Research Associates, "It Takes More Than a Major: Employer Priorities for College Learning and Student Success," Association of American Colleges and Universities, accessed June 8, 2018, https://www.aacu.org/publications-research/periodicals/it-takes-more-major-employer-priorities-college-learning-and.

IBM, "Leading through Connections: Insights from the Global Chief Executive Officer Study," IBM (2012), 21.

Inzlicht, Michael, and Obhi, Sukhvinder, "Powerful and Cold-hearted," *New York Times* (July 25, 2014), https://www.nytimes.com/2014/07/27/opinion/sunday/powerful-and-coldhearted.html?ref=opinion&_r=1.

IKEA, "Welcome Inside Our Company," accessed June 7, 2018, https://www.ikea.com/ms/en_US/this-is-ikea/company-information/index.html.

Isaacson, Walter, "How Steve Jobs' Love of Simplicity Fueled a Design Revolution, *Smithsonian Magazine* (September 2012), https://www.smithsonianmag.com/arts-culture/how-steve-jobs-love-of-simplicity-fueled-a-design-revolution-23868877/.

Kahn, William A., "Psychological Conditions of Personal Engagement and Disengagement at Work," *Academy of Management Journal* 33, no. 4 (January 1, 1990): 708.

Kennedy, John F., "Untitled Speech" [Undelivered], Trade Mart, Dallas TX (November 22, 1963), https://www.jfklibrary.org/Research/Research-Aids/JFK-Speeches/Dallas-TX-Trade-Mart-Undelivered_19631122.aspx.

Keswin, Erica, "Use Stories from Customers to Highlight Your Company's Purpose," *Harvard Business Review* (June 22, 2017), https://hbr.org/2017/06/use-stories-from-customers-to-highlight-your-companys-purpose.

Ketchum, *Leadership Communication Monitor* 2016 (2016), http://www.ketchum.com/pt-br/special-report/leadership-communication-monitor-2016.

Kirby, Julia, "Beware the Baboon Boss," *Harvard Business Review* (May 22, 2009), https://hbr.org/2009/05/baboons.

Kouzes, Jim, and Posner, Barry, *The Leadership Challenge* (New York: John Wiley & Sons, 2012).

Kouzes, James M., and Posner, Barry Z., *The Truth about Leadership: The No-Fads, Heart-of-the-Matter Facts You Need to Know* (Hoboken, NJ: John Wiley & Sons: 2010).

Lang, Annamarie, and Bradford, Thomas, "Where Are Your "Ready-Now" Leaders?" *Development Dimensions International* (February 20, 2013), http://www.ddiworld.com/ddi/media/white-papers/whereareyourreadynowleaders_wp_ddi.pdf.

"Life Expectancy at Birth," World Bank, accessed June 6, 2018, https://data.worldbank.org/indicator/SP.DYN.LE00.IN?end=2015 &start=1960.

Lin, Bing C., Kain, Jason M., and Fritz, Charlotte, "Don't Interrupt Me! An Examination of the Relationship between Intrusions at Work and Employee Strain," *International Journal of Stress Management 20*, no. 2 (2013): 77–94.

LinkedIn, "2016 Global Report: Purpose at Work," LinkedIn (2016), https://business.linkedin.com/content/dam/me/business/en-us/talent-solutions/resources/pdfs/Global-Report-on-Purpose-at-Work.pdf.

Loew, Laci, "State of Leadership Development 2015: Time to Act Is Now," Brandon Hall Group (August 2015), http://www.ddiworld.com/DDI/media/trend-research/state-of-leadership-development_tr_brandon-hall.pdf?ext=.pdf%2520.

Loew, Laci, "Study Shows Leadership Development Rated below Average or Poor in More than One-Third of Organizations," *Training* (May 28, 2015), https://trainingmag.com/study-shows-leadership-development-rated-below-average-or-poor-more-one-third-organizations.

Lubin, Joann, "How to Be a Better Boss? Spend Time on the Front Lines," *The Wall Street Journal* (February 9, 2012), https://www.wsj.com/articles/SB10001424052970203824904577211295 1446826014.

Luna, Tania, and Perringer, Leeann, *Surprise: Embrace the Unpredictable and Engineer the Unexpected* (New York: Tarcherperigee, 2015).

Lutz, Ashley, "How Trader Joe's Sells Twice as Much as Whole Foods," *Business Insider* (October 7, 2014), http://www.businessinsider.com/trader-joes-sales-strategy-2014-10?IR=T.

Lutz, Ashley, "Nordstrom's Employee Handbook Has Only One Rule," *Business Insider* (October 13, 2014), http://www.businessinsider.com/nordstroms-employee-handbook-2014-10?IR=T.

Lyft (@lyft), "Our Mission Is to Reconnect People through Transportation and Bring Communities Together" (March 16, 2015), https://twitter.com/lyft/status/577558134698348544?lang=e.

Madden, Mary, and Jones, Sydney, "Most Workers Use the Internet or Email at Their Jobs, but They Say These Technologies Are a Mixed Blessing for Them," Pew Internet and American Life Project (September 24, 2008), http://www.pewinternet.org/files/old-media//Files/Reports/2008/PIP_Networked_Workers_FINAL.pdf.pdf.

Mankins, Michael, "Is Technology Really Helping Us Get More Done?" *Harvard Business Review* (February 25, 2016), https://hbr.org/2016/02/is-technology-really-helping-us-get-more-done.

Mankins, Michael, Brahm, Chris, and Caimi, Greg, "Your Scarcest Resource," *Harvard Business Review* (May 2014), https://hbr.org/2014/05/your-scarcest-resource.

Manyika, James, Lund, Susan, Auguste, Byron, and Ramaswamy, Sreenivas, "Help Wanted: The Future of Work in Advanced Economics," McKinsey Global Institute (March 2012), https://www.mckinsey.com/~/media/McKinsey/Featured%20Insights/Employment%20and%20Growth/Future%20of%20work%20in%20advanced%20economies/Help_wanted_future_of_work_full_report.ashx.

Mark, Gloria, and Bren, Donald, "Too Many Interruptions at Work?" *Gallup* (June 8, 2006), http://news.gallup.com/businessjournal/23146/too-many-interruptions-work.aspx.

Martinez, Amy, "Tale of Lost Diamond Adds Glitter to Nordstrom's Customer Service," *The Seattle Times* (May 11, 2011), http://old.seattletimes.com/html/businesstechnology/2015028167_nordstrom12.html.

McCarthy, Niall, "A 40 Hour Work Week in the United States Actually Lasts 47 Hours," *Forbes* (September 1, 2014), https://www.forbes.com/sites/niallmccarthy/2014/09/01/a-40-hour-work-week-in-the-united-states-actually-lasts-47-hours/#4022e569f5e4.

Mesmer-Magnus, Jessica, Glew, David J., and Chockalingam, Viswesvaran, "A Meta-analysis of Positive Humor in the Workplace," *Journal of Managerial Psychology* 27, no. 2 (2012): 155–190, https://doi.org/10.1108/02683941211199554.

Minter, Adam, "Somebody's Making Money off of All Our Junk," *Bloomberg* (August 28 2017), https://www.bloomberg.com/view/articles/2017-08-28/the-self-storage-business-is-booming-here-s-why.

"More than Half the Homes in U.S. Have Three or More TV's," Nielson (July 20, 2009), http://www.nielsen.com/us/en/insights/news/2009/more-than-half-the-homes-in-us-have-three-or-more-tvs.html.

Murphy, Mark, "Interruptions at Work Are Killing Your Productivity," *Forbes* (October 30, 2016), https://www.forbes.com/sites/markmurphy/2016/10/30/interruptions-at-work-are-killing-your-productivity/#6708a8981689.

Nadella, Satya, "Satya Nadella: The C in CEO Stands for Culture," *Fast Company* (September 21, 2017).

Nadella, Satya, "We Sat Down with Microsoft's CEO to Discuss the Past, Present and Future of the Company," interview by Krzysztof Majdan and Michał Wasowski, *Business Insider* (April 20, 2017), http://uk.businessinsider.com/satya-nadella-microsoft-ceo-qa-2017-4?r=US&IR=T.

Naisbitt, John, *Megatrends* (New York: Warner Trends, 1984), 25.

Nasri, Grace, "Solving Information Asymmetry: How Today's Companies Are Empowering Consumers and Creating More Efficient Markets," *Huffpost* (November 9 2013), https://www.huffingtonpost.com/grace-nasri/solving-information-asymm_b_3870302.html?guccounter=1.

The New Palgrave Dictionary of Economics, ed. *Steven Durlaf and Lawrence Blume* (London: Macmillan, 2008), 841.

Nyberg, A., Alfredsson, L, Theorell, T., Westerlund, H., Vahtera, J., and Kivimäki, M., "Managerial Leadership and Ischaemic Heart Disease among Employees: The Swedish WOLF Study," *Occupational and Environmental Medicine* 66, no. 1 (January 2009): 51–55.

O'Connor, Kara, "Out of Time Residents Not Happy about Post," *The Hour* (September 15, 2010), http://www.thehour.com/wilton/article/out-of-time-residents-not-happy-about-post-8295123.php.

Oxford Economics, "Global Talent 2021: How the New Geography of Talent Will Transform Human Resource Strategies," *Oxford Economics* (2012).

Perelman, Michael, "Henry Ford Double's His Worker's Wages," Delancey Place (January 29, 2016), https://delanceyplace.com/view-archives.php?p=2991.

Pine II, Joseph B., and Gilmore, James H., "Welcome to the Experience Economy," *Harvard Business Review* (July–August 1998), https://hbr.org/1998/07/welcome-to-the-experience-economy.

Pink, Daniel H., "Revenge of the Right Brain," *WIRED* (January 1, 2005), https://www.wired.com/2005/02/brain/.

Pink, Daniel H., *To Sell Is Human: The Surprising Truth about Moving Others* (New York: Riverhead Books, 2012), 83–89.

Popken, Ben, "Zappos Saves Best Man from Going Barefoot at Wedding," *Consumerist* (May 19, 2011), https://consumerist.com/2011/05/19/zappos-saves-best-man-from-going-barefoot-at-wedding/ .

Porath, Christine, "Half of Employees Don't Feel Respected by Their Bosses," *Harvard Business Review* (November 19, 2014), https://hbr.org/2014/11/half-of-employees-dont-feel-respected-by-their-bosses.

Pfau, Bruce, "What Do Millennials Really Want from Work? The Same Things the Rest of Us Do," *Harvard Business Review* (April 7, 2016), https://hbr.org/2016/04/what-do-millennials-really-want-at-work.

Quigley, Jeana, "Do You Care about Onboarding? You Should," *Bamboo HR* (April 23, 2014), https://www.bamboohr.com/blog/onboarding-infographic/.

Quirk, Mary Beth, "Zappos CSR's Kindness Warms Our Heart," *Consumerist* (January 17, 2011), https://consumerist.com/2011/01/17/zappos-customer-service-reps-kindness-warms-our-cold-hearts/.

Rehak, Judith, and *International Herald Tribune*, "Tylenol Made a Hero of Johnson & Johnson: The Recall That Started Them

All," *The New York Times* (March 23, 2002), https://www.nytimes
.com/2002/03/23/your-money/tylenol-made-a-hero-of-johnson-
johnson-the-recall-that-started.html.

Reingold, Jennifer, "What the Heck Is Angela Ahrendts Doing at
Apple?" *Fortune* (September 10, 2015), http://fortune.com/2015/
09/10/angela-ahrendts-apple/.

Ricci, Judith, Chee, A. E., Lorandeau, A. L. and Berger, J., "Fatigue
in the U.S. Workforce: Prevalence and Implications for Lost Productive Work Time," *Journal of Occupational and Environmental
Medicine 49*, no. 1 (2007): 1–10.

Robinson, Ken, "Do Schools Kill Creativity?" TED (February 2006),
https://www.ted.com/talks/ken_robinson_says_schools_kill_
creativity.

Roggio, Armando, "The Zappos Effect: 5 Great Customer Service
Ideas for Small Businesses," Practical Ecommerce (March 11,
2011), https://www.practicalecommerce.com/The-Zappos-Effect-
5-Great-Customer-Service-Ideas-for-Smaller-Businesses.

Samarrai, Fariss, "Human Brains Are Hardwired for Empathy,
Friendship, Study Shows," *UVA Today* (August 21 2013), https://
news.virginia.edu/content/human-brains-are-hardwired-empathy-
friendship-study-shows.

Schwartz, Tony, and Porath, Christine, "Why You Hate Work," *New
York Times* (May 30, 2014), https://www.nytimes.com/2014/06/01/
opinion/sunday/why-you-hate-work.html.

Shen, Lucinda, "United Airlines Stock Drops $1.4 Billion after
. Passenger-Removal Controversy," *Fortune* (April 11 2017), http://
fortune.com/2017/04/11/united-airlines-stock-drop/.

Siegel & Gale, "Simplicity at Work: Demonstrating the Positive
Impact of Simplicity on the Workforce" (2017), https://simple
.siegelgale.com/acton/attachment/9371/f-03e7/1/-/-/-/-/Simplicity
%20At%20Work.pdf.

Sims, Peter, *Little Bets: How Breakthrough Ideas Emerge from Small
Discoveries* (New York: Random House, 2012).

Sinar, Evan, Wellins, Richard, and Paese, Matthew, "What's the Number 1 Leadership Skill for Overall Success?" *DDI* (February 23

2016), https://www.ddiworld.com/global-offices/united-states/press
-room/what-is-the-1-leadership-skill-for-overall-success.

Sinek, Simon, "How Great Leaders Inspire Action," TED Talk
(September 2009), https://www.ted.com/talks/simon_sinek_how_
great_leaders_inspire_action.

Solomon, Lou, "Many Leaders Shrink from Straight Talk with
Employees," *Interact* (February 2015), http://interactauthentically
.com/new-interact-report-many-leaders-shrink-from-straight-talk-
with-employees/.

Solomon, Lou, "Two Thirds of Managers Are Uncomfortable
Communicating with Employees," *Harvard Business Review*
(March 9, 2016), https://hbr.org/2016/03/two-thirds-of-managers-
are-uncomfortable-communicating-with-employees.

Son, Sabrina, "Effective Employee Retention Strategies for the Retail
Industry," TINYcon (August 11, 2016), https://www.tinypulse
.com/blog/effective-employee-retention-strategies-for-the-retail-
industry.

Sorenson, Susan, and Garman, Keri, "How to Tackle U.S. Employees' Stagnant Engagement," Gallup (June 11, 2013), http://
news.gallup.com/businessjournal/162953/tackle-employees-
stagnating-engagement.aspx.

Spira, Jonathan, B., and Feintuch, Joshua, B., "The Cost of Not Paying
Attention: How Interruptions Impact Knowledge Worker Productivity," BaseEx (2005), http://iorgforum.org/wp-content/uploads/
2011/06/CostOfNotPayingAttention.BasexReport.pdf.

The Staff of the Corporate Executive Board, "The Role of Employee
Engagement in the Return of Growth," *Bloomberg* (August 13,
2010), https://www.bloomberg.com/news/articles/2010-08-13/the-
role-of-employee-engagement-in-the-return-to-growth.

"The State of Enterprise Work," Harris Poll, Workfront, accessed
June 8, 2018, https://www.workfront.com/resources/the-state-of-
enterprise-work.

Sturt, David, and Nordstrom, Todd, "Yes, You Should Celebrate
Employee Appreciation Day," accessed June 7, 2018, https://
blog.octanner.com/appreciation-2/yes-you-should-celebrate-
employee-appreciation-day.

Sweeney, Deborah, "3 Ways Handwritten Notes Impact the Workplace," *Forbes* (April 24, 2012), https://www.forbes.com/sites/deborahsweeney/2012/04/24/3-ways-handwritten-notes-impact-the-workplace/#30fcbf22b4fd.

Taylor, Frederick Winslow, *The Principles of Scientific Management* (New York: Harper and Brothers, 1911).

"THANKS, BUT NO THANKS: Survey Reveals Strangest Forms of Workplace Recognition; Research Also Finds Two in Three Employees Would Leave Their Job If They Didn't Feel Appreciated," Robert Half, accessed June 7, 2018, http://rh-us.mediaroom.com/2017–04–12-THANKS-BUT-NO-THANKS-Survey-Reveals-Strangest-Forms-of-Workplace-Recognition-Research-Also-Finds-Two-in-Three-Employees-Would-Leave-Their-Job-If-They-Didnt-Feel-Appreciated.

Tripp & Tyler, "A Conference Call in Real Life," *YouTube* (September 21, 2017), https://www.youtube.com/watch?v=kNz82r5nyUw

Truffaut, Francois, *Hitchcock: A Definitive Study of Alfred Hitchcock* (New York: Simon & Schuster, 2008).

Twaronite, Karyn, "Global Generations: A Global Study on Work-Life Challenges across Generations," *EY* (2015), http://www.ey.com/Publication/vwLUAssets/EY-global-generations-a-global-study-on-work-life-challenges-across-generations/$FILE/EY-global-generations-a-global-study-on-work-life-challenges-across-generations.pdf.

"The United States in 1900," Digital History, accessed June 7, 2018, http://www.digitalhistory.uh.edu/disp_textbook.cfm?smtID=2&psid=3175.

Useem, Jerry, "Power Causes Brain Damage: How Leaders Lose Mental Capacities—Most Notably for Reading Other People—That Were Essential to Their Rise," *The Atlantic* (July 2017), https://www.theatlantic.com/magazine/archive/2017/07/power-causes-brain-damage/528711/?utm_source=nhfb.

USPS, "About the United States Postal Service," accessed June 6, 2018, http://about.usps.com/who-we-are/leadership/about-usps.htm.

USPS, *Strategic Information Plan 2006–2010* (September 2005), https://about.usps.com/strategic-planning/stp2006–2010/welcome.html.

Valukas, Anton "Report to Board of Directors of General Motors Company Regarding Ignition Switch Recalls," Jenner and Block (May 29, 2014), http://s3.documentcloud.org/documents/1183508/g-m-internal-investigation-report.pdf, 2.

Van Dyne, Linn, and Pierce, Jon L., "Psychological Ownership and Feelings of Possession: Three Field Studies Predicting Employee Attitudes and Organisational Citizenship Behavior," *Journal of Organizational Behavior 25* (2004): 439–459.

Vozza, Stephanie, "10 Unique Ways Leaders Bond with Their Employees," *Fast Company* (September 18, 2015), https://www.fastcompany.com/3050651/10-unique-ways-leaders-bond-with-employees.

Wiley, Carolyn, "What Motivates Employees According to over 40 Years of Motivation Surveys," *International Journal of Manpower 18*, no. 3 (1997): 263–280.

Woods, David, "Poor Communication between Managers and Employees Wastes Time and Impacts Productivity," *HR* (January 15, 2010), http://www.hrmagazine.co.uk/article-details/poor-communication-between-managers-and-employees-wastes-time-and-impacts-productivity.

Wooden, John, "First, How to Put on Your Socks," interview by Devin Gordon, *Newsweek* (October 24, 1999), http://www.newsweek.com/john-wooden-first-how-put-your-socks-167942.

Yaeger, John, "John Wooden" (October 1, 2009), http://donyaeger.com/john-wooden.

Zappos, "About Zappos Culture," accessed June 7, 2018, https://www.zappos.com/core-values.

ACKNOWLEDGMENTS

The journey toward success is not a straight line, and neither was the process of writing this book. This project (my first book) has been humbling, exhilarating, and exhausting—and often on the same day. It's something I envisioned doing for a very long time. Now that the vision is a reality, finding words to adequately express the depth of gratitude that I have is surprisingly challenging.

So many people have touched the creation of this book. I've been influenced, shaped, and improved by a tremendous number of people: writers, leaders, teachers, clients, colleagues, and friends. I'm grateful to them all. Within that group, there are some who deserve special mention.

First, a huge thank-you to the tens of thousands of participants in the various leadership seminars I've been privileged to lead. Your willingness to share the good, the bad, and the ugly of what worklife is really like has taught me more about organizational leadership than any graduate program ever could. Special thanks to the leaders whose real stories appear in this book. I've changed certain details to preserve confidentiality.

This book wouldn't have been possible without the team at Eagle's Flight. I'm honored to have worked with them for more than 20 years. They've been incredibly supportive in fostering my professional growth. It's a place where I've gotten to live connection, communication, and collaboration daily. Special thanks to these colleagues past and present: Kristin Abell, Sue Bitton, Rick Boersma, Ian Cornett, Cynthia Davis, Oliver Dawson, Mike DeQuetteville, Diane Essel, Krista Foreman, Paul Goyette, Carl Harkrider, Sandra Herriot, Matt Hill, Roger Joseph, Sue Krautkramer, Keith Lewis, Paulette LoMarro, Bill Martin, Todd McCallum, Lorraine McCrossan, Paul Morris, Nicola Mount, Tim O'Regan, Christy Pettit, Jana Poppe, Nancy Priest, John Reid, Dave Riveness, Jennifer Schmidt, Karen Sonoski,

Bob Speers, Debi Speers, Blair Steinbach, Kevin Stenhouse, Kristin Stewart, Kim Wassal, Kate Webster, Sue Wigston, Brady Wilson, John Wright, and Julie Wylie. Phil Geldart: your vision of how to engage adults to take action has always inspired me. Thank you for creating such a remarkable organization.

Lisa Bodell and the team at Futurethink have been a constant source of encouragement and motivation. Lisa: thank you for modeling the way as an author, leader, and all-around dynamo.

Tony Schwartz and The Energy Project have forever altered how I understand leadership and performance. Tony: the beauty of your writing comes from the depth of your character. You inspire me. It's an honor to be your colleague and friend.

I'm so lucky to have Tess Callero as my agent. From the moment we met, Tess has believed in the vision of this book and has been a tireless advocate ever since. Jeanenne Ray, Kelly Talbot, Susan Geraghty, and the team at Wiley have been true professionals and partners in shepherding the book through the publishing process.

Marina Tersigni designed all the images in these pages. Marina: thank you for your vision and flexibility.

Samie Al-Achrafi, Nina Bainbridge, Dave Barry, Stephen Butler, Victoria Cliche, Andy Cohen, Fiona Coleman, Iain Edward, Hilary Gee, Terence Gilheany, Sue Gray, Bill Lienhard, Sarah Lock, Daniel Ludevig, Ousmane Power-Greene, Paula Quinn, and Paul Winke: thank you for always being so positive and inquisitive about this book's progress. Your friendship and care has meant more than you can imagine.

To have colleagues who are keen to read a whole manuscript and give detailed feedback is a gift worth its weight in gold. Elena Petricone, Mike Scott, Mike Torrie, and Scott Wyler: I'm so moved by your willingness to dig into the nitty-gritty of these ideas and pull them apart so they could get better. This book wouldn't be nearly as good if it wasn't for you.

Launa Schweizer gave feedback as well and has been in my writing corner for well over a decade. She's read through drafts of my other book ideas that have been dreadful, and somehow she found kind things to say to help me grow as a writer. Launa: your feedback is so good it should get its own book contract. You're an amazing writer and an even more amazing friend.

I'm a big believer that all leadership development starts with personal development. I've been lucky to have tremendous mentors and friends who have supported and challenged me to become a better man. These include Jeff Altman, Paul Bolles-Beaven, John Broucek, Joseph Dicenso, George Faison, Alan Gilburg, Seth Harwood, Boysen Hodgson, Kell Julliard, Josh Knox, Greg Liotta, Rich Menges, Mish Middelmann, Terry Mollner, Harold Norris, Tom Pitner, Jonathan Polgar, Matt Sislowitz, Andy Towlen, Alex Von Bidder, Jon Wilson, JD Wolfe, Gary Zaremba, and Robert Zeller.

I'm moved to acknowledge some of the thinkers who have had a profound effect on how I see the world: Don Beck, Arthur Carmazzi, Jim Collins, Viktor Frankl, Daniel Goleman, Daniel Kahneman, Jim Kouzes, Daniel Pink, Jerry Porras, Barry Posner, and Ken Wilber. If you spotted them lurking in these chapters, you're right.

My family—Gilberte, Paul, Sarah, Park, Ann, Joanna, Tom, Joan, Carol, Serge, Chandra, Theodore, Lucas, and Kaia—have supported of all my various endeavors through the decades. I hope this book finally explains what it is that I actually do for a living.

My daughter, Miranda, has been a great teacher of empathy and connection. Miranda: thanks for challenging me to step out of my comfort zone and practice fewer golden rules and more platinum rules. Your sensitivity and care for others inspires me.

My son, Alexander, is a role model of clear and open communication. Alex: thank you for the courage to give honest feedback on how I can be an even better dad. I've grown a tremendous amount because of you.

Mary Clark has been my partner and teacher of collaboration for 20 years. It's been said that leaders should surround themselves with people smarter than they are. Mary's brilliance is matched only by her unbridled enthusiasm and willingness to keep showing up. Mary: thank you for being such a rock through all of these years of change and growth. I'm lucky to be on your team. And thanks for saying yes to starting a 24/7 child-care center together. The kids are turning out pretty well.

ABOUT THE AUTHOR

A sought-after keynote speaker, facilitator, and coach, Alain Hunkins is a leadership expert who connects the science of high performance with the performing art of leadership. Leaders trust him to help unlock their potential and expand their influence, leading to superior results, increased engagement, higher levels of retention, and greater organizational and personal satisfaction. He has a gift for translating complex concepts from psychology, neuroscience, and organizational behavior into simple, practical tools that can be applied on the job.

Over the course of his more than 20-year career, Alain has worked with tens of thousands of leaders in more than 25 countries and has served clients in all industries, including 42 Fortune 100 companies. He delivers dynamic keynotes, seminars, and workshops covering a variety of leadership topics, including communication, team-building, conflict management, peak performance, innovation, motivation, and change.

In addition to *Cracking the Leadership Code* (Wiley), Alain's authored more than 400 articles and has been published by the Association for Talent Development, CEO Refresher, and the American Management Association.

With his Master's in fine arts in acting from the University of Wisconsin–Milwaukee's Professional Theater Training Program and a BA in English from Amherst College, Alain also serves on the faculty of Duke Corporate Education, ranked number 2 worldwide in 2019 by *Financial Times* on its list of customized executive education programs. Alain has also lectured at University of North Carolina's Kenan-Flagler's business school and Columbia University.

A certified co-leader for ManKind Project International, a nonprofit whose mission is to help men lead lives of service to their families, communities, and workplaces, Alain resides in Northampton,

Massachusetts, with his wife and two children. For resources on how Alain can help you and your organization, please visit

- www.alainhunkins.com
- @AlainHunkins
- linkedin.com/in/alainhunkins

INDEX